Intimacy:
A 100-Day Guide to Better Relationships

Douglas Weiss

DISCOVERY PRESS

INTIMACY: A 100-DAY GUIDE TO BETTER RELATIONSHIPS
by Douglas Weiss
Published by Discovery Press
719.278.3708
heart2heart@xc.org
www.drdougweiss.com

This book or parts thereof may not be reproduced in any form, stored in a retrieval system or transmitted in any form by any means—electronic, mechanical, photocopy, recording or otherwise—without prior written permission of the publisher, except as provided by United States of America copyright law.

Unless otherwise noted, all Scripture quotations are from the Holy Bible, New International Version. Copyright © 1973, 1978, 1984, International Bible Society. Used by permission.

Scripture quotations marked NKJV are from the New King James Version of the Bible. Copyright © 1979, 1980, 1982 by Thomas Nelson, Inc., publishers. Used by permission.

AUTHOR'S NOTE: The testimonies of individuals in this book are fictitious and created from composites of clients who share similar issues. Names and identifying information have been changed to protect confidentiality. Any similarity between the names and stories of individuals described in this book and individuals known to readers is coincidental and not intentioned.

Cover design by Judith McKittrick Wright

Copyright © 2001, 2003 by Douglas Weiss
All rights reserved

Library of Congress Catalog Card Number: 2001089206
International Standard Book Number: 978-1-881292-53-1
(paperback)

20 21 22 23 24 — 21 20 19 18 17
Printed in the United States of America

DEDICATION

I dedicate this book to my teacher of intimacy, my heavenly Father, and to my teammate in intimacy, my beautiful wife, Lisa, and also to all the travelers with a destination toward intimacy that I have met and will yet meet.

Contents

Introduction
Searching for Genuine Intimacy *1*

PART ONE: DIMENSIONS OF INTIMACY

1 The Awesome Power of Spiritual Intimacy 7
2 Soul Mates—the Joy of Emotional Intimacy . . . 17
3 Physical Intimacy—a Lifelong Celebration 29

PART TWO: ROADBLOCKS TO INTIMACY

4 The Anger Enemy 47
5 Flossing Away Relational Plaque 67
6 Dealing With Sexuality 77
7 Money Matters 93
8 Is Your Marriage Based on Emotion? 134

PART THREE: THE 100 DAYS

9 Day by Day—
   Daily Exercises to Build Intimacy 151
10 Date Your Spouse or Go to Therapy! 177
11 Finding Sexual Agreement 202
12 Blessed Are the Consistent 227

PART FOUR: THE 100-DAY LOG

13 Beginning Your One Hundred Days 239

   Appendix: Feelings Exercise *341*

   Notes *344*

INTRODUCTION

Searching for Genuine Intimacy

Genuine intimacy is the cry of our nation. Many individuals search through multiple marriages trying to find the vital connection their souls long for. Still louder shouts the silence of the man or woman who has been married for decades and feels alone in that partnership. Many feel they have done everything right at home and with their spouses, yet there is little or no intimacy.

Far too many partners feel like roommates—as if they are just getting by emotionally. If fulfillment is promised, then why is it that few couples enjoy that impassioned connection? What do a few sparkling relationships have that seems to escape the larger population? These questions and more are what this book will review and answer.

I have lived in the laboratory of other people's marriages for many years. In addition, I myself have journeyed from the inability to be intimate to a place of deep intimacy and great fulfillment with my wife, Lisa.

Early in my married life I had the feeling that I was surrounded by walls. I desperately wanted to step out from behind those walls but could not find a way to connect to my wife. God in His graciousness drew me into the field of marriage and family counseling where I gained much understanding. Still, no one explained, "These are the steps to intimacy: 1, 2, 3." The mystery of intimacy and the skills required to build and maintain it continued to elude me—as it does so many others in my field.

It is in the laboratory of real marriage, real crisis, real love and genuine desire for intimacy that we will solve the mystery. Part of the solution can be discovered in a series of principles that can be applied daily. I've counseled couples whose relationships were so distant that they had not enjoyed sex for more than a decade. When these same couples applied the principles in this book, within six weeks not only had they rekindled their sexual relationship, but they actually started to like one other again for the first time in years.

Intimacy is really not a mystery at all—it is a process. Intimacy is the fruit of being in this process. Allow me to explain it another way: Wealth is a process. You work. You save. Maybe you invest. But to those who follow the basic principles of wealth and apply them, regardless of how they feel about them, wealth happens to them. The same applies to your health. Under normal circumstances, the process of eating right and exercising keeps you healthy. Those who do what they want, eat what they want or spend what they want often do not achieve optimal health or wealth.

The same is true with intimacy. Those who do what they want emotionally with their spouse do not achieve optimal intimacy. The following pages will guide you into the process and the practical application of intimacy. Since intimacy is a process, I strongly believe that after one hundred days of applying these skills you will reap such dynamic and satisfying benefits that you will never want to abandon these principles of living and the deeply satisfying intimacy with your spouse that they can bring—ever!

I have practiced these exercises in my relationship with my wife. Lisa and I have been married for fifteen years, and as we have applied these principles to our marriage we have continued to grow closer and stronger together. I believe the greatest gift to our children is a strong, vibrant and lovingly intimate marriage. I wouldn't ask you to do something that I don't practice myself. Throughout the years, these principles have given life to my wife, to many of my clients and to me. As you practice the power of intimacy, I pray that you and your partner will experience the abundant life that Jesus has promised each of you in your most intimate relationship—your marriage.

> Intimacy is really not a mystery at all—it is a process.

The next one hundred days can breathe life back into your marriage, but you must work at it. Determine to spend this time mastering the basic skills necessary to enjoy satisfying and enduring intimacy with your spouse.

PART ONE

Dimensions of Intimacy

ONE

The Awesome Power of Spiritual Intimacy

The most uniquely powerful picture of spiritual intimacy on earth is revealed in the oneness of the Godhead, glimpsed through Scripture. The Word (Jesus Christ) and God were one in complete harmony, unity and accord from the very beginning of time. That same oneness and togetherness are a part of God's will for us in our marriages.

> In the beginning was the Word, and the Word was with God, and the Word was God.
> —JOHN 1:1

I love reading the Bible and feeling the very keen sense that the Author, the Holy Spirit, has intimacy as a personal objective for its readers from beginning to end. God made man and woman in the garden not only to fellowship with each other but to fellowship as a couple with Him.

In the beginning God walked with Adam and Eve daily—until sin severed the union. Imagine as a couple having God the Father teaching you to love, commit and feel equally loved and understood. But the Holy Spirit does not leave us only with the picture of how God intended intimacy to be. He also pens a great word picture of Christ and the church.

The picture is of the hero and Savior, the Lord Jesus Christ, who loved and died for His bride so that she might be with Him forever. This word picture closes with Jesus coming back for His bride and hosting a great banquet to celebrate their eternal intimacy.

God is a romantic, and He is definitely interested in the issue of intimacy. That is why it is so important that we begin this study about intimacy by reflecting on the scripture, "In the beginning was the Word, and the Word was with God." Without God, intimacy is short-lived and incomplete. Even if it were possible for a husband and wife to achieve emotional and physical intimacy, their lives would feel incomplete without spiritual intimacy—living as individuals and as a couple in relationship with the all-loving God.

My personal spiritual journey started with the love of God being poured into me through the salvation of our Lord Jesus Christ. Without His consistent love and gentleness, I would know of nothing to write on these pages about intimacy. He is my greatest teacher on giving and receiving love and intimacy.

The scripture that declares this message loud and clear to me is Psalm 127:1: "Unless the Lord builds the house, its builders labor in vain." This can be no truer than for the couple who desires intimacy within their marriage without actively involving God in the process. As this scripture indicates, they would definitely be laboring in vain.

You may be a born-again Christian believer. But you may be someone who has never accepted the love of God into your life.

If you have never encountered God personally, I encourage you to take a moment and ask Jesus Christ to show you His love and His forgiveness for all the sins that have separated you from Him. Only then will you experience true intimacy from the master of intimacy Himself, Jesus Christ.

Nevertheless, spiritual intimacy is not an automatic attribute of all who believe. I have spent countless sessions with believers who don't understand even the basics of spiritual intimacy. Some individuals and couples struggle painfully with the concept of intimacy with the Father.

> God is a romantic, and He definitely is interested in the issue of intimacy.

In this chapter, I will outline some of the basics of spiritual intimacy for individuals and couples. In addition, chapter 9 provides a very practical application of this information to help you and your spouse experience spiritual intimacy in your day-to-day lifestyle.

HONESTY IS THE ONLY POLICY

Honesty is so basic to spiritual intimacy that I must address it as the first issue. Intimacy can never be increased where dishonesty and deception exist.

Many individuals have what I call an "image relationship" with themselves. They work at crafting their image so much that they themselves buy it hook, line and sinker. Such image crafters usually focus on the wonderful parts of themselves, such as their gifts or shining qualities. Their self-styled image may be charismatic, outwardly displaying wonderful virtues such as caring, sincerity, spirituality and intelligence. They often appear nearly perfect.

When I was a young Christian in Bible college I couldn't even walk out of the dorm room unless everything matched. I was quite an image to behold—a young, clean-cut, well-dressed Bible school student and choir member. Nevertheless,

I only had an image relationship with myself. I was completely unaware of my real heart condition or even how I truly felt. I appeared righteous and was always ready to convince anyone that I was OK. The only problem was that I wasn't real. I was well schooled in all the religious rhetoric; I could spout off dozens of memorized Bible verses to fit the moment, but I couldn't have a relationship to save my life.

> Honesty about how you feel, honesty about your perceptions and honesty with who you are is central to spiritual intimacy.

What does this have to do with spiritual intimacy? Everything if you're a Christian desiring intimacy. In truth I was a hurting human being who used religion to protect my heart, and it took God years to tear down that self-image so that I could begin to experience genuine intimacy.

Self-honesty is very important. Not one of us human beings is perfect or even close to it. If you take any one of us away from the normal comforts of daily life and place us in an unusually stressful situation, such as an all-day layover in an airport or being stuck in bumper-to-bumper traffic, less than wonderful things will often come out of our hearts.

It's absolutely wonderful to be human, isn't it? We are imperfect by our very design. If we could be perfect, then we wouldn't need a Savior, would we? Growing beyond false religious images and discovering who you really are is just the beginning of spiritual intimacy.

Are you thinking that this really doesn't apply to you? Try this exercise to find out. Think of your three greatest flaws. Now take a minute and come up with seven more. I find that in doing this, many of us can come up with one or two—but ten? Who even imagines that he could have ten faults? Take a moment at this point and write down ten of your worst faults and see how long it takes.

The longer it takes for you to come up with ten faults, the more important self-honesty is going to be for you on your journey toward spiritual intimacy with your spouse. By the way, when you're writing down these faults, don't cheat and ask your spouse to help.

Honesty about how you feel, honesty about your perceptions and honesty with who you are is central to spiritual intimacy. Later, as you go through the exercises in the latter part of this book, you will begin to discover more and more about the real you than you may have thought possible.

The great news is this: You won't be doing this alone. God will be with both you and your spouse, walking together with you throughout this journey.

Recently at a lunch meeting a woman asked me how a man could be taught to see the real beauty of a woman when he first meets her. I responded that it was not possible. How can you appreciate the complex caverns of a woman's soul at a moment's glance? It takes a journey of decades for a man to behold the beauty of a woman. The fragrance of a woman's many passions for life, love and relationship, her waves of emotion and her valleys of woundedness and fear could never be understood during a superficial encounter.

Intimacy is an exciting journey with a wonderful destination. The adventure of intimacy's discovery makes the traveling so much fun for you and your spouse. Honesty is one signpost on the way to spiritual intimacy. You must be honest with yourself, with God and with your spouse.

IT TAKES WHOLEHEARTED COMMITMENT

Like honesty, intimacy also requires commitment to yourself, to God and to your spouse. Intimacy rarely happens by accident, and it is even more rare that it can be sustained over a lifetime without genuine commitment.

I am personally very committed to intimacy. At times, I think I wear my wife, Lisa, out about it. I want to know her thoughts, feelings, beliefs and fears. I want to savor the scent of her personality, the moments of her fury and the playfulness of her spirit. I am committed to intimacy with both my God and my wife—and this commitment is not halfhearted. You can look into my life to see that my behavior supports my commitment to spiritual intimacy.

> Spiritual intimacy begins in an intimate relationship with Jesus Christ.

Truth is always easily found in a person's behavior; that's where an individual's commitment will always show up. For me it's one of the things that makes working with people so much fun. A person who wants to lose weight designs a plan and then follows through. A person seeking wealth plans to earn, save and invest to reach his or her goals and then works the plan. Spiritual intimacy is not any different. An individual who wants to experience spiritual intimacy with both God and a spouse can create a plan. As he or she follows through, the level of commitment will be revealed in the outcome.

Intimacy on all levels requires commitment, whether it be spiritual, physical or emotional. No amount of reading about intimacy can give you genuine intimacy. You must make a commitment and then follow through with it.

As you walk through the various aspects of intimacy, your commitment will be challenged. Your determination to follow through will become an essential tool in obtaining the intimacy you seek. In the next one hundred days, as you and your spouse complete the exercises offered in this book, your entire life can be dramatically changed.

It will take focus, commitment and hard work, but in one hundred days I believe you can experience intimacy on every level and maintain this intimacy for the rest of your life together.

BUILDING YOUR HOUSE

Spiritual intimacy is the cornerstone upon which all genuine intimacy can be built. For "unless the LORD builds the house, its builders labor in vain" (Ps. 127:1). That's why spiritual intimacy is the cornerstone of this 100-day guide to intimacy.

Spiritual intimacy can be broken down into two categories: personal intimacy with the Father and marital intimacy with the Father. Let's investigate.

THE FIRST STEP OF PERSONAL INTIMACY

Spiritual intimacy begins in an intimate relationship with Jesus Christ. The temptation to be religious, to practice religious forms and expressions devoid of genuine relationship, is ever present in all of us. Intimacy is never about religion—it is never a list of dos and don'ts. Intimacy only arises from a dynamic connection to the living person of God through Jesus Christ.

No one on earth can tell you how much food makes you full. It doesn't even seem rational. Could you imagine going to a restaurant and two-thirds of the way through your meal your waiter stops you and says, "Excuse me, but you're full, so stop eating now"? Is that not the most ridiculous thing you have ever heard? I certainly know when I am full, and I know when I am hungry. It's funny, but when I am hungry I can act a little differently.

Here's my point: No matter how sincere or knowledgeable

a spouse, teacher or Bible scholar may be, they can never tell you how much prayer, Scripture reading or praise and worship of God you need on a daily basis to be full. Similar to eating, they can only encourage you to eat enough.

Therefore, you must ask yourself, "Is my spirit being fed enough through worship and praise, prayer and God's Word to be filled?" I can't tell you how much is enough, but you do need to eat daily from God's banquet to maintain spiritual intimacy. So if you're spiritually full most days, great! But if you're spiritually hungry and acting selfish, rude or impatient, then you may need to make some changes. Examine yourself. What is the fruit of your spiritual tree? Galatians 5:22 says, "But the fruit of the Spirit is love, joy, peace, patience, kindness, goodness, faithfulness, gentleness and self-control. Against such things there is no law."

From personal experience, I can tell you that I need to have intimacy with God daily in my life to maintain intimacy with my wife. My flesh loves to be rude and selfish, so I need a certain balance of worship and praise toward God along with prayer and meditation of His love letter to me (the Scriptures).

Make a plan to feed yourself daily. Remember, it's not *religion*, it's *relationship*. No person needs to preach me into eating lunch! When I get hungry I eat! So commit to behaviors that make you spiritually full. Don't be like the man in Proverbs 19:24: "The sluggard buries his hand in the dish; he will not even bring it back to his mouth!"

Imagine that you're dining in a fine restaurant. The gentleman at the next table has a wonderful meal laid out in front of him, but he is too lazy to put the food in his mouth. Wouldn't you wonder what in the world was wrong with him. To top it off, you learn that the fabulous meal was *free*! He didn't even have to pay for it to eat it. He simply had to eat.

I think you get the point. Jesus Christ paid the price of spiritual intimacy for us all. Every day He prepares a banquet of spiritual delights so that we can be filled. All we have to do is show up and eat. I encourage you to a make a plan for yourself so that every day you can be filled through the spiritual intimacy that was freely given. Eat up—it's free!

MARITAL INTIMACY

Much like personal spiritual intimacy, marital intimacy requires a commitment from each spouse to work together *spiritually*. God walked with Adam and Eve in the garden. He did not walk with just one of them but with both of them jointly. As we saw earlier, this is also true of the Godhead. John 1:1 says, "In the beginning was the Word, and the Word was with God, and the Word was God." Togetherness and spirituality are truly concepts that are linked in the Bible.

> From personal experience, I can tell you that I need to have intimacy with God daily in my life to maintain intimacy with my wife.

Do you want to take a spiritual journey with God the Father and with each other? As we've noted, the first step in this togetherness concept is commitment. But don't think ahead to the practicalities and methods of this commitment just yet. Doing so might only serve to stir up religious fears. Instead, just tell each other how committed you are to spiritual intimacy in your marriage.

At this point, take a moment to close this book and talk to your spouse about spiritual intimacy. Don't merely address methods; instead, affirm your commitment to each other and to spiritual intimacy. Since spiritual intimacy is the cornerstone, don't proceed any further until you have both agreed to take this journey together. Use the chart below to record the results of your conversation.

Marital Spiritual Intimacy

Count me in on marital spiritual intimacy. I don't know what we will do yet, but I am committed.

He said: ❏ Yes ❏ No   She said: ❏ Yes ❏ No

Today's date: _____

It's important that both spouses agree to marital spiritual intimacy before a plan is designed to implement your goals. The Bible says, "Do two walk together unless they have agreed to do so?" (Amos 3:3).

Now that you both agree to be committed, you can work out the details together later on when we offer practical suggestions for you as you take this intimate journey with God and your spouse.

> **Intimacy has been an awesome discovery as I've experienced God and my wife, Lisa—who is God's precious daughter.**

Perhaps you haven't prayed together in years or maybe decades. Maybe you have sat side by side at church together for years but have never opened a Bible together. No matter where you are in your relationship, with God all things are possible. Choose to be optimistic, to believe that God desires genuine, satisfying and delightful intimacy for you and your spouse. Later on you will begin to learn how to walk out your commitment.

Intimacy has been an awesome discovery as I've experienced God and my wife, Lisa—who is God's precious daughter. I love growing together spiritually as a couple in the exciting adventure of intimacy.

TWO

Soul Mates: The Joy of Emotional Intimacy

Emotional intimacy is a vital part of your one hundred days to intimacy. It engages the soul, touching, connecting and finding a place of security and permanence in the other where you can rest. It's an aspect of intimacy that is simply delicious. Once you add skills and consistency, you can savor meal after delicious meal of the many enjoyable aspects of your spouse's soul.

My precious Lisa's soul is so delicious and fun that I truly ache when I don't get to connect with her. If I am traveling, and hectic schedules throw us into different time zones so I don't get to connect with my beloved, I really feel unsatisfied.

Lisa is my mate, spirit, soul and body—all three dimensions—and we're friends for life. I'm sharing this with you because I want to whet your appetite for this level of intimacy.

To experience intimacy that touches the depths of human longing doesn't happen by accident. Lisa and I diligently work at nurturing, connecting, honoring and reflecting positively to one another's soul. We've been doing the exercises in this

100-day guide for more than a decade, and I can personally say, they work!

NURTURING EACH OTHER

Nurturing another individual's soul is an effortless gift for some. They glide through their daily activities encouraging the hearts of people they meet all day long. But extracting a kind word from others requires an act of Congress.

Remember the punch line: "I told you I loved you the day I married you. If that changes I'll let you know." We laugh at such thoughts when we hear them. But as a therapist who treats couples, I can tell you that a man or woman who is not nurtured by a spouse becomes a very different person than the one who is nurtured.

I liken the soul of a person to a sponge inside the body. This sponge needs regular watering (or praise) to stay soft and alive. If a spouse decides, for whatever reason, to withhold that praise, the sponge begins to dry out. Over the years and decades if the sponge is not nurtured, that person will become brittle inside. The sponge gets hard and seems to break easily. This will show up in sarcasm, anger, bitterness, rigidity and a lesser ability to give love to the spouse who is withholding the nurturing.

What is nurturing? It is the skill to place praise and affirmation into another person's heart. In the case of a marriage, nurturing is the ability to put that praise and affirmation into the heart of your spouse.

Many of us intuitively understand our responsibility to nurture when it comes to our children. "I love you!" "Great job!" "You're really smart, creative, handsome or beautiful!" The accolades just seem to roll from our hearts and mouths. Rarely does a day go by when my two children don't receive numerous nurturing comments from Dad and Mom. We love to see their little faces light up as we nurture them, clap for them and praise them.

Many of us accept the nurturing of our children as part of our God-given role in their lives. We want ours to be the primary nurturing voices in their lives. We know that if we build them up they become healthier psychologically and more resilient in the face of life's many challenges as they mature.

> To experience intimacy that touches the depths of human longing doesn't happen by accident.

Believe it or not, the same is true of your spouse. Think about it for a minute. God only has children. He doesn't have any adults on planet earth. He is infinite, and we are fortunate to live eighty to one hundred years. Yet, in His eyes we are still just children. I think we make way too much of being *adults*. I am still a big child—how about you? I still need my heavenly Father's help with my life. I am not in control. He is. I am not all-knowing. He is. I am just fine with being a "child" of God forever.

Do you feel that this attitude of "being a child" is ridiculous, that adults don't need nurturing? Let me challenge you with what I discovered in the Father's love letter, the Bible.

At the baptism of Jesus, the Bible says, "And a voice from heaven said, 'This is my Son, whom I love; with him I am well pleased'" (Matt. 3:17). What God chose to say and record about this event gives us insight into His heart.

We see a second snapshot of God the Father talking with Jesus on the Mount of Transfiguration. Matthew 17:5 says, "While he was still speaking, a bright cloud enveloped them, and a voice from the cloud said, 'This is my Son, whom I love; with him I am well pleased. Listen to him!'"

In our modern-day vernacular, God might have said, "This

is My boy. I love Him, and I am so happy with Him!" How interesting! Of everything He could have chosen to say to Jesus, He intentionally nurtured Him. Jesus wasn't needy or psychologically impaired. He was a person, and God can't help but nurture people.

If nurturing Jesus was a priority to God, then nurturing others should be a consistent part of our relationships as well.

Nurturing is the skill or ability to put praise and affirmation into our spouse's heart. Many of us did not grow up with parents who modeled this ability toward each other. Some of us grew up with little or no praise at all from our parents. Many of us cannot recall one positive thing that our mother or father said to us. They may have lacked the skill or were simply negligent in this area of nurturing our souls.

Even fewer of us can recall our father affirming our mother by saying something like, "Your mom is so smart." "Doesn't your mom look really pretty today?"

Neither have many of us heard our mother affirming our father by saying, "I love your dad. He's so generous to others!" "Your dad is really a fun person to be with!"

Personally, I can't recall such positive modeling of adult nurturing in my own family, either. Nevertheless, my past has not and will not determine my present or my future.

I could make more excuses than most people not to apply these behaviors. I was conceived in adultery. I never met my biological father. My legal father was an alcoholic. I was placed in foster homes, experienced abuse and later became multiply addicted. But since Christ came into my heart, excuses went out. Now I truly believe that Christ enables me to succeed in all I do, just as the scripture reads: "I can do everything through him who gives me strength" (Phil. 4:13).

I can and have learned a new set of skills. You too have learned skills throughout your own lifetime. No doubt you have received some level of education, and you have also chosen to do many things differently than your parents did. Learning to nurture others can be just one more thing that you can educate yourself about and create differently for yourself in Christ Jesus. Trust me, if I can learn how to nurture—and my educational experience did not teach me this—then anyone can.

Later on we will discuss in detail how to learn to nurture through very specific and tested principles—principles that have been proven over the past ten years. I honestly believe that we will be accountable for how well we have treated our spouses while on this earth.

I was in a car accident not very long ago, and three questions immediately came to my mind as I lay on the ground wondering if I would survive. Deep down in my heart of hearts, I believe that when I die, I will have to answer these questions.

1. "What did you do with Jesus?"
2. "What did you do with the spouse I gave to you?"
3. "What did you do with the children I gave you?"

I want to get As for my response to all three questions. Don't you?

Most people hope and pray that our children will grow up and find future spouses who will be kind and affirming. Our feelings toward our child's spouse are based upon whether he or she is willfully neglectful or consistently loving and kind toward our loved one.

God is also a father, and He is the father of your spouse. He loves and values your spouse so much that He died for him or her. Now, how do you think God would feel toward you if He knew (and He does) that you were willfully neglecting to nurture and affirm His child—your spouse?

This perspective gives the situation a new twist—at least it does for me. I don't nurture or celebrate Lisa, my wife, based upon how good she is to me or her mood for the day. I base my actions upon who she is to God.

My heavenly Father loves it when I love and nurture Lisa, even when she is in a less-than-wonderful mood. I am responsible to God to nurture her for His sake, not hers. So as you learn the skills you can become a great nurturer. It is a skill that anyone can learn.

CONNECTING EMOTIONALLY

Connecting is fundamental to having and maintaining emotional intimacy. Many of us grew up unskilled emotionally. As a teenager in my home, I can remember that we seemed to express only three emotions. The first emotion we communicated was anger. The second emotion we were allowed to display was "really angry." This was when doors were slammed or something was thrown. The last permitted emotion was what I call "other." *Other* meant, "Leave me alone!" "I'm going for a walk, a drive or a drink." This emotion found some other way to avoid or not process what we felt.

> It is critical that you understand how to express your feelings.

I grew up truly emotionally illiterate. I felt as if I had all these feelings locked up inside of me, but I only had these three exit doors: door number 1—*anger*, door number 2—*really angry* and door number 3—*other*. I went all the way through Bible college and partially through seminary before I really understood that I didn't have a clue as to what I was feeling inside.

I admit that at times I thought it rather odd that I was in this great counseling program but still wasn't being taught how to know and express my own feelings. Many of us have grown up without the ability or skill to identify our feelings.

It is critical that you understand how to express your feelings. Your feelings are like a large engine-powered ocean liner. This engine provides the ship's energy. It pushes it in whatever direction the rudder directs. The rudder is our rational mind. Our emotions have great energy and pressure our minds. If not properly understood, emotions can drive us in such a way that they cause us to crash and be destroyed.

OVERCOMING EMOTIONAL CONSTIPATION

Emotions are powerful. If they have only three outlets as mine did, it can cause "emotional constipation." *Emotional constipation* is when a person has many more feelings than he or she has the skills to express or identify. This constipation will show itself differently in various people. Some fly into rages, while others pout or stop talking to their spouse for days at a time. Regardless of how this constipation manifests, it never moves a couple toward intimacy.

This constipation can be a roadblock to connecting emotionally. Suppose I am in a marriage with only three feeling options: angry, really angry and other. Now suppose that I also marry someone with only three emotional options: angry, really angry and other.

Now the fun begins. Let's suppose that one day I really feel rejected, and I have to decide how to express my "rejected" feeling. After thinking a little bit I may decide that angry would be the best "door" to pick for my rejected feeling. My wife, on the other hand, may feel alone and unimportant, but she chooses the "other" door to express these feelings.

When I come home from work, I'm showing anger (door number one). She is expressing door number three ("other") for her feelings of being alone and unimportant. Now we are off to the races.

This is the emotionally constipated way of communicating.

We are unable to identify our real emotions, but we are still trying to get our points across. If your relationship has ever been there, you know that it can take hours or days to sort through the confusion.

If you don't have the ability to identify your own emotions, then how can you share them with your spouse? You can miss the blessing of sharing yourself emotionally with your spouse, not because of spitefulness, but simply because you honestly don't know how.

Again, this goes back to a skill that was never developed. The good thing about this problem is that the solution is simply a skill issue that can be learned! It took a little time for me to learn my own feelings, but once I did, our miscommunication problem happened much less. I truly can't remember when we had our last big emotionally constipated disagreement.

Once you complete this skill-building program you will be able to better identify your own feelings and effectively share them with your spouse. You will truly be amazed at how emotionally connected you can become in a very short period of time when you are faithful to do the exercises provided in the back of this book. You will find that overcoming emotional constipation will dramatically help you to build and maintain connectedness or emotional intimacy.

We all need emotional connectedness—and I do mean *need*! Weary is the soul that has no one with whom to share. We all need someone who will hear us. Being able to share yourself and to be heard are basic, legitimate God-given needs. Your need for emotional connectedness is no less legitimate than your need for food and water. When you genuinely accept this as truth you will be able to take responsibility to make sure that your own needs and your spouses' needs are met on a regular basis.

I remember when Tom and Kathryn, an older couple from the Northeast, attended their first counseling session with me. Tom was an engineer for over thirty-five years. He was a godly man who loved the Lord, his wife and his children. If you knew Tom, you would probably agree that he was a pragmatic, smart man who knew his Bible well. After all the children grew up and left home, Kathryn decided they needed to come for counseling. She was not feeling nurtured. She might have phrased it like this: "I feel dry inside. I don't really know what is going on inside of Tom. He doesn't talk to me."

> You can miss the blessing of sharing yourself emotionally with your spouse, not because of spitefulness, but simply because you honestly don't know how.

I knew exactly what Kathryn was trying to communicate. Tom did not know how to share his feelings with her. Now, in Tom's defense, he grew up on a farm in Missouri as one of seven children, five of whom were boys. He grew up poor and worked hard. His family didn't discuss their feelings, just what farm work needed to get done. His parents were good people, but they left Tom with no emotional skills.

Tom went off to college, worked his way through an engineering program and enjoyed a successful career at an engineering firm. Unlike psychology, the field of engineering never requires you to discuss your feelings or to develop emotionally during the learning process. In Tom's career feelings were irrelevant.

On the other hand, Kathryn had grown up freely expressing her feelings. As one of three sisters, she talked about her feelings all the time. When Kathryn married Tom she was full of love and devotion. She felt alone in the earlier years of the marriage until she had her children. Then she threw herself into raising her son and daughter. Tom provided well, and they functioned well together as parents and church members.

Now that the children were gone, Kathryn was again feeling as disconnected and alone as she felt in the earlier years of her marriage. She couldn't face looking at twenty-five or more years of feeling alone in marriage again.

Tom loved Kathryn, but he didn't understand what she needed. I tried to help. "Kathryn is like the engine of your car, Tom," I told him. "You wouldn't let your engine go without oil, would you?"

> By honoring emotions, you assert that they are a real, valuable, precious part of the person you love.

Tom said no. A good engineer couldn't imagine such a thing.

"If you let your oil go, eventually your engine will make all kinds of unpleasant, strange-sounding noises. Eventually it would just freeze up and stop working, wouldn't it?"

Tom said, "Of course."

I explained that his wife needs to have emotional oil in her engine to run properly—the way God intended. "Tom," I continued, "if you don't give her the oil, eventually funny noises will happen, and one day the engine will just quit."

After equipping Tom with the skills he needed to connect emotionally with his wife, they were well on their way to emotional intimacy. Tom realized that not only did his wife have emotional needs, but he also needed to connect and share. What a positive difference connectedness made in Tom and Kathryn's lives.

HONORING EMOTIONS

To acquire the skills necessary for emotional intimacy we must shift the way we think about emotions. We must learn to honor them. By honoring emotions, you assert that they are a real, valuable, precious part of the person you love. These feelings are an essential part of your spouse's being.

As human beings we can think and behave differently than we feel, but we can't feel differently than we feel. Here is an illustration to help you understand this better. Think of a person at work whose behavior irritates you deep down inside. When you're with him, you act and behave appropriately so that no one knows how you really feel. If that person were to come into your office and ask you to tell him honestly how you "feel" about him, you would be honest and share the truth. At that point he would know about you and your feelings toward him.

I say this to illustrate that our emotions are who we are. If I feel tired, then I am tired. That is who I am at that microsecond of time. Now here is the tricky part. Feelings may be real, and a real part of who I am, but they are not necessarily truth, and they change constantly.

Early in my career as a therapist I authored my first book, and things seemed to be going well for me at the time. We were in the process of shooting two large national television shows per month, and financially everything was solid. One night I remember crawling into bed, and as is our custom, we began sharing our feelings.

"I want to share a feeling that makes no sense," I told Lisa. "It isn't true, but for whatever unknown reason, I am feeling it today. I feel unsuccessful."

Lisa honored my feelings as a feeling and didn't try to fix it, change it or rationalize it away.

The unsuccessful feeling was just a feeling—nothing more,

nothing less. All of our feelings change constantly. Most of us can barely recall even a few of the feelings we had a week ago.

Learning to honor your spouse's feelings places you in a precarious balance. When you hear your spouse's feelings, you must honor them immediately. They are precious offerings to you at the time of sharing. However, you must resist the temptation to change, alter or rationalize away what he or she may be feeling at the moment. Our spouses will not feel any one particular feeling forever. Feelings change, and being honored and heard are very important.

Men in particular have more difficulty just sharing feelings instead of trying to solve problems. But as you grow in the skill of sharing, hearing and honoring the feelings of your spouse, the quality of emotional intimacy soars. When I feel safe and honored as I share my feelings, I am more likely to keep sharing them with others as well.

When you decide to honor your spouse emotionally on a regular basis, you will begin to see your spouse as the best person on earth to be with. I know that I can share any feelings with Lisa and still feel accepted by her. When she honors my emotions, it makes me feel special, important and loved by my wife.

Your spouse and his or her emotions are ever changing. Honoring your spouse's emotions without feeling the need to fix them or fix the situation will produce enormous positive fruit in your relationship. So make a decision to travel through the next one hundred days together honoring your spouse's emotions and cherishing the person he or she is on the inside.

THREE

Physical Intimacy: A Lifelong Celebration

The world we live in is definitely a physical one, and God certainly knew what He was doing when He created Adam and Eve. He made these crowning masterpieces of His work to be able to walk, talk, taste, smell, see and hear the physical world He created for them.

The physical world is a great place. I love to climb the mountains and see the jagged rocks, the icy brooks and smell the pines in Colorado where I live. I love the fact that I can hug and play with my children.

I realize that the physical world has its limitations since sin entered the world through Adam. We have sickness, diseases and just plain old bad days because of the bodies in which we live. Still, our bodies are a wonderful gift for experiencing intimacy with our spouses.

NONSEXUAL INTIMACY— THE POWER OF TOUCHING

We can experience incredible intimacy through the thousands of nerves placed in our physical bodies. Each of us needs to be hugged daily to feel good about ourselves. Touch is so important that infants who lack physical affection do not thrive.

Psychologists generally agree that as humans we need—not just want—physical touch. Nonsexual touch is extremely important.

This is especially true in a marriage. A couple who regularly touches one another by holding hands, hugging, kissing and giving an occasional pat on the back has mastered this much-needed nonsexual physical intimacy.

Even men need to be hugged, kissed and enjoyed physically by their wives. Did you grow up without any of your physical intimacy needs being met? Many people do. If so, you may have a deficit in the area of physical touch, as well as a skewed perception of the value of physical touch. Fortunately, God often puts an individual who hasn't been touched together with a spouse who likes to be touched and likes to touch. This gift is not always received well and can even be a source of contention. This was exactly the case in the following story.

Mary Alice is a fifty-six-year-old secretary who has worked most of her life. She grew up in a Mennonite home in Pennsylvania where everyone did his chores, got good grades, walked the straight and narrow road and, of course, went to church. She really couldn't remember hugs or kisses from her family as she grew up.

Mary Alice worked in a local office in town and met Daniel, a fine Christian man who sold insurance. Danny, as everyone called him, grew up quite differently. He was hugged, touched regularly and kissed often, even throughout his teenage years. Hugging Mom, Dad, sister or brother was normal for Danny.

Danny and Mary Alice fell in love and married after a couple years of dating. Soon into the marriage it became obvious that they thought very differently about physical intimacy. Sex was OK with Mary Alice because she believed that was her Christian duty toward her husband, but she wanted no part of Danny's desire to hug, kiss and be playful.

If Danny hugged Mary Alice, she froze up. When he kissed her, not only would she not respond, she would actually recoil. She could not initiate a spontaneous touch, hug or kiss toward Danny. He didn't understand his wife's coldness; however, he knew that she loved him.

> Even men need to be hugged, kissed and enjoyed physically by their wives.

Three years went by and Mary Alice told him that she felt the only reason he hugged her and wanted her attention was for sex. Although he adamantly disagreed, she sincerely believed she knew "the real truth." After their second child came along, Danny gave up on trying to be physically close with his wife. He stopped asking for hugs and kisses and was no longer physically playful. He was faithful to her, but deep down he began to get angry.

He told me, "I felt an ache I couldn't get to." He got massages occasionally at the health center, which seemed to scratch his itch to be touched for awhile, but the anger didn't go away.

Danny stayed married, stayed faithful and stayed mad. He had been experiencing touch deprivation for almost three decades, and felt increasingly vulnerable to get into an affair in order to get his touching needs met.

His issue wasn't sex; it was touch. Through counseling, Mary Alice was convinced to try nonsexual touch. Under the guidelines that Danny could not use it to initiate sex, she felt safe to experiment physically. Eventually Mary Alice not only accepted Danny's need for legitimate nonsexual touching, but she began to discover her own needs for touch as well.

Mary Alice made the turn when she realized, "Why should he get all the touching? What about me?" This couple was on their way to restoring physical nonsexual intimacy. Danny was genuinely grateful for the spontaneous kisses of his wife. Mary Alice repeated to me what he told her: "My husband wants to say thank you for giving him a new wife." We laughed and thanked God for the healing that took place in their lives.

Touch deprivation is painfully real today in marriages. Some couples touch only during sex. How sad when God has given us the wonderful gift of our physical bodies with which to enjoy each other. Touch is a great way to express intimacy. Fewer things are better than a time of cuddling or massaging or scratching your spouse's back.

Physical touch is important not only for your marriage, but also for the quality of your children's marriages. Are you modeling the kind of affection to your spouse that you want your sons and daughters to give and receive in their marriages?

At this point, evaluate the place of physical touch has in your relationship with your spouse. Spend some time together discussing your answers.

1. Is physical touch mostly associated with sexual advances?
2. Do you have consistent patterns of hugging, holding hands and kissing?
3. Do you ever just hang out and touch each other?
4. Does one person give much more touch than the other?
5. Does one person do almost all the initiation of touch?

6. Have your children laughed lately because of a spontaneous show of your affection to your spouse?
7. Is touch a much-needed area for improvement in your marriage?
8. Are you committed to working on physical touch in your relationship for the next one hundred days?

SEXUAL INTIMACY— THE MARITAL HOLY OF HOLIES

Sexual intimacy is the ability to engage your spouse spiritually, emotionally and physically. It is the holy of holies of your relationship. Sexual intimacy allows us to know and be known in a way that no other person knows us.

> Fewer things are better than a time of cuddling or massaging or scratching your spouse's back.

Sexual intimacy can be the greatest connection that a man and woman can experience here on earth. This pleasuring and exploring of each other is God's will and God's design.

Have you ever thought about the thousands of changes your body goes through during the sexual act? Your organs become enlarged, fluids change, nerves are excited and pleasure is experienced at an almost traumatic rate. God designed this. He designed our bodies so that we could enjoy the ultimate pleasure within a marriage. This was His idea, and I personally think it was one of His better ones!

Sexuality is such an integral part of who you are. Sharing yourself physically, emotionally and spiritually is the deepest level of intimacy that you can experience with your mate.

Sexual intimacy is the ultimate way of giving of yourself to another.

I will discuss some biblical and practical truths about sexuality to optimize sexual intimacy between a husband and wife later in chapter 11 of this book. Also in chapter 6 we will talk about sexual issues that can limit a couple's sexual connectedness.

GOD'S BEST SEX

God created sex for procreation, but He also designed it for our enjoyment as well. Sexuality is a core part of each person's God-given role here on earth. God intended that sexuality be experienced exclusively in marriage. His Word is full of cautions about lust, sexual fornication and adultery. Sexual sin is a part of the Ten Commandments: "You shall not commit adultery" (Deut. 5:18).

> Sexual intimacy can be the greatest connection that a man and woman can experience here on earth.

God sees sex as sacred and holy, having the innate power to bond a husband and wife into a unit to raise godly children. When sexuality is experienced within these proper guidelines, any couple can enjoy great sexual satisfaction.

When I speak at conferences on God's best sex, I am continually floored at how uptight believers are about sex. Just saying the word sex from the pulpit can bring all kinds of funny looks. When I share that almost everyone in the Bible (except a few people) had sex, to my amazement I discover that few people have ever even considered such a thing. Many don't think of Moses, Isaiah and Peter as sexual beings. Even the mother of our Savior, Mary, had sex with Joseph after Jesus was born and produced other children. Throughout time, saints of God have enjoyed sex. Many of them had the same kinds of conversations and experiences with their spouses that you have had. It's liberating to realize that many godly people have enjoyed sexual intimacy!

Where do you believe God is when you are having sex with your partner? When I ask that question at conferences, it surprises people. Does He close His eyes? Does He put black patches over certain areas of your anatomy? No. Of course not! He can see, and He is not ashamed of you or your sexuality. He made it for the both of you to help you to enjoy one another.

God is not hung up about sex. Nothing in the Bible even suggests that God does not want a married couple to have a good time.

THREE-DIMENSIONAL SEX

God's best sex within the marriage relationship is what I call "triune" or "three-dimensional sex." It involves regular physical, spiritual and emotional intimacy with your spouse. If you do not share spiritual and emotional intimacy, yet expect fireworks within your sexual relationship, then you are just kidding yourself. Anything less is simply one-dimensional sex.

One-dimensional physical sex is what I call "squirt gun" sex. It's simply two bodies having physical sex, but their spirits and souls are not connecting.

Three-dimensional sex is what I call "atomic bomb" sex. The intensity of all three dimensions of your beings touching and experiencing sex is explosive and will make you want to be spiritually and emotionally close regularly. This kind of sex will keep you together for life, and it gets better and better over the years.

If you would like to experience sexual intimacy at a three-dimensional level, follow the three guidelines detailed below (complete the emotional and spiritual exercises daily).

Principle 1—Eyes open

When you and your spouse are being sexually intimate, keep your eyes open, beholding each other. During sex your brain sends the highest level of endorphins and enkephalins to the excitement center of your brain. It is the highest chemical reward your brain gets for anything. This reward attaches to whatever you are looking at and creates what I call "sex glue." Psychologically you will attach to what you are looking at.

> God sees sex as sacred and holy, having the innate power to bond a husband and wife into a unit to raise godly children.

Some couples keep their eyes closed, disconnect or fantasize about something else during this intimate time of sexual intimacy. This limits their sexual connecting. Sexual connecting is God's will, but your spouse provides what you need to connect. Practice this. It may feel unfamiliar at first, but before long you may begin to experience what some of my clients have called "the best sex of our life!"

Principle 2—Lights on

Keeping some kind of light on during sexual encounters is also important, for it allows you to see each other. If women really understood that whatever a man looks at while having sex is what he bonds to, they would never again feel plagued by concerns over body image. You see, it doesn't matter what imperfections he may see. He will bond to what he looks at. No matter what your body type is, he will like it.

Isn't that great? God knew what He was doing. If you do it right and bond to your wife, thirty years later when she walks into a room with jeans and a T-shirt on, you will say, "Thank

You, Jesus!" So I encourage you both to keep some lights on and maintain eye contact.

PRINCIPLE 3—NURTURING CONVERSATION

During sexual intercourse, be as open and vulnerable as you can be spiritually, emotionally and physically. During this time nurture your spouse with phrases such as, "I love you. You are special, handsome, beautiful and a great lover." Such words will go straight into your spouse's very heart of hearts. Sexual intimacy is fertile soil into which to plant the flowers of praise and celebration in your spouse. When you get really good at nurturing each other, the good feelings that flood your spirit and soul will blow you away as your body is being pleasured by your lover and spouse. This is the kind of sexual intimacy God intended.

You won't have to beg your spouse to be sexual if this is the time when you flood him or her with praise. I've never had one client who practiced these three principles during sexual intimacy who ever went back to lights off, eyes closed and no conversation.

That shut-off type of sexual interaction is "fast food" sex. It may qualify for sex (food), but it is nothing compared to what you can have. You can enjoy a "five-star meal" with sexual intimacy as you practice these principles during your sexual encounters.

EMBRACING YOUR SEXUAL PERSONALITIES

Issues pertaining to sexual preferences, sexual appetites and sexual differences often come up during marriage counseling sessions. At these times I like to bring up what I call "sexual personalities."

Our sexual personality is often very similar to our nonsexual personality. If you marry a woman who drives the speed limit, doesn't take many risks and is pretty conservative in her beliefs and behaviors, don't expect her sexual personality to be exotic or bizarre. She probably won't be what you created in your imagination as a teenager. She will be herself.

Men, take a minute here and think about this. Is your wife more conservative in her approach to life, or more appetite driven? Is she a risk taker? Is she loud? Whatever her personality is outside the bedroom, it will most likely be her personality inside your bedroom, regardless of your preconceived notions of what she should be. She is who she is. Accepting her sexual personality will give you a better perspective of your precious spouse.

> If you marry a woman who drives the speed limit, doesn't take many risks and is pretty conservative in her beliefs and behaviors, don't expect her sexual personality to be exotic or bizarre.

Ladies, if you married a man who likes to take risks, drives fast, lives on the edge and is creative in his work and life, then these characteristics may also be a part of his sexual personality. If such traits do not reflect his personality outside the bedroom, then I doubt that he would be different in the bedroom.

Having laid that groundwork, now the fun begins! Often men or women who take risks and have more aggressive personalities are attracted to more stable spouses who do not seek the limelight. You can see how these personalities compliment each other in most areas of life. When it comes to sex, both the husband and wife will desire sexual expression that is congruent with their personalities.

Your partner's personality is a gift that can balance your

sexual intimacy as a couple. Accepting each other as a gift is important in this process of negotiating what your sexual expression can be. Both personalities are challenged to grow and yet stay true to themselves. Genuine balance can take years to negotiate. This is especially true when a couple polarizes, which occurs when each demands to be right instead of both personalities growing sexually into oneness.

We will get more specific about solutions and negotiations with sexuality later in the guide. For now I simply want to make you aware of sexual personalities and how they rarely differ from our nonsexual personalities.

UNDERSTANDING THE STAGES OF SEXUAL DEVELOPMENT

All of us continue to develop sexually throughout our entire lives. Some of us experience healthy, informed growth. Unfortunately, for others sexuality has suffered because of being misinformed about sex as they developed.

Let's look at three basic developmental stages of sexuality. Depending on the individual's emotional or behavioral development, an adult can sexually be in any one of these three stages. When we discuss a "sexual child" or "sexual adolescent," we are referring to an adult who exhibits behaviors or attitudes from this stage. This is very important, for not everyone who is an adult physically is automatically an adult spiritually, emotionally, financially or sexually.

STAGE ONE—SEXUAL CHILDHOOD

An adult whose behavior and emotions are consistent with that of a child's, regardless of his or her age, will have beliefs about sex that are childlike. An adult who behaves as a child doesn't really understand that he or she is a sexual being.

Such individuals tend to avoid sexual responsibility in their marriages. They rely on their spouse to initiate all sex and often put it off as much as possible. Adults who behave as children feel nonsexual. They are uncomfortable, awkward and even ashamed when discussing sex. The notion that others might think that they are having sex would be very disconcerting, even if they have children. They neither want to read about it nor learn about it. They refuse to grow, experiment or explore sexually.

> Adults behaving as sexual children make it difficult for their spouses to reach higher levels of sexual intimacy. If you find yourself in these descriptions, try to reach beyond your fears and awkwardness so that you and your spouse can enjoy sexual adulthood together.

The husband or wife in stage one whose behavior exhibits a sexual child gets very emotional and unreasonable when sex is discussed, even in a therapy session. Adults at age twenty, thirty, forty or older can be stuck at stage one as a sexual child. If this individual doesn't want to talk about sexuality, he or she won't, and that's that!

Adults behaving as sexual children make it difficult for their spouses to reach higher levels of sexual intimacy. If you find yourself in these descriptions, try to reach beyond your fears and awkwardness so that you and your spouse can enjoy sexual adulthood together.

STAGE TWO—SEXUAL ADOLESCENCE

Those at stage two, the adolescent stage of sexual development, are all too willing to be sexual. They enjoy sex, but sex is primarily about them having a good time. Sexual adolescents are much more focused on their own pleasure.

This individual refers to the sex act as "it," "some" and other object-type terms. When sexual needs are not met when this person feels they ought to be, he or she may pout or get angry.

The husband or wife at the sexual adolescent stage rarely considers the thoughts, feelings or sexual needs of the other spouse. In addition, the sexual adolescent is not beyond using emotional or physical bullying to manipulate the partner into having sex.

Those stuck at stage two are often disconnected emotionally and spiritually during the sex act. They are capable of one-dimensional sex only, and believe that more is better.

Sexual adolescents can damage their spouse and actually train them not to enjoy sex. The husband or wife who is behaving as a sexual adolescent can grow beyond this stage, but it usually takes work to promote his or her heart and beliefs to sexual adulthood.

STAGE THREE—SEXUAL ADULTHOOD

Mature sexual adults accept their sexuality. They understand that sex is a normal ongoing and committed part of an adult marriage. They accept their fair share of sexual initiation in the marriage. Sexual adults give themselves spirit, soul and body and receive their partner's sexuality as well.

A sexual adult couple recognizes that they will enjoy sex thousands of times throughout a lifetime together. Mature sexual adults learn to communicate their sexual needs, desires and preferences, and they can be creative during sexual encounters within the limits of their personalities. Feelings about sexuality can be discussed without shaming, blaming or belittling the other spouse.

Manipulation is unnecessary to get sexual needs met.

Sexual adults can keep their word and follow through with their sexual promises and agreements.

Sexuality can be a real blessing when both husband and wife are in stage three as sexual adults. They can talk about sex, negotiate with each other about sex and hear each other during a sexual dialogue.

Of course, reaching sexual adulthood—as with spiritual, emotional or financial adulthood—takes time, correct information and a willingness to grow. As we read earlier, all things are possible in Christ Jesus. He can carry us from stage one through stage three into sexual adulthood. His grace, love and patience are with us as we ask Him to change us, and they are available to all who ask.

God can help you to attain sexual adulthood. Even if your sexual journey has been challenging, your soul will rest when both you and your spouse are at stage three of sexual adulthood.

Mature sexual adults learn to communicate their sexual needs, desires and preferences.

Don't use this information about the stages of sexuality as ammunition to aim at your spouse. Instead, use it for your own self-awareness. If areas of your spouse's sexual struggle have been revealed, use this information as points of prayer, not points of manipulation.

In my own life, I laid down my sexuality before the Lord Jesus Christ and made Him Lord of it. It was at that point that I realized I was really free. When I have issues about sex, I don't talk to my wife first. I talk to my God. He is able to change me or change her or change us both. This is the quickest way to remove sexual blocks and hindrances between couples.

Both you and your spouse need to yield your sexuality to God as you mature sexually. You are probably going to have sex for the rest of your life. Sexual intimacy is a journey, not a destination. As you walk out that journey together, learning to balance your sexual personalities, personal preferences and sexual maturity, you will soon discover that you never arrive. Sexual intimacy is a constantly evolving, wonderful journey of exploring and celebrating each other all the days of your life.

Please, pray with me.

> Jesus, I want what You want for my spouse and me sexually. I want to be as sexually mature as You can make me. Please intervene in my life and marriage, and open my eyes of understanding to sexually love, accept and nurture my spouse. Amen.

PART TWO

Roadblocks to Intimacy

FOUR

The Anger Enemy

Small infractions caused by a couple's sins and unresolved conflicts during the course of a marriage create roadblocks to intimacy. The onslaught of trauma experienced by other couples causes deep, destructive rifts.

Neglect and abuse, which accompany addictions to alcohol, drugs, sex, food and work, can seriously damage the spouse married to an addict. Lies, empty promises and the rollercoaster rides that typify these addictive marriages create truly indescribable pain.

The scarring of physical and mental abuse causes more than just a buildup of painful events—it often causes legitimate rage. The effects of sexual infidelity, rape and child abuse will most certainly traumatize any marriage, even those appearing to be very religious. Although such things "should" not happen in Christian marriages, I know they do.

On the other side of abuse is neglect. Neglect is more common in Christian marriages seeking help. Prayerlessness in a

Christian couple's relationship is definitely a form of neglect. I cannot tell you how many women have come to my office over the years complaining about the lack of connection with their spouse.

Refusing to share your heart, coupled with an absence of prayer and praise over the decades, will create a silent anger, an internal rage within your spouse. This serious roadblock stunts the growth of trust and intimacy and can create real problems down the road for the couple who remains together.

Adulterous situations throw a spouse into a traumatic situation that he or she must then attempt to handle. To expect the spouse in an adulterous situation to simply move on and put the matter behind him or her minimizes the trauma. Adultery affects the spirit, soul and body, creating deep wounds in one or both spouses.

This type of wounding requires time to heal. Saying "I am sorry" will not make the pain disappear. I have personally experienced several traumas throughout my life prior to my marriage. My soul was wounded before I became married. So I am personally aware of how trauma affects the ability to be intimate.

In many relationships, trust has been broken, decency has been violated and healing must take place in the soul of the wounded spouse. This individual is thrust into a paradoxical situation. Unfortunately the person whom he or she loves the most may also be the one with whom he is most angry and for good reason. This is an internal controversy that says, "I love you" and "I'd like to pound you!" all at the same time.

If you are a wounded spouse, the perpetrator is responsible for your feelings. Yet, the responsibility to heal is yours. If I happened to walk outside and a sniper randomly shot me, I would be responsible to heal and repair from the damage of this event. I'm the one who would have to do what the doctor or physical therapist advised if I wanted to be restored. The following story will help make my point more clear.

Jake and Fran are a couple who had been married for over forty years. He drank some, and on a couple of occasions he physically abused Fran and sexually forced himself on her, which is rape. They had children, and Jake became a workaholic. As a salesman he traveled three to five days a week, abandoning his wife with the children.

While Jake was traveling, he had several affairs that Fran found out about much later. Jake had a born-again experience after their last child left home to attend college. He changed completely and began to live a genuine Christian life of integrity. Jake stopped traveling, and he and Fran began working at improving their marriage. Although both were Christians (she had prayed for him for years), they struggled with intimacy.

Jake protested, "She just won't forgive me for the past. I am a new creature now!" He cited 2 Corinthians 5:17, "Therefore, if anyone is in Christ, he is a new creation: the old has gone, the new has come!"

Fran continued to feel stuck in her past feelings. She verbalized her forgiveness, but she still felt that she couldn't totally trust him and didn't appear to want to connect intimately with him.

Fran's past wounding needed to be healed before intimacy could take place. Such pain goes far deeper than merely seeking forgiveness for past offenses. This spouse needed support, not criticism, to get through this.

Alan and Barb were another wounded couple that needed healing.

Alan and Barb are a Christian couple with a middle-class income. In the earlier days of the marriage, Barb was an out-of-control shopper. Today she says, "I was definitely a shop-a-holic! I didn't even need the stuff that I would buy. I just shopped to try not to feel anything and to make myself feel better."

Barb constantly berated Alan, who was in his twenties at the time, because they couldn't afford the bigger car, a larger house and couldn't live like some of their forty-year-old friends who traveled all the time. She would shame him and was constantly critical of him. She conveyed the messages "You're not good enough," "You'll never measure up," "I'm not proud of you."

> Regardless of the past, healing can take place. It requires work and patience, but the results are nothing short of marvelous.

Alan really took these messages to heart! He spent more than fifteen years climbing the ladder to success and rarely received praise for all of his hard work. Alan and Barb were both Christians during their entire marriage. Years later, Barb was convicted about her spending behavior, which she felt was an addiction. She went to therapy and group counseling and had not relapsed with shopping for a long time.

From the outside everything looked good. But on the inside Alan was distant, continued to mistrust his wife and did not feel loved by her. He stated he has tried many times to forgive her, but he still battles with outbursts of rage during which he will say regretful things to her and stay distant from her for days.

Alan had hidden anger. The wounds his wife inflicted on him had built up inside over years. He was understandably angry about the painful events that took place in his marriage. He loved his wife, but didn't feel as if he really liked her. Alan didn't want to deal with the trust issues he had involving Barb. He felt sorry following blowout arguments and truly wanted to know his wife the way Christ wants him to. Nevertheless, he kept hitting what he called "the walls." "I just can't let her in," he said in our counseling sessions.

Is Alan truly not forgiving Barb, or is he trying to punish

her? I don't believe he is doing either. Alan experienced trauma throughout his years of marriage because of his wife's behavior and has internalized legitimate anger. This hidden anger (hidden even to Alan) is now a roadblock to intimacy with his wife, whom deep down he truly loves.

Anger is a familiar problem in many marriages, and it must be taken seriously as you strive to be intimate with your spouse. Only when wounds inside a relationship are identified and addressed biblically can healing begin to take place. When wounds are healed, a totally new level of intimacy can follow.

A spouse may have entered into a marriage with wounds from the past, and new wounds may occur during the marriage. In other marriages, both partners may be wounded. For example, when a husband and wife survive the same car accident, each may have his own physical bruises, bandages and pain. As they sleep together in the same bed, when one turns over the other cries out in pain. Emotional pain responds the same.

Silent anger about your wounds can block intimacy, even when you long for it in your marriage. You can be healed from inner pain, regardless of the source. Once you identify the roadblock and take responsibility for your own healing, you can begin to move forward once again.

I have seen many courageous men and women identify and receive healing from the wounds that their spouses have inflicted on them. All forms of abuse, neglect, infidelity, addictions and shame can be successfully overcome with the desire to do so.

Regardless of the past, healing can take place. It requires work and patience, but the results are nothing short of marvelous. As a Christian counselor I have witnessed the healing of deep wounds and broken marriages. I have watched as couples reclaimed intimacy and once again became vibrant and sexually passionate. We serve a great God, and as a colaborer with Him, all things are possible.

The following exercise, called "cleansing the temple," is designed to help you get free from past hurts and wounds. I have witnessed tremendous grace come into the hearts of those who follow this exercise.

CLEANSING THE TEMPLE

This exercise can remove a lot of the pain that you may carry in your soul. This pain may be from your family of origin and caused by neglect, abuse or abandonment. It may be from childhood sexual abuse or rape. Some pain carried in your soul is from your spouse. In some marriages, spouses traumatize one another or deprive one another to such a degree that their anger seems overwhelming.

> Although I didn't cause this mess I was in, I was still 100 percent responsible to clean it up.

Anger can build up in your soul until the size of your wound makes intimacy extremely difficult. Even though you did not cause the wounds, you are now responsible to receive healing for them. Similar to walking outside and getting shot by a sniper, you are 100 percent responsible to receive healing from your wounds, even though the sniper is 100 percent responsible for causing the wound.

In our culture, victim status is power. This power is wielded through manipulation to make other people pay, or it is used as an excuse to abdicate responsibility for yourself or the direction of your life.

I can attest as much as anyone else to the fact that life can be painful and some people enjoy creating pain for others. I was conceived in adultery. My conception caused a divorce in my mother's first marriage. She then married my legal father, who was an alcoholic, and they divorced after having three girls. My three half-sisters and I were placed separately into several foster homes for the next few years. My mom eventually took us back out of the foster homes in our early adolescence. I was abused at about fourteen years of age. I could go on, but I think you get the point. My soul has seen some painful days.

Even as I child I realized that, although I didn't cause this mess I was in, I was still 100 percent responsible to clean it up. I believed that God would be with me in my healing process, but I had to be obedient and not allow the pain from the past to justify not becoming all that I could be.

If you need to be healed from similar issues, what I am about to ask you to do is going to require difficult work. I could not be as intimate and open with my wife, Lisa, today had I not cleaned up the past anger I harbored during the early years of our marriage. If you have wounds that others have afflicted upon your life, follow through with the homework assigned.

The cleansing the temple exercise has its roots in the biblical examples in which Jesus cleansed the temple. The account of this is found in each Gospel. You would do well to take a moment and study each account. The recordings in Scripture of this event are as follows.

> Jesus entered the temple and drove out all who were buying and selling there. He overturned the tables of the money changers and the benches of those selling doves.
> —Matthew 21:12

> On reaching Jerusalem, Jesus entered the temple area and began driving out those who were buying and selling there. He overturned the tables of the money changers and the benches of those selling doves.
> —Mark 11:15

> Then he entered the temple area and began driving out those who were selling.
> —LUKE 19:45

> In the temple courts he found men selling cattle, sheep and doves, and others sitting at tables exchanging money. So he made a whip out of cords, and drove all from the temple area, both sheep and cattle; he scattered the coins of the money changers and overturned their tables. To those who sold doves he said, "Get these out of here! How dare you turn my Father's house into a market!"
> —JOHN 2:14–16

Each of these accounts contains the principles of the cleansing the temple exercise. First we will review the four major principles, and then we will walk through the practical application. The following scripture will be our text for this exercise.

> When it was almost time for the Jewish Passover, Jesus went up to Jerusalem. In the temple courts he found men selling cattle, sheep and doves, and others sitting at tables exchanging money. So he made a whip out of cords and drove all from the temple area, both sheep and cattle; he scattered the coins of the money changers and overturned their tables. To those who sold doves he said, "Get these out of here! How dare you turn my Father's house into a market!"
>
> His disciples remembered that it is written: "Zeal for your house will consume me." Then the Jews demanded of him, "What miraculous sign can you show us to prove your authority to do all this?" Jesus answered them, "Destroy this temple, and I will raise it again in three days." The Jews replied, "It has taken forty-six years to build this temple, and you are going to raise it in three days?" But the temple he had spoken of was his body. After he was raised from the dead, his disciples recalled

what he had said. Then they believed the Scripture and the words that Jesus had spoken.
—John 2:13–22

BIBLICAL PRINCIPLES

Principle 1—He knew the temple needed to be cleansed.

In most accounts of Jesus cleansing the temple, the *temple* refers to a physical building in Jerusalem. But in John's account Jesus refers to His body. John 2:18–21 says,

> Then the Jews demanded of him, "What miraculous sign can you show us to prove your authority to do all this?" And Jesus answered, "Destroy this temple, and I will raise it again in three days." The Jews replied, "It has taken forty-six years to build this temple, and you are going to raise it in three days?" But the temple he had spoken of was His body.

This is the first insight into the fact that Jesus was changing the dwelling place of God from the physical temple to the temple of a human being. Paul develops this thought a little later when he records that Christian believers are God's temple.

> Don't you know that you yourselves are God's temple and that God's Spirit lives in you? If anyone destroys God's temple, God will destroy him; for God's temple is sacred, and *you* are that temple.
> —1 Corinthians 3:16–17, emphasis added

God's plan all along was to dwell inside of us. We are His holy temple. This being true, temples can become defiled through many avenues, including manipulation, abuse and neglect from others. When we get defiled through life, our temple gets defiled also and needs to get cleaned out as well.

It's interesting that Jesus, the owner of the temple, was the one who took full responsibility to clean His own temple. He could have made the moneychangers and sellers of doves who were the perpetrators in the story clean up their own mess, but He didn't. He cleansed the temple.

We are the possessors of our temple. If your temple gets defiled through the abuse of others, you are the one who must clean it up. You are actually the only one who can clean your temple.

Even if it was your spouse who has caused the defilement, he or she cannot clean it out of your temple. Your partner can say he is sorry, but that doesn't get rid of the muck or defilement that has been placed inside your soul. You must clean up the mess. By cleaning His own temple, Jesus sends a clear message to us: We are responsible to clean our own temples as well.

Principle 2—He identified the sin that caused the defilement.

John's rendition of this Gospel event was as follows: Jesus stated, "Get these out of here! How dare you turn my Father's house into a market!" (2:16). In Luke 19:46, Jesus' words are slightly stronger: "'It is written,' he said to them, 'My house will be a house of prayer;' but you have made it 'a den of robbers.'" Mark 11:17 and Matthew 21:13 are very similar.

Jesus made it very clear to them why He was cleansing the temple. They were taking something holy and misusing it to profit themselves. Most of the people who have hurt you have no concept of your holiness or preciousness. You have felt used or abused during the incidents in which you were wounded. You will need to identify the sin or damage that has been done to you by those who have defiled your temple.

Principle 3—He engaged His anger at the injustice.

Jesus was able to engage His anger at the injustice both verbally and physically. Turning over the tables probably created quite a scene. I am sure that is why the Jews challenged His authority to create such a ruckus.

Jesus wasn't merely having a bad day. This was an act of His will. It was a well thought out act of obedience. This is an important point to understand, because it will take an act of your will to clean your temple. Once you walk through the rest of the exercises, I believe that it will become an act of obedience as well.

How do I know this was a premeditated act on Jesus' part? Look at John's account of the cleansing of the temple. "In the temple courts he found men selling cattle, sheep and doves, and others sitting at tables exchanging money. So He made a whip out of cords" (John 2:14–15). This passage gives us the sense that Jesus was looking around and witnessing the peoples' mistreatment of His holy temple. Then, in verse 15, He gets a bunch of cords, and He takes the time to make a whip. Now I don't know how long it took Jesus to make a whip, maybe minutes or hours, but He had already decided to use that whip when He entered His temple to cleanse it.

As we proceed with this exercise, you will need to make choices to prioritize your time to prepare for cleansing your temple. Those who go about this intentionally and purposefully have received great breakthroughs in their lives.

Principle 4—The temple was restored to its original order.

The story of Jesus cleansing the temple offers a picture of how to heal the wounds inside your temple. After Jesus engaged His righteous rage, His temple was cleansed. Only Jesus had the power to cleanse His own temple. No other prophet or king had done so before Him or after Him. He alone could clean His house. In the same way, we alone can clean our own temples.

I have encountered many wounded souls over the past decade while working with couples and individuals in both inpatient psychiatric hospitals and outpatient office settings. Many of these souls experienced trauma in one form or another, and their wounds were at the very core of their beings.

An individual who has experienced a trauma has experienced it at all three levels of his or her being—spirit, soul and body. All three parts have been defiled, injured or neglected.

As I train therapists across this country, I stress the three levels at which trauma survivors have been affected—spirit, soul and body. I ask these individuals, "Why do we just treat trauma cognitively and expect people to heal? If the trauma affects all three dimensions of a person, doesn't it make sense that the healing of trauma involves all three aspects—spirit, soul and body—as well?" Their heads nod in agreement to this logic.

I share the same logic with you. People may have hurt you significantly. You may have presumed to forgive them, and you have done so. Nevertheless, the bullet is still inside. The muck and defilement are still surrounding it. That doesn't necessarily mean you didn't forgive them—it just means that you haven't cleansed your temple yet.

The concept I am about to suggest to you may seem foreign or uncomfortable at first. My experience with cleansing the temple has been nothing short of miraculous. Sexual abuse survivors heal very quickly after this exercise. Women who have been sexually betrayed by their husbands move through the stages of grief and forgiveness much more quickly than those who refuse to cleanse their temple.

If your spouse or anyone else has injured you, keep an open mind and try this exercise. Only after you've gone through it will you know whether or not it's been effective.

THE "CLEANSE THE TEMPLE" EXERCISE

1. Write an anger letter.

The first step in the cleansing of your temple is to write an anger letter to the person who has hurt you, but don't send it. Imagine this person in the room with you, but he or she is unable to talk or move. You can say whatever you need to say to him or her in this letter. This is not a letter to suppress your feelings, but rather to vent all the thoughts and feelings of hate, disgust and anguish that have been robbing your soul. Neither is this an "I forgive you" letter. That will come later. This is the place where you rid yourself of the anger that has been a part of your soul.

2. Get warmed up.

In Jesus' situation He made a whip for Himself. I don't recommend whips, but a padded baseball bat or tennis racket could be helpful. First, warm up your body. Take your bat and hit a mattress or pillow with small hits. Then use medium, large and extra large hits. Do this three times. Warm up your voice as well. Shout *No* each time you hit the pillow. Use small, medium, large and extra large *Nos* with your voice. This may feel awkward, but removing this buildup of pain from your soul and spirit feels almost like having a baby. That is why it's important to be warmed up physically.

While you're warming up, make sure you are home alone. Disconnect the phone so that you are not disturbed.

Note: Before doing this, if you have a heart condition or other medical condition that warrants talking to your medical doctor first, please do so.

3. Read your letter aloud.

After your physical warm-up, take the letter you wrote to your offender and read it aloud. If your offender's name is Toby, then you would read as follows: "Toby, how could you have done this to me? I trusted you!..."

Of course, Toby is nowhere around. You certainly don't need to do this with him or her around. You are simply in a room alone just reading the letter aloud.

4. ENGAGE YOUR ANGER PHYSICALLY AND VERBALLY.

After reading your letter, pick up your bat. Hit the bed or pillow and symbolically let "Toby" have it. You can yell, scream and cry, but release the infection that has been robbing you. You can symbolically tell him that his secrets are not controlling you any more. He was to blame! You have no limits as to what you can say to your offender. For once, let go of all the emotional control that is keeping this wound infected. Let it out!

> Carrying pain inside causes you to protect yourself from being hurt. In the process, you also protect yourself from being intimate.

This can last from fifteen minutes to an hour. Your body will let you know when you have completely put this behind you—spiritually, emotionally and physically.

Someone has given you something toxic, and you have been unhealthy ever since. After you remove it from you, you will feel so much better. You're worth getting it all out!

COMMENTS

When you do this cleansing exercise, only work on one offender at a time. If three different people have offended you, then you will need to complete three different sessions. *Do not* try to go through this exercise just once for all the different people who have offended you. Each "bullet" needs to be taken out separately.

If several people have caused you trauma before or during your marriage, make a list of them. Start with the least painful trauma and work your way up to the larger offenses. In this way, you will get better skilled at the exercise and will know what to expect.

You may have different experiences and gain helpful insight as you work through your list. I've known men and women who thought offender number three was the worst, and yet an offender whom they considered less significant actually was a much larger venting experience for them.

Remember, you're cleansing your temple so that over the next one hundred days you can experience the absolute best intimacy possible. Carrying pain inside causes you to protect yourself from being hurt. In the process, you also protect yourself from being intimate.

As you read through this exercise together, it is not imperative at this point that you discuss with each other to whom you need to write a letter.

Cleansing My Temple

I feel there is some work for me to do for cleansing my temple.

His response: ❏ Yes ❏ No

Her response: ❏ Yes ❏ No

If you checked yes to the above question, take a moment to discuss when you can be home alone to do your own Cleansing the Temple exercise. In the space below, determine the days and times when each of you can have the house alone. The sooner this takes place, the better it will be for both of you.

By making a commitment to set aside the time to do this work, you will be much more likely to follow through with it.

Monday	A.M./P.M.
Tuesday	A.M./P.M.
Wednesday	A.M./P.M.
Thursday	A.M./P.M.
Friday	A.M./P.M.
Saturday	A.M./P.M.
Sunday	A.M./P.M.

If you are on the fence as to whether your spouse needs to be on the list of those who have hurt you, follow this simple rule of thumb. Imagine that all offenses can be categorized in levels from one to ten, with ten being the most severe. Responses to these offenses are categorized in the same way. When your spouse does something that really should be responded to with a level two emotional response, and you consistently give responses at an emotional level seven or eight, you probably have some unresolved anger.

In most cases, if you have any doubt, then it is better to go through the Cleansing the Temple exercise regarding your spouse in order to find out for sure if you have unresolved anger. It's far better to discover the truth than to leave emotional blockages inside that can affect your ability to be intimate.

FORGIVENESS

This next stage of healing is only for those who have already cleansed their temple. It should be completed about five days after you have completed the anger work of cleansing the temple regarding a particular offender.

Five days or more after finishing your anger work you should be feeling much better. It is similar to how you feel after getting over a cold. You can feel that the junk in your lungs is gone, and you can breathe clearer and easier now.

Several clients have shared that after doing the Cleansing

the Temple exercise with a focus on their mom or dad, the next time they visited their parents they didn't get all knotted up or tight inside. After completing this exercise most people can reenter the relationship without pain.

The next step to healing is forgiveness. I am not suggesting that you look up your violators and tell them you forgive them. Rather, I am talking about doing another therapeutic exercise so that you can see how far along in the process of forgiveness you really are with this person.

The following exercise is very effective, and most are able to choose to forgive their offenders. The Bible is full of teachings on forgiveness. It might be helpful to get a concordance and look up all of the verses listed under the word *forgiveness*. Start with Matthew 6:14–15:

> For if you forgive men when they sin against you, your heavenly Father will also forgive you. But if you do not forgive men their sins, your Father will not forgive your sins.

Work your way through the entire New Testament regarding forgiveness. I realize that for some individuals, healing and cleansing will need to come first before they are truly able to forgive from their heart. For a whole book on the subject of forgiveness, I would recommend a book by John Bevere, *The Bait of Satan* (Charisma House). This book goes into great detail about the importance and value of forgiveness.

This exercise guides you through the process so that you can forgive and have a place in time to mark when your offense was released from your soul. Walk through this exercise with all those on your offender list. It might include your dad and mom, your spouse and any others who have hurt you.

This exercise has three steps to it. So select one offender and go through the process. Do this exercise while you are home alone. You will need two kitchen chairs.

THE FORGIVENESS EXERCISE

1. ASSUME THE ROLE OF THE OFFENDER.

Place the two chairs facing each other. Pick a chair and sit facing the other chair. We'll call the chair in which you are sitting, "Chair A."

While you are sitting in chair A, role-play your offender. You are now this person. As you role-play this individual, have him or her apologize and ask for forgiveness for all that they have done to you. They are hypothetically confessing to you in the other chair (chair B). If I were doing this exercise about my dad, I would sit in chair A as I role-played my dad. I would verbally own his sin, apologize and ask for forgiveness for the things I did and didn't do to Doug in chair B.

As I play my dad, I might say, "Doug, I need you to forgive me of..." Now since I am playing my dad, I can say what he needs to say to me in order to own and apologize for his sin against my life.

2. ROLE-PLAY YOUR RESPONSE AS THE ONE OFFENDED.

Now I have played my dad as he asked forgiveness for several offenses against Doug, who was symbolically sitting in chair B. Yet as the one offended, I heard my dad own his sin and ask forgiveness for it. Now I can start step two.

I begin by physically moving to sit in chair B, now role-playing myself.

After hearing my dad ask for forgiveness, I now decide how I will respond. Above all be honest. If you are not ready to forgive your offender, tell him or her.

You could say, "I'm just not ready to do this yet, but I will try again in a few weeks."

Whatever you do when you play yourself, don't be a phony or do what you think you *should* do. Do what is real.

If you are able to forgive your offender, then tell him or her. In our example, Doug is now talking to Dad in the opposite chair.

I could say, "Dad, I forgive you."

I could really release him from his abuse and neglect of my soul and the impact his actions had on my life.

If you forgave your offender, move to step three. If at this time you are not able to forgive your offender, get out your calendar and set up a date in about three to four weeks when you will try this exercise again. Do this every month to measure your progress until you are able to forgive.

3. ROLE-PLAY THE OFFENDER'S RESPONSE TO FORGIVENESS.

In our example, Doug has forgiven Dad. Now I physically get up and sit down in chair A again, and play the role of my dad. Now it is Dad's turn to respond to Doug's forgiveness.

Dad (role-played by Doug) might say, "Thanks, Doug." When Dad is done talking to Doug the exercise is over.

Let's review:

1. Start in chair A as the offender asking for forgiveness.
2. Now sit in chair B as yourself, and honestly respond to your offender's request for forgiveness.
3. If you have forgiven him or her, go back to chair A and play the offender responding to the forgiveness.

COMMENTS

This can be a very emotional exercise for those with extremely abusive backgrounds, so have a box of tissues nearby. In addition, make sure the phone, doorbell or anything else will not interrupt you. It will be important for you to stay focused.

Do this exercise only after you have completed the Cleansing the Temple exercise. Many individuals attempt to forgive before they heal. Jesus cleansed the temple before He issued the words, "Father, forgive them" (Luke 23:34). Cleansing comes first, then forgiveness.

In all these exercises, each offender gets his or her time in the chair with you. You must role-play each one and receive an individual apology from each. Don't role-play more than one offender in a day.

Releasing your offenders will free you if you complete your Cleansing the Temple work first. I have personally experienced much freedom through these exercises given to me by God. I didn't read about these exercises somewhere and Christianize them. They are exercises the Lord gave me in the process of healing myself so that I can heal others also.

> The door will swing open to an entirely new and refreshing way of life.

As you do these exercises and move through forgiveness, especially toward your spouse, you can once again feel free to give, trust and build. That's what it is about—removing all the roadblocks to intimacy. As you do this, the door will swing open to an entirely new and refreshing way of life.

Let's pray together:

> Lord, help me to process my woundedness and to apply these exercises to my life. Comfort me, Lord, and lead me to still waters where I can drink of the intimacy that You have for me. In Jesus' name, amen.

FIVE

Flossing Away Relational Plaque

Every morning, no doubt you faithfully brush your teeth. But what a feeling you can get if you forget to brush! You end up having that unclean feeling in your mouth called *plaque*. Plaque buildup is particularly unpleasant.

In many ways our bodies reflect great spiritual and practical truths. Over time, relationships, especially marriages, can build up what I call "relational plaque." It's usually caused by little acts of neglect—and sometimes large offenses—that couples experience over the years. Poorly managed, these offenses create the plaque within relationships.

Many people today, Christians included, have a problem with the word *sin*. Instead of using the word *sin*, we speak of "a family of origin issue" or "a personality trait." Selfishness, rudeness, taking advantage of another person and lying are all sins!

Sin begins to trickle into a marriage, and if not owned or identified by the person sinning, it will create distance in the relationship. This buildup of sin—or plaque—is not always very obvious. It continues to multiply if continual repentance and forgiveness are lacking in the relationship.

When I counsel with new couples in my office, I often ask them the standard question: "So what brings you here today?"

> In a healthy marriage, each person will be asking for forgiveness at least weekly.

Sometimes a couple will look at me and then look at each other and shrug their shoulders. Invariably one of them will say something such as, "We're just not getting along." The following couple's story is a case in point.

Nancy and Kevin are a clean-cut couple with an upper middle-class income and strong Christian beliefs and practices. They were married young and had children shortly thereafter. Now in their midthirties, Kevin has many challenges in his career, and Nancy runs a part-time business. They have three teenagers.

Kevin and Nancy began to feel that they didn't really like each other very much anymore. They really couldn't point to a particular event that caused this feeling; there just seemed to be a wall between them. They couldn't seem to connect and were just going through the motions of work, school, PTA and children's activities.

"We love each other," they both said, "but we just don't know how to get our marriage back on track where we like each other."

In allowing Nancy and Kevin to continue to talk about their day-in and day-out activities, it quickly became apparent that little healthy structure had remained in their marriage. Neither seemed aware of the effect one person's choices or behaviors had on the other.

I asked Kevin and Nancy when was the last time they asked for forgiveness for sinning against the other. I wish you could have seen their faces drop! From their mutual expressions, I could tell what they were thinking, *What do you mean by sinning against each other? We're Christians!*

Sometimes reality is overwhelming for Christian couples, especially when they have been lulled into a state of unawareness of their sins. Teaching Nancy and Kevin that some of their behaviors and attitudes were sin, and that sin had to be confessed, dealt with and forgiven, was like turning a light bulb on. This great couple really did love each other, but they drifted away from the basic truth that they still sinned.

You may think a lot like Kevin and Nancy. Your attitudes and actions may subtly say, "Nobody sins around here!" I challenge you to think of the last time you asked for forgiveness for a sin you committed (whether willful or not) against your spouse.

If it's been more than days or weeks, you may be excusing away the sin in your relationship. I sin in my relationship with my precious Lisa. Sometimes I'm rude, thoughtless or selfish. But I have made a commitment in my heart that if I sin against anyone, it is my biblical duty to confess that sin to him or her. Till the day I die I will be a sin-afflicted, imperfect human being. As I grow in Christian maturity, I expect to sin less and less. Nevertheless, I should still confess it when I do.

In a healthy marriage, each person will be asking for forgiveness at least weekly. In no way do I plan to sin. But if I do, I must go to my wife and say, "Lisa, I sinned against you by being selfish. Will you forgive me?"

She usually responds by saying, "I forgive you."

BUILDING UP RELATIONAL PLAQUE

Now you're probably asking yourself, *What do plaque and sin have to do with each other?* Couples who don't own sin for what sin really is will develop relational plaque over time. It can take years.

Eventually, a husband and wife will both become aware of the distance that has developed between them, distance caused by unconfessed sin. They are no longer as honest as they once were. Silently they keep score of things they never talk about. Entitlements or "you owe me" attitudes begin to grow as well as other dysfunctional or unhealthy behaviors because of unconfessed sin.

> For plaque not to build up in a relationship we need to be honest about being wrong.

Let's discuss a little further how this happens in a relationship context. Suppose a husband and wife go out for a social event. During the evening the husband makes a few sarcastic remarks and put-downs directed toward his wife. In most cases his wife will just suck it up and may not even mention the hurt he caused her (plaque begins). If she does bring it up, he may belittle the pain and rationalize it by saying, "I didn't mean anything by it." Hence he is not owning his sin or the affect it had on the person he loves the most (more plaque builds up). From this isolated incident you can see how easy it is for plaque to build up.

Let's use another example. A husband and wife are out and about having an enjoyable day of running errands and shopping together. At lunch, the husband feels close to his wife and clearly communicates his desire to be sexual that night. They get home, eat dinner and continue to do a few other things around the house. The husband needs to run another errand and clearly communicates that he will be right back. Instead of waiting up, the wife heads directly to bed and goes to sleep.

He comes home exactly as he said and is hurt that he cannot be sexual and that she didn't even give him a chance to talk about it. Plaque begins to build up. The next day he mentions about how he thought they were going to be sexual last night, and she laughs it off. She says, "That will teach you to go to the store." More plaque builds up.

In both of these cases the spouse did not own his part in the wrongdoing. The other spouse is stuck with a sticky feeling. The spouse may feel as if he or she can't discuss his feelings about the hurtful experience anymore. Here is where plaque builds up.

For plaque not to build up in a relationship we need to be honest about being wrong. This is true both for the husband who put down his wife and for the wife who did not clearly communicate her lack of sexual interest.

Saying "I'm sorry" isn't quite the same as saying "I sinned against you by putting you down." When you lightly say, "I'm sorry," the other spouse may be thinking, *I'll bet you're sorry!* Never attempt to minimize your offense by apologizing lightly when you're wrong. Own all of what you have done and any consequences you know that have occurred because of this offense.

When asking for the forgiveness of sin becomes a part of a couple's regular interaction, they are on their way to a plaque-free relationship. You may need to literally practice asking each other for forgiveness so that it becomes a regular habit. Take your three greatest sins toward your spouse and write them down. Practice saying to your wife or husband, "I have sinned against you by _____. Can you forgive me?"

Practice doing this daily for a week to feel more comfortable with the language and the process of forgiving each other so that you can begin to put it to regular use. This will not only keep relational plaque to a minimum, but it will also allow you to experience the refreshing taste of honesty and integrity in your relationship. It can also facilitate greater intimacy because sin will no longer be separating you from the holy of holies with each other.

Some relationships have been building up relational plaque for years. Because our goal in the next one hundred days is to move closer to each other, we must address historical plaque that could be blocking the intimacy you and your spouse are seeking.

A helpful exercise for dealing with historical plaque is called "an owning." Let's walk through it step by step. It is very important that you follow the directions carefully. If you decide to do an owning, make sure that you both agree to follow the guidelines specifically.

AN OWNING EXERCISE

1. Make a list of the sins you "own."

We humans have a tendency to sin, and being married, we have a tendency to sin against each other. The only way to deal with sin is to own it, confess it and be forgiven of it by God and by our spouse. Therefore, in this step we will deal with simply the "owning it" part of our sin.

Husbands and wives, *separately* review your relationship history, including your relationship before marriage. Individually make a list of the sins *you* committed toward your spouse. Some of these sins are actions, others are attitudes and some are promises that you haven't fulfilled. This is *your* list to make. *Do not* ask for your spouse's help in developing your list of sins.

If you are struggling with what to write, pray. Ask God to reveal your sins to you. You will find that long-forgotten actions and attitudes will come into your mind. When this occurs, God is helping you so that you might find healing. Be as painstakingly honest with yourself as possible in making your list.

Before we go any further, you need to discuss whether or not you are committed as a couple to this process of owning your past sins against each other. Note your decision on the below space.

    _____   As a couple, we decided to own our past sins to each other.

    _____   As a couple, we decided not to own our past sins to each other.

The owning is a scheduled event. As a couple, when would you like to have your individual list completed? Please place a date in the below space.

Our goal to be finished with our owning lists is _____.

Do not discuss your list with each other for any reason prior to actually doing the exercise. This is extremely important.

2. READ YOUR "OWNING" LIST TO YOUR SPOUSE.

At an agreed-upon time when you and your spouse can be alone, sit in chairs facing each other. You may feel the need for support from a counselor, pastor or very safe lay person. This is permitted.

If you plan to do this at home and have children, make sure they are not at home during step two. In addition, take the phone off of the hook or turn on the answering machine. This can be a very emotional exercise, so keep a box of tissues nearby.

When you are seated facing each other, have your personal list of sins available. The first person reads off one of his sins to the spouse. For clarity, let's suppose the husband starts; we will call him Harry.

Harry states, "I need you to forgive me for _____."

The wife has only two options at this point. She may respond in one of the following ways:

    1. "I forgive you for that."
    2. "I need some time on that one."

Again, these are *her only two responses*. During the exercise, if anyone begins to give feedback or ask questions, *please stop the exercise*. Let me give you two examples of how to do it correctly:

Harry: "I need you to forgive me for embarrassing you in front of your sisters at Christmas last year."

Alice: "I forgive you for that."

Harry: "I need you to forgive me for embarrassing you in front of your sisters at Christmas last year."

Alice: "I need more time on that one."

These are the only two options Alice can have to Harry's request for forgiveness. Anything else is unacceptable. If you have a pastor or counselor involved, that individual should stop the person who wants to respond any differently. Alice is not required to forgive Harry of every sin during the exercise, but they both must stick to the two-response format.

During this exercise, you are both going to feel very vulnerable. If one spouse uses this time to injure the other, it means that the couple is not ready to do this exercise without someone else present. If this happens to you, agree on who needs to be present and schedule a later time to resume.

Here is an example of what you *should not do*.

Harry: "I need you to forgive me for embarrassing you in front of your sisters."

Alice: "I am not ever forgiving you for that."
"I still hate you for that."
"I forgive you, but you were a real jerk."
"*Why* did you do that anyway?"

I hope you get the point. If you are going to do this owning exercise, it must be done correctly. So in our example, Harry stated his sins, then Alice responded. Next it is Alice's turn to ask for forgiveness. Here is what it looks like so far with Harry's response.

Harry: "I need you to forgive me for... (sin #1)."

Alice: "I forgive you."

Alice: "I need you to forgive me for... (sin #1)."

Harry: "I forgive you."

Harry: "I need you to forgive me for... (sin #2)."

Alice: "I need more time on that one."

Alice: "I need you to forgive me for... (sin #2)."

Harry: "I need more time on that one."

I think you get the idea that you rotate back and forth. Inevitably, one spouse's list will be longer for whatever reason, and this is normal. Then just allow the person with the longer list to continue to ask for forgiveness with the other spouse continuing to respond appropriately.

Note: While going through and responding to your spouse's sins, be honest. If you are not able to forgive something at this point in time, be honest and just say the appropriate response, "I need more time on that one." It is better to be honest in this exercise than to lie to yourself or your spouse regarding where you are on an issue. Lying to each other never deepens intimacy.

3. WAIT AT LEAST SEVENTY-TWO HOURS BEFORE DISCUSSING YOUR RESPONSES.

When each person is done with his list, take some time apart for a little while, an hour or so is appropriate. *Do not talk about the exercise!* Give yourself at least seventy-two hours before you talk about the things mentioned in this exercise. You both will be too emotionally raw to discuss this exercise immediately.

The goal for an owning is not to be forgiven, but to own our side of the street. In most cases, about 90 percent of our sins are forgiven. The percentage that is not forgiven by either spouse is that person's own issue; they need to work this through. It doesn't mean a spouse is less kind, generous or un-Christian because he or she needs more time to heal or process before forgiving.

Most couples find the owning exercise a great way to clean up the old layers of built-up plaque. Countless couples I have worked with believe this exercise alone gave them hope for achieving the intimate relationship they desired.

> To stay plaque-free you must remain consciously aware of when you sin toward your spouse.

Sin that is not owned or that goes unconfessed is a plaque builder. To stay plaque-free you must remain consciously aware of when you sin toward your spouse. Immediately ask for forgiveness so that plaque does not build back up in your precious relationship.

I know I will sin. I expect that I will continue to sin. Although I hope it grows less, I still need to humble myself and ask forgiveness of my spouse, my children and others. As you do, continue this exercise in your relationships to stay free from the plaque of sin.

Plaque is a terrible thing to have in a relationship. Nevertheless, the blood of Christ has the power to forgive sin. As you forgive and are forgiven, God's grace can enter into your marriage for the rest of your days.

SIX

Dealing With Sexuality

Sexuality is at the core of all of us. Sex should be a beautiful exchange between loving spouses. Unfortunately, some of us never developed a healthy and strong sense of sexuality because of past histories marked with issues such as sexual abuse or sexual addiction. Some marriages are also plagued with intimcy anorexia, which is the active withholding of spiritual, emotional and sexual intimacy. Such sexual baggage can create roadblocks to sexual and nonsexual intimacy in a marriage.

THE IMPACT OF SEXUAL HISTORIES

Most people probably have had some sexual history prior to marriage. If you abstained from sex prior to marriage, this is ideal. I praise God that you kept yourself just for your mate. However, I have met few couples for whom this was true of both spouses.

Your sexual history is exactly that—yours. Still, your

premarital sexual behaviors may now be creating hindrances to your sexuality in your present relationship. Some premarital sexual behaviors may have been choices you made, while others may not have been choices at all, but the result of sexual abuse. First, I will discuss the sexual experiences that were your choices. Sexual abuse and other experiences over which you had no control will be discussed in a latter portion of this chapter.

Before you were married you may have had sex. If you are a Christian, you may have experienced a good degree of guilt over such sexual encounters. You may have become a committed Christian later on in life after many sexual experiences. Or you may have been a Christian who was educated by prevailing sexual attitudes and not fully awakened to Christian beliefs regarding the whole issue. Now, as you mature as a Christian, you view your earlier sexual choices as sin that was destructive to the lives of those you touched.

Even before I became a Christian, at times I had a clear sense that what I was doing wasn't right. I didn't know why it wasn't right, but I realized that at some level sex without a commitment was wrong. What I didn't understand during my youth was that being sexually active was damaging me, damaging my relationship with God and damaging my future marriage. I was completely unaware that my sexual behavior was causing great damage to my soul. I had learned to equate sex with accomplishment. The sex act was symbolic of my achieving something. This made sex a goal—an objective. And to reach my goal it turned people into objects. Honestly, I can't count the wives who have shared with me that they feel this way in their marriage because of the approach their husband takes during their sexual experiences.

Another very damaging behavior I learned in the world was the way you get sex. I learned to manipulate women, to lie about my feelings toward them and to put more emphasis on sex than on friendship. I learned to manipulate through touch, humor and whatever else was necessary to reach my goal. This damaged others and me immensely, because I totally missed the real goal of sexuality, which was to connect with one person for life.

Relationships for me only had value if sex was part of the mix. Such erroneous concepts not only hurt my future marriage, they also damaged my ability to experience genuine sexual intimacy.

> Being sexually active was damaging me, damaging my relationship with God and damaging my future marriage.

Let's go a little further into my sexual history. I was negatively impacted by pornography early on in my sexual history. Viewing some form of pornography at one point or other in their lives damages many men. Pornography is extremely harmful. It teaches young men many wrong things about sex.

I did this to myself. I didn't and can't and won't blame anyone else for my sin. It's mine. What these experiences brought to my soul was greater secrecy. Somehow I concluded that if anyone really knew what I was doing, there would be no way that person could love me. I felt dirty, worthless and phony. So I couldn't really let anyone into my heart of hearts; therefore, I couldn't really be intimate with anyone.

I use my story to illustrate the impact your sexual history has on your most important relationships. Your relationship with God gets damaged. I remember hours and hours of repenting as a young Christian, because now I knew better but continued to behave the old way. My relationship with myself was damaged because I couldn't trust myself and didn't like myself for what I was doing. My relationship with my future wife was going to be damaged because of all the junk inside of me, which needed to be cleaned out.

If you have a sexual history, evaluate what your experiences taught you about sex and measure that against what God's Word teaches. You can and must heal from the robbery of that sin, which attempts to keep you from the best sex of your life with your spouse.

> Many of us are too ignorant to know what is best for us.

My story is a man's story; however, I have listened to countless women through endless tears share their sexual histories with me. Wives confessed that their self-loathing revealed the lack of wisdom regarding their sexual choices. They gave away their sexuality to men who hurt them by shaming them into performing behaviors with which they didn't feel comfortable. Such encounters left them feeling isolated and less valuable than the good people in their lives, or with what I call the "damaged goods syndrome." Once diminished by humiliating sexual encounters, they began to believe that they were unlovable and that it no longer mattered what they did. So they continued to make mistake after mistake.

These women have painful sexual histories, and the damage is just as traumatic for them as it is for the men. They unknowingly damaged their relationship with God, with themselves and with their future spouse as well.

Such painful baggage brought into a marriage is damaging on several levels.

KEEPING A SECRET PLACE

You feel that if you were totally honest you would be rejected. Therefore, you keep a secret place that you believe your spouse can't know about, can't love and can't accept about you. This secret place damages the spiritual, emotional and sexual intimacy within the relationship because you are not 100 percent available for intimacy. A certain percentage of yourself remains hidden.

Learned Manipulation

The approaches you learned to get sex or avoid it are usually the only methods you know to bring into the relationship. Manipulation, such as lying and insensitive attitudes toward your spouse's sexuality, creep into the marriage.

Comparing Previous Partners

The sexual expectations to which you may have become accustomed can now be totally inappropriate for the sexual personality of your spouse. You may have experienced multiple sexual partners along with their unique sexual personalities. You can project the memory of another's sexual personality onto your spouse. Outwardly, you may not say anything, but inwardly you may question why your spouse can't sexually be more like someone else.

Projecting past sexual personalities onto your present spouse is the result of sin. It was sin for you to be involved with your past sexual partners, regardless of whether or not you knew better at the time. Sin exposed you to various sexual personalities and sexual fantasies. This sin can block you from accepting and appreciating the great sexual personality of your spouse.

Let's take a moment to talk about wants and needs in your relationship. I love a God who knows what you need better than you do yourself. In your distorted, sin-filled youth, you may have wanted a woman sexually to be a risk-taker and adventurous. Such sexual personalities tend to come with a lot of baggage that you probably wouldn't want in your life. What you may need is a woman who hasn't been sexual with anyone else, who loves you and for whom you will never have to spend one minute wondering if she has been unfaithful.

I am so grateful that God knows what we need. Many of us are too ignorant to know what is best for us. I have talked with many men and women who defile their marriages with the sexual expectations created by sin. They loudly complain about what they want from their spouses because of their earlier exposure to sexual sin.

Your sexual memories, whether you like it or not, are the unfortunate consequence of the sins to which you exposed yourself. Your memory is your problem. Don't project it onto your spouse.

Often couples defile their present marriage with a past sinful experience or expectation. If your spouse is pressuring you because of a sinful past by comparing you to it, ask him or her to talk to God to deal with that expectation.

One of the reasons you married your spouse is because you liked his or her personality. Now you need to practice being grateful for your spouse and for his or her sexual expression. Your partner may not have the same past as you do. As you journey together you can create your own special sexual history together.

YOUR OWN SEXUAL HISTORY AS A COUPLE

As a married couple, not only do you have sexual histories with others prior to marriage, you have also created your own sexual history within your present marriage. For some, this history is mostly positive despite a few minor bumps that need to be worked out. For others who may have been married for decades, there may seem to be more bumps through the years than anything else.

Some husbands and wives had to learn, as all of us do, through trial and error, but communication was good, and you managed to pull through. Other couples have experienced major setbacks within their relationships that have created spiritual and emotional roadblocks to sexual intimacy.

Some couples have experienced marital sexual abuse or what is now called "mate rape." The wife clearly didn't want to have sex, but the husband forced himself on her. Other partners have been sexually rejected so often that they no longer even want sex. Some couples I have counseled have been involved in watching pornography together and even have had others who were sexually involved with them. Many couples have had affairs, prostitutes or homosexual encounters during their marriage, which are all now a part of their marital sexual history.

> You need to practice being grateful for your spouse and for his or her sexual expression.

The sexual histories of some couples are laden with more baggage within their marriages than before. Years of being sexually shamed, ridiculed or put down can substantially limit spiritual, emotional and sexual intimacy. Couples with these issues within their marriage will have more difficulty working through the blockages to intimacy than most. Nevertheless, it will be necessary to receive healing to improve your intimacy.

I don't believe in minimizing the role of your past sexual history. The past is valid, real and important to be owned. As you take responsibility to heal from the past, your likelihood of spiritual, emotional and physical intimacy in the future is improved.

Sometimes religious people say, "The past is the past. Forgive it and move on." Oftentimes the person saying it is the offender, not the recipient. If a person gets shot and a bullet remains in his body, you wouldn't tell him to forgive first, would you? No. First you would get him to a doctor to remove the bullet. Even if he cried out to the offender, "I forgive you" while in pain, he would still need to have the bullet taken out.

Once the "bullet" (your sexual past) is taken out, you can begin to heal and really release the past. Even if you have been wounded to the core of your sexual being by your spouse, given information and time, you can heal and begin to move on.

OVERCOMING SEXUAL ABUSE

Sexual abuse creates a roadblock to spiritual, emotional and sexual intimacy. I have reviewed an enormous amount of research related to sexual abuse. The statistics range widely. The most common figures available report that about 30 percent of females and 10 percent of males are sexually abused before the age of eighteen. That breaks down to about one out of three women and one out of six men.[1]

When you look over a congregation of believers, no matter what the doctrine or worship style, these statistics still apply. Christians are similar to all other groupings of people and have similar sexual issues.

We will discuss the sexual abuse that has occurred prior to adulthood. Some children are abused in an ongoing manner. For others it is a one-time event by a parent, sibling, neighbor or stranger.

When the abuse occurred, the individual's sexuality was objectified and taken advantage of by another. The person who took advantage of the child's sexuality is a sexual offender, regardless of his or her relationship to the child.

This offender is 100 percent responsible for the offense. I underscore this fact, because this three dimensional-type trauma—involving the spirit, soul and body—is so devastating to a child or teen that he or she naturally blames himself for it. It is the only way a child can categorize this behavior to make sense of it. The truth of the matter is that it takes total insanity for someone to abuse another sexually, and it will never make rational sense—especially to a child.

Sexual abuse affects each victim differently. For some victims, it brings on a lifestyle of *hypersexuality*, or a tendency to be sexual all the time. The effect of sexual abuse on another might be *hyposexuality*, where the individual is not sexual at all. Some men and women who have been sexually abused struggle with depression, eating disorders, rages and the inability to enjoy healthy relationships. Many suffer with addictions throughout their lives.

Many books and journal articles have been written on the effects of sexual abuse. For some individuals it appears that the abuse has not affected them much at all. They appear to be more resilient to the adverse affects. Some are affected by the abuse for a period of time but seem to work through the issues. Still others who have been sexually abused desperately need healing in their soul to process the pain and the memories. This person may need professional help to work through these past events. All are valid responses to this trauma.[2]

If you fall into this last category, your offender has already stolen many years of your life. I strongly encourage you to seek professional help to get the healing you need. I am a survivor of sexual abuse, and I believe that talking about it to someone else tremendously reduces the shame it causes. I made a decision to work through my misconception of sexuality and to deal with the rage it caused. My healing process allowed me to put the past in the past and not to let it control my worth, value or sexuality.

Just remember that you didn't cause or ask for sexual abuse to happen. You are in no way responsible for what happened. Nevertheless, you are 100 percent responsible for your healing. I know it's possible! I have seen many others throughout my years as a practicing counselor find healing from sexual abuse and its effect on their marital relationships.

As you heal—spirit, soul and body—you will have more of yourself to give to your spouse and to your children. If this applies to you, outline what you feel you need to do, and pray and ask the Lord to free you from the past by directing you into the path of healing that you need.

THE HIDDEN SHAME
OF SEXUAL ADDICTIONS

Sexual addiction is a killer of spiritual, emotional and sexual intimacy for married couples. Between 29 and 39 percent of Christian men in local churches are sexually addicted, according to statistics. This suggests you will have a significant number of sexual addicts in church congregations of any size or denomination.[3]

Sexual addicts are usually men; however, women have joined the ranks as well. Most sexual addicts are survivors of sexual abuse. According to statistics, between 80 to 85 percent of sex addicts have been sexually abused.

The other side of this picture is what I call the "biological sex addict." I counsel with many biological sex addicts, Christians included. The biological sex addict often grew up in a good home and was not sexually abused. For some, their first experience with sexual intercourse was on their wedding night, but they are still sexually addicted.

What often triggers the sexual addiction for this biological sex addict is the discovery of pornography during the early teen years. Generally they couldn't talk to anyone about it because they knew it was wrong. They began to engage in self-sex behavior while viewing the pornography. You recall our earlier discussion regarding sexual release providing your brain with its greatest chemical reward. Many men and women obtained this reward while looking at pornography often hundreds and sometimes thousands of times before ever experiencing their first real sexual encounter with a person.

> Sexual addiction does not only affect the sex addict.

The "sex glue" that should be cementing the marriage of these individuals has cemented them neurologically to the fantasy world associated with pornography. Now as an adult, they have mastered disconnected, lust-driven, objectifying sex. In their fantasy world, women always want sex, are willing to do anything during sex, will work harder than the man for his pleasure and have no needs of their own. Imagine reinforcing that erroneous sexual belief system thousands of times. Do you think they're going to have happy, healthy, three-dimensional sex?

That's just the beginning of the problems this biological sex addict will encounter. This person's behavior drives him underground. He develops a secret lifestyle the wife doesn't know about that involves self-sex, porn movies, sex magazines and hours spent on the Internet. He believes that if anyone knew about what he was doing that he would be rejected. This behavior can go on for decades without the wife having a clue as to what's going on with her husband. She doesn't understand why he is unable to be more than superficially intimate, why he seems so distant at times and why she can't do anything right for him some days.

Meanwhile this sex addict lives in denial. He thinks that he can handle the daily objectifying of and lusting after others, and he can dabble in pornography and still be OK. I have counseled men and women with this problem for many years. There is help and healing for the person who is a sex addict.

Sexual addiction does not only affect the sex addict. The wife of a sex addict is definitely affected by the husband's addiction. Our recent research study reported three major areas of damage a woman receives when living in a relationship with this addiction. She is most likely to suffer from depression, low self-esteem and eating disorders.[4]

From my professional experience, I can assure you that as long as the addict is active in his addiction he cannot be intimate. The addict is usually emotionally limited and crippled with guilt and shame. An addict can be a deacon, a pastor or a Sunday school teacher, but he can't be intimate with his wife on an ongoing basis.

If this might be an issue for you, or if you are wondering whether or not you are married to a sex addict, get more information and begin the process of healing. This addiction is a plague in America. I strongly believe that it is becoming the number one hindrance keeping couples from enjoying God's blessing of spiritual, emotional and physical intimacy.

ARE YOU STARVING FROM INTIMACY ANOREXIA?

Intimacy Anorexia is the withholding of spiritual, emotional and physical intimacy from a spouse. An intimacy anorexic spouse will refuse to be available to share feelings, be sexual, to pray together and will rarely be affectionate. Intimacy Anorexia is very covert. Often you may not even realize it has been going on for many years.

Intimacy Anorexia runs counter to the goal of three-dimensional intimacy. Below is an excerpt from my video *Intimacy Anorexia*, which helps identify this pattern in your relationship. Answer these questions with your spouse as truthfully as possible.

Intimacy Anorexic Patterns

❑ Yes ❑ No   1. Does it feel as if your spouse limits or withholds love from you?

❑ Yes ❑ No   2. Does it feel as if your spouse limits or withholds the amount of praise he or she gives you?

❑ Yes ❑ No   3. Does it feel as if your spouse limits or withholds the amount of sex he/she gives you?

❑ Yes ❑ No   4. Does it feel as if your spouse with-

Dealing With Sexuality

holds spiritual connection with you?

❏ Yes ❏ No 5. Does it feel as if your spouse is unwilling or unable to share his/her feelings with you?

❏ Yes ❏ No 6. Does it feel as if your spouse uses anger or silence to control the relationship?

❏ Yes ❏ No 7. Does it feel as if your spouse has unfounded or ongoing criticism of you?

❏ Yes ❏ No 8. Does your spouse control or shame you about money issues?

❏ Yes ❏ No 9. Do you or your spouse tend to keep yourselves so busy that you have little time for just you as a couple (just couple time without other family members present)?

❏ Yes ❏ No 10. If issues or problems come up in the relationship, do you tend to get blamed before your spouse owns an issue?

❏ Yes ❏ No 11. Do you feel more like a roommate than a lover in your relationship?

If you or your spouse answered yes to five or more questions, I would recommend that you seek help in this area. Intimacy Anorexia is similar to an eating disorder. It is stubborn, but there is practical help available to get out and stay out of these harmful intimacy anorexic patterns.

If your spouse is intimacy anorexic, whether it is the husband or the wife, you probably feel very alone. You may feel like roommates instead of marriage partners. The spouse of an anorexic often feels avoided, confused, dry on the inside and may feel more like the manager of the household, not the love of her or his life.

Many spouses of anorexics feel they are not valuable and have finally just given up on intimacy because deep down inside he or she knows that if it came down to being intimate or leaving the marriage, the anorexic would chose leaving.

I have counseled many women married to male anorexics, and their souls were now almost hollow from the lack of praise from their husbands. They haven't been praised in years, and some have not been sexual in months or years. They are often angry, confused and have feelings of hopelessness.

The husband of an intimacy anorexic wife often is hostile from trying to be perfect enough to be loved or to be sexually intimate. Jesus can and will walk a couple through this issue of intimacy anorexia regardless of how dry it may presently feel. I have seen this miracle of healing occur in marriages with anorexia present. This happened to the following couple.

Joel and Janet were both professionals in the mental health industry. Joel had a long history of self-sex and pornography, which began early in his teenage years. After his first year of marriage to Janet, Joel lost interest in sex with his wife. Being sexual in their marriage decreased to a couple times a month and soon to annually. By the time they set up a session with me, it had been years since they had sex together.

Joel was both a sex addict and an intimacy anorexic. He had eight of the eleven symptoms of intimacy anorexia. It wasn't only sex that he withheld from his wife. He was a deacon in his church, yet he hadn't prayed with his wife in more than twenty years. And she couldn't remember the last time he opened up his heart to her in any way.

They didn't want to divorce. They had raised their family and felt a divorce would be contrary to their faith. Joel started in his recovery from self-sex, porn and intimacy anorexia.

As he followed the eight guidelines I gave him, he learned to become spiritually, emotionally and sexually intimate. Within a short period of time, Joel was able to get sober from the sexual addiction and heal. Today Joel and Janet enjoy sexual and nonsexual intimacy regularly.

There is hope for those who struggle with sexual addiction and intimacy anorexia. If an individual will do the work of healing, miracles of intimacy can occur.

SEX ON THE NET

As people living in a culture obsessed with technology, we need to address the Internet in the context of marital intimacy. The Internet is a great tool for research, shopping and many other services. Like the television it can be used for good purposes, such as carrying the gospel around the world. It can also be used for less noble purposes.

The largest portion of the Internet is devoted to pornography. Pornography in all its forms, including magazines and videos, is a real threat to intimacy. Internet pornography is an even greater threat. Pornography on the Internet is more perverse than what you can purchase anywhere. It is available twenty-four hours a day, seven days a week, and it is also much more addictive than any other form of pornography.

In the past five years I have encountered increasing numbers of men and women who are getting into trouble through chat rooms, news groups, pornography and sex services. The Internet is trapping people from all walks of life—including missionaries, pastors, Bible scholars and Christian celebrities.

The Bible warns us to flee sexual temptation. (See 1 Corinthians 6:18.) To own a computer with open access in a home with young people is unwise. If you need or want Internet access at your home, you must protect yourself. One option available on our website www.drdougweiss.com is what I believe to be one of the best porn-blockers on the net. It is maintained by a Christian organization that has been fighting pornography for decades. There are no passwords, and you cannot delete the filter unless you hand write a letter to the company. With this in place, Internet porn cannot accidentally traumatize teenagers or adults. If you have Internet access, I strongly encourage you to download the filter today.

The Internet can be addictive not only for pornography but also for games. If your marriage's intimacy is being threatened by the Internet, you will need to address this issue together. Work together to establish boundaries to protect the precious gift of intimacy in your marriage.

In the space below write out your boundaries for the Internet.

Our Internet agreement for our marriage is:

_____
_____
_____
_____
_____

IN CONCLUSION

Sexual matters need to be addressed by both spouses. Our sexual histories, sexual personalities, sexual development, sexual addictions and intimacy anorexia can all be overcome by the grace of our God and a willingness to obey Him in our areas of need. As we address these issues, we can become more sexually mature and available for God's best sex for the rest of our lives.

As one who has made this journey myself, I can assure you that God will travel with you. You can sexually mature as a couple no matter what your age and enjoy increasingly satisfying intimacy as you grow together—and the results will last a lifetime!

SEVEN

Money Matters

Martin Luther is believed to have said that there are three conversions of a man: his heart, his mind and his purse.[1] I think he had a good understanding of the complex role that money plays in a person's life.

Money is a very personal issue. Most of us are extremely independent in our thinking and resist accountability. But living in a very materialistic, image-driven culture makes money an issue that each couple must address at some point in their marriage.

As a young Christian married couple grows together, it faces many decisions that must be made together. Each spouse has his or her own family history of managing and spending money, and each partner has his spending and money management history. Over time, each spouse will develop a history of spending, managing and hopefully saving and investing within the marriage.

In a marriage, each spouse approaches the handling of

money from a developmental role. A husband or wife can be a financial *child*, a financial *adolescent* or a financial *adult*. If both husband and wife are at different developmental stages financially, coming into unity as a couple can be a huge hurdle to surmount.

> Few couples start out understanding the complexities before them, especially those involving money matters.

A young Christian married couple will make enormous money management decisions. Which partner will manage the money is one major question couples need to address early in the relationship. Here are some questions that every couple must tackle:

- ❏ What do we believe and how do we behave in regard to debt?
- ❏ How much debt is reasonable?
- ❏ What do we believe about spending and the use of credit cards?
- ❏ What do we believe about tithing?

As each couple moves through a myriad of financial decisions, they begin to create a financial system. This system evolves over time and is rarely clearly communicated, and even more rarely agreed upon, by both spouses. Yet the system is very present—functioning in the couple's day-to-day life.

Budgeting, saving, planning for retirement and leaving an inheritance to future grandchildren are all huge financial issues that each couple faces somewhere in its financial journey together. The Bible speaks of the importance of such matters. Proverbs 13:22 says, "A good man leaves an inheritance for his children's children."

Few couples start out understanding the complexities before them, especially those involving money matters. The challenge of financial issues can present a great opportunity for personal growth, closeness and spiritual discipline. These challenges can also present roadblocks to spiritual, emotional, physical and sexual intimacy.

In counseling with couples, I have found money to be a paramount issue at which couples often can get stuck.

Money can build up or tear down intimacy in a couple's relationship. We must confront this head-on as with so many of the other issues we have addressed thus far. Reading through this chapter may be easier for some couples than others. Some husbands or wives were trained in financial issues, and others are just gifted at understanding the complexities of finances. This section contains truths to help make money matters work for you as a couple instead of letting them pull you apart.

THE POWER OF AGREEMENT

Earlier we referred to Amos 3:3, which says, "Do two walk together unless they have agreed to do so?" This principle is powerful, especially when addressing money matters. Financial disagreement can create much havoc and pain for a husband and wife. Even if a financial decision wasn't the best, if a couple agrees together then they both adjust quite well from an intimacy perspective.

Money and its issues are part of a learning process, and mistakes will happen. I don't think I've ever met a couple professionally or personally who has not made some financial mistakes. If you're expecting not to make financial mistakes, you may be placing your expectations way too high.

Can you expect to be informed, wise and prudent in your

money decisions? Absolutely! Will you be perfect throughout forty or more years of marriage? Absolutely not! At some point a husband may make a bad stock decision that causes loss of money. A wife may purchase a new piece of furniture that costs more than their budget can handle. So in the process of discussing the principle of agreement, agree that mistakes with money will occur in your lifetime. One partner will forget to deposit a check and the other partner will overdraw the account, or one partner will make a purchase he or she feels is a great deal only to later discover money was lost. Can we agree mistakes will happen?

Agreeing on Financial Matters

I, _____, agree with my spouse that financial mistakes will probably happen to us through our lifetime together. (Sign and date)

1. _____ Date _____
2. _____ Date _____

This marks the beginning of your agreement on money matters. I know it may seem like an unusual way to start a discussion on money, but I have encountered too many couples with expectations of financial competency that are too high. Then when the finances are not handled perfectly, scapegoating, blaming and harmful behaviors can rob the husband and wife of the intimacy God wants them to experience.

I have discovered that God uses finances to teach me faith, to increase my dependence on Him and to enlarge my relationship with my precious wife, Lisa. We have weathered some interesting storms financially, and some of the storms were not even of our own making. Lisa and I have one steadfast principle that has keep us solid through thick and thin. Lisa and I agree to agree.

We had determined that we will not be in disagreement about any aspect of our financial affairs. We won't spend over a certain amount independently. We won't even increase or decrease our savings or investments or do household improvements without first being in total agreement. If we don't agree, we don't do whatever it is we are thinking about.

I have found that Lisa is God's gift to me in so many areas, and money is one of them. If she is not in 100 percent agreement with a money issue, then we agree that it is not necessary to make that decision yet. If we make a poor decision that we both agreed upon, then we both absorb the consequences without blaming or shaming each other. We both become wiser, and we refine our decision-making process pertaining to money matters.

Let me give you an example about a financial agreement. Every year Lisa and I go out for a New Year's Eve dinner. It is our tradition to set aside that time to review several aspects of our relationship. One of the aspects of our relationship is our personal financial goals for the new year. We may decide to focus the following year on debt reduction, spending in certain areas or investments and savings. One year we agreed to pay off all our debts including our mortgage, which meant that personal spending that year would be kept to a minimum.

Later during that same year I felt a real desire to purchase a new car. My car had been paid off for a few years, and it was about six or seven years old. I started looking at car magazines and would drive by and stop at car dealerships—all the things guys do when they start shopping for a new vehicle. We could definitely afford to buy a car. That was not an issue at that time in our life. But I was forgetting that we had agreed to make no large purchases that year. When my wife reminded me of our agreement, I knew she was right. I didn't like it and may have even argued, but I had given my word and could not break our agreement.

Agreement is primary for navigating through the

complexities of money matters. This is why Lisa and I discuss it first, for without agreement, money issues can generate disunity instead of intimacy.

Sign your names below and the date that you agree to agree on your financial journey together for a minimum of one hundred days as you work together toward intimacy.

I agree to agree financially with my spouse.

_____ Date _____

_____ Date _____

COMING TO GRIPS WITH FINANCIAL HISTORIES

Financial histories begin within your family of origin. How your family did or didn't handle money has a major influence on your learning curve about money. The following story can help you to see this more clearly.

> I have found that Lisa is God's gift to me in so many areas, and money is one of them.

Kurt and Darlene are an upper middle-class couple who earned $200,000 a year together. Kurt grew up very poor. He spoke openly about moving frequently as a child and leaving behind unpaid bills. He wore hand-me-downs from his two older brothers. As soon as they could, all the boys worked various odd jobs such as cutting the grass, newspaper routes and harvesting in the summer. Kurt was smart, intuitive and could sell anything.

Kurt grew up promising himself that he would never again be poor. He worked hard and earned lots of money, but Kurt had learned nothing about the value of paying bills, nor did he have boundaries around spending. In his family, if Mom or

Dad had money, he remembers them spending it. He didn't recall conversations about savings or retirement accounts in his parent's conversations.

Darlene, on the other hand, grew up in a two-income family. Dad was a real estate lawyer, and Mom was a certified public accountant. Both parents worked hard, saved, invested and were able to retire shortly after Darlene was out of college. They had lots of talks about money around the table. Discussions about stocks rising and falling were common at Darlene's home.

When Darlene started to work at the local ice cream store, she opened her own bank account on which her mother was a cosigner. Together she and her mom worked on paying her tithes and saving money for a car. Darlene met Kurt one year after college and married a year later.

They both worked until the children were born, and then Darlene stayed at home. Darlene managed the money because Kurt really didn't want to be bothered. Darlene and Kurt came in for counseling because of their differences over the way they dealt with money. The primary issue was that if Kurt wanted to buy something, he would just go ahead and buy it. Three-wheelers, motorcycles and endless hunting gear became a real point of contention with Darlene. Kurt was earning a high income, but he spent the money just as quickly as he made it.

They argued and fussed about the finances for most of their eight years of marriage. They had little savings, and the small amount they had was what retirement Kurt's company provided. The only financial plan they had was Kurt makes the money and Darlene pays the bills.

Needless to say, Kurt and Darlene are not that uncommon when it comes to financial histories prior to marriage. I myself grew up in a very poor family and had absolutely no financial training from my parents. Lisa, on the other hand, grew up in a more financially stable situation and was taught about saving money. When we met, I was a poor Bible college student without a car, and she was employed and knew how to save money, buy a car and had great credit.

We all bring into our marriages the financial influences from our family of origin. I want to make clear that we cannot blame families for our financial problems. I personally have had to get the information and training to become financially responsible, and anyone else can do the same. There are plenty of Christian books on the subject of finances that you can find in any Christian bookstore.

YOUR FAMILY OF ORIGIN'S INFLUENCE

Without blaming, you do need to address your family of origin's influence on your financial history.

Family of Origin Financial History

1. How were financial decisions made in your family?
2. Who controlled or managed the money?
3. What were you taught about tithing?
4. What seemed to be the family's attitudes and behaviors about:

   a. Debt?

   b. Large purchase spending?

   c. Recreational spending?

   d. Saving money?

   e. Investing/retirement?

5. How did your mom and dad communicate about money in general?
6. How did they handle financial crises?
7. What did you learn, both positively and negatively, about money from your parents?

8. In the space below, describe your family's financial influence as best as you can.

His family's financial influences:

_____
_____
_____
_____

Her family's financial influences:

_____
_____
_____
_____

9. You both have financial histories that involve influences from your family of origin. Plan a time with each other to discuss these findings from your family of origin.

   Our appointment date to discuss this together is _____

You may have a financial history as a single adult prior to marriage. I have prepared some questions for both you and your spouse to help you understand that history. After answering these questions, make a time to discuss these findings.

FINANCIAL HISTORY OF HUSBAND PRIOR TO MARRIAGE

1. As a single person, how did you manage your money?
2. Did you tithe money earned prior to marriage?
3. Did you save money?

4. What was your attitude toward money? Did you consider your money to be your own or God's?
5. How did you pay for your first car?
6. With whom did you discuss money matters, and how did you educate yourself financially prior to marriage?

FINANCIAL HISTORY OF WIFE PRIOR TO MARRIAGE

1. How did you as a single person manage your money?
2. Did you tithe money earned prior to marriage?
3. Did you save money?
4. What was your attitude toward money? Did you consider your money to be your own or God's?
5. How did you pay for your first car?
6. With whom did you discuss money matters, and how did you educate yourself financially prior to marriage?

After you are married, you continue to express yourself through your finances, spending, debt, savings, investing and tithing. Discuss the following questions together as they relate to areas of your past financial history that you would like to change. If money management has been a weak area in your relationship, you may need to ask a pastor or counselor to join you. Some husbands and wives find it helpful to write their answers separately and then to come together in a public place such as a restaurant to discuss them.

OUR PAST FINANCIAL HISTORY

1. As a husband and wife, what have been your beliefs and behaviors regarding tithing?

2. What is your general attitude and behavior toward money? Do you consider it to be God's money or your own?
3. As a couple, what have been your attitudes, behaviors and agreements about large purchase spending? Debt? Recreational spending? Savings? Investing? Holiday spending? Budgeting? Retirement?
4. Who primarily manages the money and why?
5. What have been your financial goals in the past, and have you met these goals?
6. Historically, what emotions arise around the discussion of money? From the husband? From the wife?

After you answer these questions separately, they are to be discussed. See if you can create an accurate account of your financial history together. It is important for you to be aware of how you think about money as a couple. You also need to discern any roadblocks that may be hindering you from experiencing the best intimacy possible.

I realize that some of the issues you will need to address and not sweep under the rug can be sensitive and challenging. Your journey to intimacy demands self-growth from both you and your spouse in a variety of areas. Be encouraged! Once these major issues are addressed, you will be forever freed from repeating the same past mistakes.

HOW FINANCIALLY GROWN UP ARE YOU?

As individuals, we develop physically, sexually, socially and financially. How you have grown and developed financially as an individual is vitally important when discussing your financial situation as a couple. You briefly discussed the influence of your family upon your marriage. Now, let's look at how far you have come in your own individual financial development.

Let's outline three stages of development as a financial person. Each of these stages will be identified and their characteristics discussed. These stages are not to be used as points of shaming or blaming the other spouse but as paradigms for self-understanding.

> Financial children live in a magical world where everything seems to work out for their benefit.

Paradigms can be very helpful for understanding yourself. They provide insight into what stage you are in and where you need to go. The following section is intended to help you to gain understanding about yourself, not necessarily about your spouse. If you choose to discuss this section as a couple, discuss the insights that you have gained about yourself, not what you have learned about your partner.

As in all human development, there appears to be three phases or stages. The first stage of any development in any human dimension, whether physical, psychological, emotional, spiritual or financial is the *child* phase. The second phase of development is the *adolescent* phase. The last phase, of course, is the *adult* phase of development. Let's look at developing as a financial person in light of these three stages.

Financial child

A financial child is a husband or wife who absolutely refuses to have anything to do with finances. If you don't say no too often and you give this person his or her candy and toys, he is happy.

An adult who is a financial child feels overwhelmed and confused when money issues are raised. He or she may completely delegate the checkbook to the other spouse and will place the full responsibility of their financial future on the spouse's shoulders. Taxes are too complicated, bank statements don't make sense and investing is what rich people do, or so the financial child believes.

There are husbands and wives who stay at this stage of financial development all of their lives. They marry young and allow their spouse to do all the financial planning, asking only for a spending allowance. Spending is not difficult for a financial child; it's the credit card bills that are confusing.

Financial children live in a magical world where everything seems to work out for their benefit. Christians who are financial children may spiritualize their stunted development by claiming they are "trusting the Lord" to handle the finances. A financial child lives in the here and now only. They do not intelligently address important future financial issues.

This behavior may work out in your favor if you happen to marry a financial adult or someone who likes total control of the money. However, if something should ever happen to the spouse who handles all the finances, often the financial child doesn't even know where the checkbook or insurance policies are located.

The male financial child may be the one who makes the money, but his wife controls the checkbook. He gets his allowance and has to check in with his wife to spend beyond his allowance. He lets his wife and accountant figure out everything and provides the obligatory signatures. He really doesn't like the system, but it's better than learning it for himself. An occasional blowup might occur if there is a toy he can't afford, but overall he goes with the adult's financial plan of action.

Financial adolescents never consider the consequences of their purchases.

A female financial child is very similar. She might have her own checking account or credit cards, but must use them within the limits set by the adult. She receives her weekly or monthly stipend and has to make requests for any larger sums of money. She doesn't have any idea what she and her husband earn together, where her investments are or how much life insurance they may carry. She asks few questions and wants to know as little as possible at tax time when it is time to sign the forms. She is generally happy and doesn't concern herself with other financial decisions.

This lifestyle can work for the financial child, but eventually the spouse fills with resentment. The burden of shouldering all of the financial concerns, retirement plans, bill payments and unplanned expenses can be overwhelming. Resentment and disrespect for the financial child can build over the years. Eventually the financial adult's unresolved feelings toward the financial child can erect a roadblock to intimacy.

Financial adolescent

The financial adolescent is different in attitudes and behaviors from the financial child. Similar to adolescents in general, the world totally revolves around financial adolescents and their needs. A financial adolescent is characterized by an enormous sense of financial entitlement.

The money present in the marriage is theirs, irrespective of who worked for it. It is not mutual money but "my money." If the financial adolescent wants something he should have it. Not only should he have it, he should have it "now!"

Financial adolescents never consider the consequences of their purchases. They try to keep up with the Joneses and create a mountain of debt. They want to look good and feel better than everyone around them.

Financial adolescents are emotionally volatile regarding financial issues. They feel threatened when their judgment is questioned. They will make you pay emotionally if you don't agree with them when they want you to.

Unlike a financial child, a financial adolescent does not accept boundaries around money very well. If you put limits on their credit card, they will simply get another one that you don't know about.

When it comes to money, financial adolescents will lie if they need to. Christian financial adolescents will just not tell you the whole truth. Living with a financial adolescent feels volatile and unsafe. As a spouse, you are more likely to experience financial betrayal. This betrayal may be in spending, creating debt or in borrowing money without your knowledge or agreement.

Financial adolescents resent any financial control in their life. If they are Christians, they keep God outside of their box when it comes to the decision-making process of spending and incurring debt until a major crisis happens and they need God's help to get out of it.

The male financial adolescent is often a financial tyrant. He keeps the wife on a "need-to-know basis." This means that if the financial adolescent thinks she should be informed, he will tell her. If he deems she doesn't need to know about a financial matter, then he doesn't tell her.

As a Christian, he may overspiritualize his role as "the man." Emotional abuse will occur if his judgment is questioned or if his desire for something new is challenged. He may prefer his wife to be emotionally and financially dependent on him so he cannot be challenged. Her natural inclinations toward present and future security are ignored or rejected.

> Money isn't for you alone. It becomes a part of a spiritual realm as well. Your money is God's.

His plans for retirement are simple: He'll worry about that later. Often he has been plagued with a history of careless spending, ongoing debt and at times has been neglectful of the needs of his wife and family.

A financial adolescent wife shares many of the same characteristics as the adolescent husband but often expresses them in a more passive way. If she works, her money is "hers" and his money is "theirs," which means it is hers as well. Like her male counterpart, she often keeps up with the Joneses. She has an insatiable appetite for the best makeup, makeovers, cosmetic surgery, clothes and massages.

She lives in hot pursuit of a really good bargain or of making something of hers better. Her emphasis on savings may be deceptive. Her belief of saving forty dollars while spending ninety can be a way of rationalizing the years of frivolous spending.

If she has credit cards, both hers and the family cards are maxed out. When questioned about this, she retorts, "You don't understand" or another shaming remark directed at the male gender.

Often she is not directly honest and open about her spending. She refuses to "be treated like a child." Therefore, monitoring her spending or expecting accountability from her is impossible. She can be sweet, charming and even quite spiritual, but don't confront her about her money or her right to spend it.

As her spouse, you will pay dearly emotionally and often sexually if you question or limit her spending. She lives for the day. Retirement and savings are her husband's worries and something he should do for her. She shares the same attitudes of entitlement with her male financial adolescent counterpart.

Living with a wife who is a financial adolescent can be unpredictable. The spouse of the male or female adolescent often feels more hopeless than angry. Feelings of aloneness are very real for the man or woman married to a financial adolescent.

FINANCIAL ADULT

Few, if any, of us are born as financial adults. Most of us have made our mistakes during our financial adolescence and stumbled into financial adulthood as a result of a tumultuous process. The cost of our financial adulthood education is high, but the results can be tremendous with the time we have left.

In financial adulthood your understanding about money shifts entirely. Money isn't for you alone. It becomes a part of a spiritual realm as well. Your money is God's. Not only tithes and offerings, but the rest of it as well. You are a financial adult when you are consciously aware of your stewardship of the money you earn and feel accountable to God for it.

Financial adulthood is distinguished by a genuine effort to be financially responsible. The financial adult is committed to paying bills on time. If that cannot happen, the truth is clearly communicated.

A financial adult knows he or she is not perfect and still makes mistakes. The financial adult seeks out information when making large purchases.

The future is a reality for the financial adult. He or she regularly plans for investments and savings. The financial adult takes retirement seriously and doesn't look to the government, a company or Santa Claus for security.

Reasonable debt is considered intelligently with pad and paper along with a plan to pay it off. Financial adults consider reckless debt and keeping up with Joneses as distasteful and shortsighted.

Living with a financial adult is a true blessing from God. Someone who has both feet on the ground financially is a huge asset to a marriage. If two financial adults marry each other they are usually happy and plan together for early retirement and college funds for the children, along with Christmas and recreational spending.

Both husband and wife financial adults share the same

values and behaviors. They make informed choices, not based on feelings, but on sound financial principles. Secrets are not necessary in a relationship with financial adults. They are able to have firm boundaries financially and accept accountability and seek out wise counsel when needed.

If you are a couple seeking to develop and maintain intimacy on all levels, you must address money issues. This is true whether you are a financial child, adolescent or adult. Financial agreement must be your next step to intimacy. Only when you aim to live as financial adults can you truly bless each other and your children.

This discussion is designed to help both husband and wife discover yourselves. If you need to grow in this area, then make it a point of prayer and ongoing study. God will be with you. The journey may be interesting, but He will give you wisdom.

> If any of you lacks wisdom, he should ask God, who gives generously to all without finding fault, and it will be given to him.
> —JAMES 1:5

I have spent many hours as a maturing Christian asking God for financial wisdom. Over the years of being married, He has used my financially mature wife, accountants, financial advisors and all kinds of Christian financial literature, together with His holy Word, to mature me into financial adulthood. I am not perfect financially, but I feel truly blessed and reasonably responsible now with our finances. I say this to glorify God because if He can mature me despite my ignorance and willfulness, then anyone can become a financial adult.

ELECTING A MONEY MANAGER

Every husband and wife on the planet has to address the age-old question: "Who will manage the money?"

Money must be managed through every stage of a couple's marriage. In the early years of marriage, there generally isn't a lot of money to manage. One person might be working and the other attending college. Even if both are working, it doesn't take much to pay the rent for an apartment, perhaps a furniture bill and a utility or two.

Over time, with increasing mortgages, insurance and medical expenses for a growing family, the job of managing money can require more time and skill.

Early on couples tend to elect the person who either is naturally better at managing money or the person who puts up less of a fuss about doing it. No election or voting process took place. If you ask most couples when this position was determined, neither will remember the day it began. This entire process of electing a money manager remains a mystery in most marriages.

The person elected into office doesn't realize that this is a lifelong post, and rarely can he or she get a recount of the votes. Everyone just goes along with this pattern for some time. Over time, as this position demands increasing skill in accounting and investing, the money manager can become a lonely position.

The issue of who has authority over the couples' money creeps slowly into the marital dynamic. Surely the person who writes the checks is the authority, right? They miraculously become the financial authority on what can and cannot be purchased and when. True, they have more information, but who voted this person to office anyway?

It's humorous how most couples really don't consider role, authority and the length of term of the money manager. For some husbands and wives, figuring out who will be the money manager is like a game of hot potatoes. Both partners are anxious to pass it back to the other partner. Neither wants to hold the potato for more than a month or two, or at least until his desired purchase is assured.

You can easily see how manipulation, control and other issues can naturally arise as a couple determines who will fill the position. Let's briefly look at the money manager's responsibilities, roles, terms and authority.

RESPONSIBILITIES OF THE MONEY MANAGER

- ❑ Receives all incoming funds
- ❑ Writes checks for all payments due
- ❑ Records all transactions
- ❑ Reviews monthly bank records to confirm record keeping accuracy
- ❑ Mails all payments in a timely manner
- ❑ Has a reporting system to keep the other spouse informed and updated
- ❑ Makes most purchases
- ❑ Researches most purchases
- ❑ Researches and maintains health, car, house and life insurance
- ❑ Researches and maintains all savings programs for college for the children
- ❑ Researches and maintains all investments for the couple
- ❑ Plans for Christmas and vacation spending
- ❑ Distributes allowances to all family members
- ❑ Always is cheerful during financial negotiations

Role of the money manager

- ❏ Absorbs all financial stress around debt, spending and family members' desires
- ❏ Does all the job requires without taking away from marital or family time
- ❏ Keeps all the details of researching, countless phone hours on hold and purchase management a secret, and puts on a happy face
- ❏ Makes sure all family members are content
- ❏ Is willing to respectfully and tactfully fight for financial integrity and common sense spending

Money manager's term of office

- ❏ Until death
- ❏ Until an accountant, financial advisor, lawyer or others are hired
- ❏ Until other spouse wants a shot at it
- ❏ Until the office is shared by both spouses

Authority

- ❏ Just under God
- ❏ All powerful
- ❏ Questionable when the other spouse disagrees
- ❏ None whatsoever. The other spouse does whatever they want to anyway

We can laugh at ourselves for being willing to take on such a job. Remember this job is on top of a full-time job and the care of children, and it is a nonpaid position.

OK, I think we have poked enough fun at the position of the money manager. This time you are reviewing the position as a financial adult when you decide who can fill the role of the money manager.

PRINCIPLE OF AGREEMENT

In this guide we have discussed the principle of agreement more than once. Anytime a husband and wife are making a decision on how the couple or family system is going to operate, it is important to consider the principle of agreement.

Every couple develops a system of governing. Some couples choose a *theocracy* in which God is the head of the family. Both spouses are subject to Him and seek Him for wisdom and guidance. Neither person holds all the truth or all the power. Instead they both respect Christ in each other and accept that as a team they hear and obey God.

Other couples knowingly or unknowingly choose a *monarchy*. This is a popular system in which one person (often the husband) has the ultimate deciding power. He is the king of the family. The king may be a benevolent king and one who humbly listens to the wisdom, perspective and feelings of his spouse. He may truly seek God and base his decisions on the Word of God, prayer and the guidance of peace through the Holy Spirit.

But on the other hand, the king may not be a humble king. He may be proud, selfish or even addicted to something. His ability to glean insight from his spouse may be limited, or doing so may be irrelevant to him. His spiritual maturity may be limited or even non-existent, although he may attend church.

Another system of government that a couple may choose to decide upon could be a *democratic* system. In this system, at least hypothetically, each partner has a 50 percent vote or ownership in the marital system. Each couple makes his or her positions, arguments and feelings known. Each spouse feels he gets to express his positions on the matters at hand. If they disagree, they can stay in a gridlock of arguing and positioning until they agree or until the person with the most emotional energy around the issue succeeds.

Again, if both spouses include Christ in their decision-making process and seek God and His Word, this system can operate peacefully—some would say successfully. Both spouses have and give respect to each other. Both are listened to, and once a decision is agreed upon, both accept responsibility for the outcome.

> Anytime a husband and wife are making a decision on how the couple or family system is going to operate, it is important to consider the principle of agreement.

However, if the spiritual maturity of one or both partners is limited or non-existent, this system can become volatile. Continual manipulation, control and personality- or emotion-based rationales and entitlements can disrupt this style of governing quite significantly.

A last system of government is a *corporate* governing style. This couple actively agrees upon areas of responsibility. They create two department heads or two vice presidents. In this system, one department may be fully responsible for outside of the house decisions such as the yard, lawn or vacations. The other spouse may be responsible for all the decisions on the interior such as the utilities, decorating and managing the shopping. They set up corporate policies on spending and have mandatory meetings when spending more than a certain amount of money.

The department head does have unilateral decision-making responsibility over his department. He or she does not need to consult the other spouse unless a particular expenditure demands a business meeting by both departments. The greatest difficulty with this system is deciding who is responsible for what, including childcare issues. Once the corporate structure is set up and agreed upon, the system can run smoothly.

Like the previous system of governing, the success of this system depends upon the level of spiritual maturity of each department. If both are reasonably mature, this system can make for peace or harmony inside a marriage. Some couples choose this system from the beginning of their marriage, and others evolve into this system as their lives become more difficult to manage.

It's important to examine major governing themes because in money issues, the couple's true system of government will be exposed immediately. As a marriage therapist, anytime we move into the issue of finances, the couple's real beliefs and behaviors become obvious to all three of us in the room.

One of the best ways I know to illustrate this is with the example of a couple who is deciding to buy a new car. They may both weigh the issue of whether or not to buy a car now. If they decide to buy a car, whose car is it, and who decides what kind and color it should be? If one or both go to buy the car, then who handles the insurance issues, and who takes care of the ongoing maintenance of the vehicle?

In the theocratic system, both partners will sincerely pray individually and as a couple, and then go through the entire car-purchasing process seeking God's will first. In the monarchy system, the king will decide when and what to buy, perhaps choosing to delegate all the details. If he is a good king, he may seek God individually for His will on a vehicle purchase.

Within the democratic system the husband and wife may "discuss" this purchase in great detail, vote and agree on each part of the process. If they are Christians, we would hope they would involve God, His Word and prayer in the process.

In a corporate system of governing, it is the person who is in the department who makes the decision in the case. The couple agrees on whose department it falls under, and that person makes the decisions. If he or she is a loving department head, he consults the other department (his/her spouse) during the process. The department head can, however, by the power delegated to him by the corporate structure, make unilateral decisions for the company (marriage) and purchase a vehicle that seems appropriate to him.

The principle of agreement comes into play when the husband and wife actively decide their governing style. Agreement is often lacking in immature, youthful marriages, but marriages evolve into this process as a couple grows.

Now, as adults, it's time to really decide how to govern yourself. You will need to set aside some time for several discussions in order to work through this process. Both spouses must make decisions without manipulation in order for the agreement to be official.

If you neither decide on a system of governing nor participate in one, you may be setting up roadblocks to intimacy. We are seeking to remove obstacles that hinder the intimacy God desires for His children to have in a marriage. If you and your spouse fully agree on a governing system, peace can reign in a marriage regardless of the particular system you choose. As we say in America, "The people have spoken."

Smoother sailing can be ahead of you financially than the waters through which you have navigated in the past. If the organizational chart is clear, many decisions can be made without disrupting your marriage. The more peace in this area of your marriage, the greater the chance your marriage has at maintaining and growing in intimacy.

CAST YOUR BALLOT

After hours of consideration, the hour of reckoning is come. The clock is striking twelve, and the streets are clearing as both husband and wife place their votes as to how they will govern. This is a historic event. Please fill out your governing papers.

Pertaining to the marriage of Mr. _____ and Mrs. _____, we hereby certify and agree to govern ourselves primarily in a _____ form of government. Let it be hereby known by community, church and our Lord Jesus Christ that on this date of _____ we both agree without duress to conduct our governing decision-making process accordingly until further decreed by the sovereignty of our marriage. We do so by the power invested in us both by our God and by the state of _____ in holy matrimony.

Wow! I feel better already. Once you as a couple agree on the governing style, so much stress can be relieved. There are so many decisions to be made over the decades of your marriage that it is of paramount importance that you agree on a process for these decisions.

Now you need to apply this unity to several key money issues that you will face. Let's look at these key areas for optimal financial functioning as a couple.

KEY MONEY ISSUES

TITHING

Tithing is an enduring biblical principle in which an individual or couple gives a tenth of their earnings to the house of God. Theologians vary in their interpretation of the Scriptures on tithing. Some consider tithing as a part of the Old Testament law that does not apply to modern-day Christians. Others argue that tithing actually pre-dates the Law of Moses, therefore it is applicable to all of God's people throughout the ages.

Modern-day tithing is supported by the following scripture:

> Then Melchizedek king of Salem brought out bread and wine. He was priest of God Most High, and he blessed Abram, saying, "Blessed be Abram by God Most High, Creator of heaven and earth. And blessed be God Most High, who delivered your enemies into your hand." Then Abram gave him a tenth of everything.
> —Genesis 14:18–21

There are several ways to decide intelligently whether or not you should tithe and how much you should give—which usually really means how little do I have to give.

> Agreement is often lacking in immature, youthful marriages, but marriages evolve into this process as a couple grows.

I will leave the intellectual issues to others. I am concerned about the heart of the matter. I am a tither and have been all my Christian life. When Lisa and I first received income as a couple, we agreed that we would give at least a tithe to God. We have been married for more than fourteen years, and God has been more than faithful to us financially. I say this so you understand that I have a bias about this issue. I wish everyone was as richly blessed as Lisa and I are on all levels, including finances.

Lisa and I give as an expression of our love and appreciation to our Lord Jesus Christ, not only for salvation and eternal life, but also for all the immeasurable nonfinancial blessings that we have in our lives. Just putting a dollar into the offering plate would not properly reflect our love for God.

As a couple, you must truly seek God on the matter of tithing. If you are not currently or regularly tithing, discern why you do not do so. Is it something that has just evolved, or is this an active choice you've made as a couple to not give a tithe to God? If it has just evolved within your governing structure, you need to address it decisively.

As we have repeated throughout this guide, agreement is the core issue. As a first step, get informed by reading Scripture and books about tithing. Then more importantly, ask God. Pray and meditate about this matter daily for a week or more, and ask God to give you a sense of His will for your relationship. As a couple, you can both discern the will of God.

Remember, as Samuel instructed, it is better to obey God than to give sacrifices:

> But Samuel replied: "Does the LORD delight in burnt offerings and sacrifices as much as in obeying the voice of the LORD? To obey is better than sacrifice, and to heed is better then the fat of rams."
>
> —1 SAMUEL 15:22

Your obedience to Christ is the issue. If He has communicated to you as a couple that you should tithe and you refuse to obey, then you might want to consider James 4:17:

> Anyone, then, who knows the good he ought to do and doesn't do it, sins.

This is a major money matter that Christian couples especially must be united in so as not to detract from building intimacy together. Once the issue of tithing is settled by a couple, it will be one less discussion you need to have during the course of your happy marriage.

Our Financial Commitment

On this date of _____, Mr. and Mrs. _____ agree to tithe or not to tithe (circle one) ____ percent of their income to the house of God.

DEBT

Debt is also a significant issue. Debt is rarely discussed as a principle prior to decisions that demand immediate action. Most couples just let emotions dictate how much debt they will get involved in. The following story is an illustration of this.

Al and Tina married right out of college and were a typical all-American couple. When I met them, they had a thirteen-year-old son and an eleven-year-old daughter. Al and Tina were approaching their late thirties. They both worked hard throughout their marriage and had a combined income of about eighty-five thousand dollars a year.

They entered marriage with several student loans and lived in an apartment for a few years. They were making pretty good money, so they both wanted new cars. They began responsibly paying off both cars along with insurance, rent and student loans. They both carried a small credit card debt that they each kept track of separately and had a joint credit card for emergencies as well. Since both Tina and Al didn't have much furniture to bring into the marriage and were tired of the hand-me-down furniture they received from family, friends and garage sales, they decided to purchase new furniture. After plenty of shopping, they saw dining room, bedroom and living room furniture they really liked and purchased all of it on credit.

The big day came when Tina told Al they were going to have their first baby. The couple was happy, but as the months rolled by, they realized that their small apartment could no longer accommodate them.

They began to look for a house and found one they both

really loved, but the payments would take about 30 percent of their income. They obtained a mortgage, and fortunately, Al was being promoted, so they felt they could add the payments to their expanding budget. The added strain of additional bills and Tina taking off work to raise their first child made for financially difficult times. The second child came along two years later, and Al continued to get promoted at work.

Soon their children's education became a pressing issue as they considered a small private Christian school. Al and Tina continued to prosper. It was time to pay for another family car, family vacations, medical expenses and the ever-increasing load of unmanageable debt.

> Lisa and I give as an expression of our love and appreciation to our Lord Jesus Christ…Just putting a dollar into the offering plate would not properly reflect our love for God.

Al and Tina were starting to fight over many things, but finances and credit card debt became a really big hindrance to intimacy. During counseling the issue of debt surfaced quickly.

Al and Tina never really thought much about the principle of debt. They just went through life acquiring debt and not really planning for emergencies or the future. This couple's relationship was wrought with financial anxiety. Al felt extremely pressured as the sole provider, and Tina felt unsure of their ability to provide a Christian education for their children and still continue to meet their other ever-increasing needs.

Al and Tina represent probably the majority of Americans who neglect to come to a place of agreement on the principle or practice of debt. They were not in agreement on the use of credit cards. They also didn't agree in advance roughly about what percentage of debt they should carry in relation to their income. They appeared to have no boundaries as far as debt was concerned. Most of these financial issues could have been addressed in premarital counseling. Often in the early stages of marriage, debt seems so manageable that it is a nonissue and is not even discussed.

Couples like Al and Tina who make a fairly good income are borrowing from their future wealth to pay their past sometimes unwise decisions. Not only did Al and Tina need to have some conversations about debt, but they now needed to create a financial plan to reduce their indebtedness. In this manner they can have more intimacy and less friction in their marriage.

It took fifteen or more years for Al and Tina to get so into debt that finances affected their intimacy. I assured them that the solution would take time, an educated plan and active restraint on both of their parts to stick to their plan.

Debt is a money matter that every couple needs to address—the sooner the better—so that debt will not become overwhelming.

First, ask yourselves some questions. What are the principles of debt that you both agree upon? God has probably blessed your marriage by giving you both different starting and reference points regarding debt, but where can you find agreement? The following positions (or camps) can help you to clarify what you really believe.

1. Debt is evil. All debt should not happen. If you can't pay for it, you don't need it.
2. Debt is a bad thing but acceptable in the case of a house and/or car purchase.
3. Reasonable debt is acceptable.

4. Debt is a part of life, so do the best you can to stay out of the bankruptcy court.
5. Purchase as you please. God will clean up any messes that you make.

How does your camp of agreement line up with your biblical perspective of debt? After prayer, reading and discussion, agree together on whatever camp you both decide on. Now the question comes to mind as to what camp do you actually practice?

As a therapist, I can only believe behaviors. Debt is a behavior that can be traced simply to what you believe about debt. Which camp do you and your spouse operate in? If what you believe and how you behave differ, then you need to develop a plan that is congruent with your convictions. Agreement will be important as you decide on a plan for reducing or incurring future debt.

In the space below, write what you agree upon as far as the principle of debt.

Our Financial Belief

Our belief about debt as a couple is:

_____
_____
_____
_____

Now that you agree on the principle of debt, let's discuss the percentage of debt you want to have in your relationship. Personally, I do not want any debt at all. But as husband and wife, what do you both agree upon?

I personally am an advocate of living below your means and

having as little debt as possible. When God touched my heart about the debt issue I had created in our marriage, Lisa and I developed a plan. God did many miracles and removed all debt including our mortgage. It was hard work, but Lisa and I succeeded because we were in agreement.

As a couple, what percentage of your income do you ideally want to have in your current situation? Look at your debt load right now. How much of your income(s) is going toward debt, mortgage, cars, credit cards, loans or other large purchase items bought on credit? (circle one)

    10 percent   20 percent   30 percent

    40 percent   50 percent   Other _____

What is the difference between your ideal percentage of debt and your current percentage of debt? Your answer will give you a place to focus your attention.

Once you have set a goal of what your debt load should be, gather some good reading material on debt reduction and other financial matters and meet with a financial adviser whom you can trust. A pastor can review your financial goals to help keep you accountable regarding your agreement about debt reduction.

Regardless of their current debt status, some couples have agreed that this issue will not create a roadblock to their intimacy.

Debt is one of the key issues couples must address during marriage, but unfortunately, it is not the only key money matter that needs to be considered.

Retirement

Couples often neglect this money matter, especially early in the marriage. We go through our younger years without a care or thought about retirement. We are young and others are old, and we feel as if we have our entire lives ahead of us to think about retirement. The thirties move in quickly, and retirement becomes something we begin to discuss very moderately. When we cross over to the forties, pressure mounts about our future quality of life. By the fifties, we either feel excited about our financial future or really worried and just plain scared as we see our future approaching. The older we get, the more retirement issues become primary.

All couples will retire eventually unless they go to be with the Lord first. The earlier a couple addresses the issue of retirement, the less stress the marriage will feel.

A man and woman can feel more secure financially if they have thought through the issues of retirement. The basics are pretty simple to figure out for a couple.

When do you want to retire?

Take a moment here with the love of your life and discuss this. Do you want to retire at fifty, fifty-five, sixty, sixty-five, seventy, seventy-five or at eighty years of age? Any answer you both agree on is fine. The principle of agreement is as important in this decision as in any other money matter. Write down your retirement age below.

>Our ideal age to retire is _____ and _____.

That was painless enough, wasn't it? Unfortunately, this is the easiest part of retirement. The next decision has to do with your retirement lifestyle. How much money will you need to live on in retirement? Consider the basics: housing (is it paid off yet?), utilities, food, property taxes, travel and transportation. You may need to take a moment or even a week to think through these issues, but the sooner the better.

When you retire, what financial amount do you want to live on?

Two thousand dollars a month? Or $10,000 monthly? Once both of you decide on a monthly figure, together with the lifestyle you'll have, you will be well on your way to grappling with retirement issues. Write down what you both believe that you need financially a month to live comfortably.

>Monthly retirement income desired is _____.

Now take your monthly retirement income and multiply it by 12. For example, a couple thinks they will need $5,000 a month for retirement. Take $5,000 x 12 months = $60,000 annual income needed to fund your retirement.

You now have taken the second largest step in deciding your retirement goals for your marriage. Now the fun really begins. How in the world do you make $60,000 a year and not work?

This is where the financial planning part really comes in. Some couples invest in real estate during their early years, hoping to live off the income or sale of their properties. Some invest in building a company together in hopes of selling it for a significant profit at retirement. Others work nine to five and are betting on their company pensions. Some couples invest cautiously over the years in mutual funds, stocks, bonds or similar financial instruments. Still others plan on social security to get them through retirement.

What you need to do is figure out your estimated income from these various resources. Once you total these, you may have an idea of what your present retirement goals need to be.

> A man and woman can feel more secure financially if they have thought through the issues of retirement.

For example, if a couple's combined social security will be approximately $1,200 a month and their pensions together will equal $1,800 a month, then they need to plan to invest in some way to make the other $2,000 a month so they have their $5,000-a-month dream retirement.

If you are investing in mutual funds, you will need about $100,000 in a fund to receive about $800 per month as a rule of thumb. That would mean the couple in our example would need more than $200,000 invested prior to their date of retirement to earn that extra $1,800 a month.

For most couples, $200,000 or $1,000,000 are astronomical sums of money. If a couple is thirty years old and wants to retire at sixty, let's look at what they would need to invest monthly, not counting the interest they will earn.

Planning for Retirement

Thirty years old and retiring at 60 (that is 360 months) for the following amounts, without including annual interest:

$200,000 ÷ 360 months = $555 per month

$300,000 ÷ 360 months = $833 per month

$500,000 ÷ 360 months = $1,389 per month

$1,000,000 ÷ 360 months = $2,778 per month

These numbers are a little high because you would receive a percentage of profit annually depending on how you invested your money, which would reduce your monthly amount. I present this not to scare you but to help motivate you to be financially prepared for retirement.

I am not a financial advisor in any shape or form. I strongly suggest you find a licensed financial advisor who is trustworthy, and then sit down with him or her, review your goals and map out a strategy.

Like debt, it doesn't matter where you are when you begin. Couples who make a plan about retirement and review this plan at least annually can get in agreement, and it will be one less issue that could potentially block intimacy.

SAVINGS

Every married couple must also address having a savings account. What percentage of your income do you tuck away monthly for a rainy day or for health or job crisis? A couple that doesn't plan in this respect can rupture their intimacy and marriage during such an incredibly stressful time.

Keeping an available savings account is a prudent thing to do. Use the principle of agreement to decide how much savings you need as a couple to feel comfortable. The amount will reflect any other resources that you have set aside for future use.

The first savings issue: What percentage of your income do you currently set aside for savings? (circle one)

| 1 percent | 5 percent | 10 percent |
| 15 percent | 20 percent | Other _____ |

What percentage of your income do you desire to place in savings? Be sure the amount is reasonable for your current income and lifestyle. (circle one)

| 1 percent | 5 percent | 10 percent |
| 15 percent | 20 percent | Other _____ |

The next step is agreeing on when you will begin this savings plan and how it will take place. Automatic withdrawals work great for creating a savings account. With this in effect, you need not make the painful decision to write a separate check every month. The bank just moves a designated amount over into savings, and you don't have to think about it anymore.

The date we are planning to start a savings plan is _____.

The method of savings payments being made is _____.

Now you must agree on the appropriate reasons for making withdrawals from the account. If you are saving for a car and reach the purchase amount, you will experience no discord when you use the funds. On the other hand, if you are saving for a rainy day, and one spouse alone decides to withdraw the money to buy a car or another purchase, disharmony will occur that can disrupt marital intimacy.

> Budgeting is not the most fun thing you can do in a relationship, but it is essential to have open and fact-based financial communication.

As a couple, what is the purpose of your savings? (Remember, this is not a retirement or college fund.)

The purpose of our savings is:

_____
_____
_____
_____

Depending on your governing style, you have determined who has the responsibility or authority to withdraw funds from this account. Do both spouses have access to the records of this account? Do you both have to agree before funds are removed from the account? Do you want to set up an account that requires two signatures to be able to access these funds? These questions must be answered and addressed prior to a "need" that may arise.

COLLEGE

As husband and wife, do you want to fund all, some or none of your children's or grandchildren's education? Once you agree on whether or not this is a priority, you should create a plan to accomplish this goal financially. A college education is very expensive, and I don't think we can expect to see the costs go down. If you plan on setting up a mutual fund account, see a financial advisor. Make sure you agree if the account goes in your name or the child's. Understand how tax laws apply, and determine who controls the account when the child is eighteen.

Lisa and I started a college fund for our children the month they were born. We talk about "big boy" and "big girl" school (college) at least weekly. When they go to college, the funds will be ready for their use.

Every couple has to make a choice about this issue. The earlier you make the choice the better. As long as you both agree on your position regarding this issue, it should not become a roadblock to intimacy.

BUDGETING

Money matters can get complicated, and reaching your goals can feel overwhelming. Again, I am not a financial advisor, but I strongly encourage you to read many of the good Christian books available on finances and budgeting. As a marriage therapist, my focus is covering the basics so that money matters do not create blocks to intimacy.

As a couple, given your governing style, have you made a decision in the past to use a budget? Have you stayed within your plans to budget? The decision to design a budget for some couples is very easy. For others it is a real challenge.

Planning Our Budget

As a couple, do you agree to formulate a budget in the next few weeks?

❏ Yes ❏ No

If you do decide to budget, the next issue involves the basics of creating one. Again, I would refer you to any of the good Christian financial books available on the market. The basics are simple. In one column list your income. In the other column list your outgoing expenses and planned expenditures, such as dating, Christmas funds and car maintenance. Some couples just go through their checkbooks to get an idea of their expenses. Over a three-month period you can figure an average amount for utilities, food, services and other expenditures.

Creating a basic budget is a major first step. Write the date below when you compiled your basic budget.

> Our basic budget was completed on _____.

A second part of the budgeting process is a regular review. This self-monitoring process is important to regulate charges and have meaningful conversations as you transition through the various money matters that could potentially block future intimacy.

Have at least one monthly business meeting to revise your budget. Schedule this meeting on your calendar, Day-Timer or Palm Pilot. Select a time early in the evening on a weekday. Don't let fatigue become a factor in your discussions. If you agree to this, then place the day and time that best suits your lifestyle and schedule.

> Our regular meeting will take place (circle one) weekly/biweekly/monthly on _____ day of the week at _____ A.M./P.M.

Budgeting is not the most fun thing you can do in a relationship, but it is essential to have open and fact-based financial communication. This type of communication allows for greater intimacy for the couple.

Finances are one of the main areas that can block intimacy. Poor planning, poor communication and lack of financial agreement can be the archenemy of intimacy. A financial issue can bleed easily over into the emotional and sexual intimacy of a marriage.

The couple who actively takes on their financial issues is a couple who loves their marriage. You wouldn't want anyone to break into your house and steal your possessions, would you? Of course not; you would protect that which is precious.

Other than Christ Himself, your spouse is the most intimate relationship you will have over the span of several decades. Financial maturity, responsibility and honest communication can protect your great intimate marriage from the needless scarring created by money matters.

EIGHT

Is Your Marriage Based on Emotion?

A powerful dynamic that sabotages intimacy is what I call the "emotion-based marriage." Chaos, lack of follow-through and inconsistency characterize these marriages.

There are two types of emotion-based marriages. The first is what I call the "benign" form. The second form is "malignant" yet treatable. I encourage you to walk through this section—even if it doesn't apply to you—because you will probably know marriages that function this way and can better understand why.

I know a couple from another state who were both saved as adults. The husband is a professional in his career. They have two children and are very active at church. Their house is always in a state of total chaos—clothes strewn everywhere, dishes in the sink, beds unmade. They stay so busy that regular fellowship with them is difficult. They have no time for systems of intimacy such as prayer, sharing feelings, dating and finances, so everything is always in a state of flux. They seem always to be going around in the same circles, never really gaining momentum in their relationship.

This is the benign form of an emotion-based marriage system. In this system, no one is really intentionally trying to be difficult or to harm the other. They simply can't seem to "get it together."

A couple such as this one may try therapy, but they continue doing their homework for only a short period of time. When asked why they didn't follow through with it, they rarely can come up with any tangible reasons.

The entire notion of practiced consistency or principle-based thinking eludes them totally. Their decisions are made emotionally, and their schedule constantly changes often simply because they felt like doing something else instead. At that point, they are unable to remember previous commitments and totally miss events they had planned.

Such couples are often pleasant and fun to be with, at least when things are going well with them. They simply have no structure in their lives.

Progress is slow in a marriage with the benign form of an emotion-based marriage. Trying to get a commitment from this couple simply to pray together is difficult. When they get into a system for a few weeks they feel closer than ever, but they eventually stop, and then their relationship deteriorates again.

The reason for the marital deterioration is that this couple's emotions dominate the decision-making process. If they feel like doing something, they do, and if they don't (even if it is biblical), then they just don't do it. Period!

The sixties' culture raised a generation that bought into in a lifestyle of "if it feels good, do it." The concept of restraint, principles and accountability are not factored into their decision-making process.

This type of an emotion-based marriage system reeks

havoc on intimacy, since intimacy building is much more than just making up after big fights. Intimacy for a lifetime requires more than just fleeting moments of discipline. Intimacy is the result of a disciplined lifestyle. Intimacy is relational wealth that accumulates over a lifetime of invested consistent behavior. Intimacy, like wealth, doesn't just happen. It is painstakingly planned, worked for and achieved along the way while two hearts are consistently being open and available to each other.

Progress is slow in a marriage with the benign form of an emotion-based marriage.

A couple within an emotion-based system will honestly find it difficult to change. Even the benign structure meets disciplined changes with great resistance. The chaos within this system gives the couple great distraction from the lack of structure in the relationship. Crises appear from out of nowhere, such as when one or both of the partner's needs are not being met and stress appears in the marriage. Plans for the future are avoided, and a flat tire just happens. With each crisis, the cycle of the emotion-based marriage starts over once again.

The malignant form of the emotion-based marriage system is willful. In this marriage, not only are the husband and/or wife making their decisions based upon their emotions, but they also refuse instruction, information or connection from anyone in authority, including God. They are bent on doing what they want regardless of the results. If one person wants to neglect his or her spouse for days or weeks to punish that person, he will. If they want to make a financial decision regardless of the consequences, they will.

This selfishness at the cost of others becomes toxic. The

intimacy within the relationship is inconsistent and even volatile. Anger or silence is used to control the spouse and other family members as well. You know you're in a marriage like this when the major goal of the family is to keep this spouse happy.

The malignant form of an emotion-based marriage can sometimes be a result of several undiagnosed forms of emotional disorders. Addictions may be present, such as addictions to work, alcohol, drugs or sex. Professional help may need to be obtained for these issues to be resolved.

In some relationships, one spouse may have a mood disorder called *bipolar disorder* (also known as manic-depressive disorder). On some days this husband or wife will be happy, motivated, clear-thinking and fun to be around. Then, out of the blue will come one to three days of depression, moodiness and irritable behavior. Now no one in the family can do anything right, and soon everyone starts to think, *Why even bother?* After a couple of days of gloom the bipolar person cycles back and becomes cheerful. This disorder can keep an emotion-based marriage in a particularly toxic state.

If an emotion-based system is in the malignant form and addictions or mood disorders are not present, the problem may simply be a heart attitude that suggests, "I do what I want, and if you don't like it, leave." Often those with this heart attitude reject their spouse's appeal for intimacy by saying their partner is just needy or weak. The one seeking intimacy feels as though his or her spouse can't or won't let them in.

If you're reading this section, and it feels as if you are in a malignant or toxic emotion-based marriage system, you probably will need further professional help to get to the other side of intimacy with your spouse. The emotion-based marriage system can be a major roadblock to intimacy. Real problems need to be addressed. If you are in this situation, you will benefit greatly by doing the exercises in the anger chapter of this book. Do as many of the structured exercises in this guide as you can. If you feel that you need professional help, ask your pastor for a referral.

Complete the questions below to help determine if you are in an emotionally based marriage.

An Emotion-Based Marriage?

❏ Yes ❏ No 1. Does your marriage and family life feel chaotic most of the time?

❏ Yes ❏ No 2. Does it feel as if there is no consistent spiritual and emotional connection with your spouse?

❏ Yes ❏ No 3. Does money get spent regularly without anyone really knowing where it went?

❏ Yes ❏ No 4. Does it appear that you are not working toward long-term retirement plans?

❏ Yes ❏ No 5. Does it seem that some things never get done?

❏ Yes ❏ No 6. Does the way decisions get made within the marriage seem unclear?

If you answered yes to most of the following questions, your marriage may be built on an emotion-based marriage system.

A MARRIAGE BUILT ON PRINCIPLES

The opposite of an emotion-based marriage system is a principle-based relationship. Over time intimacy flourishes in this type of marriage. Principles, both biblical and practical, guide the decision-making process. A personality doesn't dominate, nor do the desires of one person in the marriage.

The relationship has structure and boundaries with consequences so that both spouses can be themselves without hurting the other. These couples make decisions based upon whether or not something is right or if it was already agreed upon, not just because of how they feel at a particular moment in time.

A couple that lives within the parameters of a principle-based relationship has the highest chance of getting and maintaining lifelong intimacy that benefits both spouses. They don't tithe simply when they feel like it—they decide to tithe and do it. They don't pray together coincidentally, accidentally or occasionally—they pray intentionally and regularly.

This couple works together to solve problems, and they don't just serve their own emotions. If they don't feel like doing something they have committed to doing, they stick with it through the initial stages of discomfort because they made a commitment.

> A couple that lives within the parameters of a principle-based relationship has the highest chance of getting and maintaining lifelong intimacy that benefits both spouses.

If your relationship is more emotionally based then you would like, don't be discouraged. As we walk through the practical applications in this guide, any couple can make great progress. Couples in an emotion-based marriage system can move into a more principle-based relationship.

It takes work to get lifelong results. Enduring intimacy is

not enjoyed by the lazy, fainthearted or undisciplined. It is a fruit produced from consistent behaviors. As you record your progress in this book, you will realize improvements can be made in the quality of your relationship in a relatively short period of time.

When you break a bone and have it set, the cast doesn't actually do the healing. It merely makes healing possible. I encourage all couples who are in emotion-based marriages to apply a "cast" to their marriage. You can do this by creating principles that will provide structure to your brokenness so that the healing process can begin.

If your marriage is emotionally based, the exercises and structures will take a determined effort at first. I strongly encourage you to try to move beyond the "if it feels good, do it" attitude. This attitude directly contradicts God's principles. The Bible says, "If you love me, you will obey what I command" (John 14:15). If you follow the commandments of Christ, you will enjoy the satisfying relationship that you and your spouse forged out of the clay of your beginnings into a marriage that gives God glory. Then you can invite others to discover what you have found—the secret to intimacy.

WHEN ONE PARTNER NEEDS TO GROW

Emotional systems can result from one or both spouses who are behaving as children or adolescents rather than adults in an area of life. It's possible to be an adult in one area of life but an adolescent or a child in another. The imbalance created by this dynamic can cause an emotion-based marriage system.

Jerry and Paula were such a case. One spouse's immaturity in one area of their relationship added a strain to their marriage and limited their intimacy.

Jerry was a pastor of a church. He was a great preacher and had personal integrity. He spent hours in prayer for those he shepherded and visited them regularly when they were sick or going through hard times.

Spiritually, anyone who knew Jerry would say he was a spiritual adult. Jerry also was an adult in his social relationships and experienced fun as he and members of his congregation fished, hunted and went to games together.

Nevertheless, in the area of finances Jerry behaved as a child. He didn't know what came in or went out of the checking account, and he would only engage in the financial process when he needed more than his regular allowance provided or to sign his tax returns. Paula handled all the finances.

When both spouses do not function as adults within their relationship, they will be robbed of intimacy.

Even though Jerry was an adult about fun, he didn't have many close friendships. He was everyone's pastor, but he really didn't have another man with whom he felt he could open up. He didn't follow through with relationships—with phone calls, getting together and being real with people outside of the church. He often felt isolated.

The areas that Jerry handled emotionally instead of in an adult manner caused Paula stress. She didn't like handling all of the finances and felt overwhelmed by trying to meet Jerry's relational needs all by herself. However, it wasn't Jerry's fault alone.

Paula, as sweet as she was, had some emotional areas in her life as well. She was an adult when it came to the social, financial and spiritual areas of her life, but when it came to sexuality she was a child. She took no sexual responsibility in the relationship. Neither Jerry nor Paula could remember one time that Paula initiated sex. Although Paula was as sweet as she could be, a perfect pastor's wife and mother, she couldn't express her feelings.

She really fought to keep others from knowing her emotionally. This added strain to their marriage and their intimacy.

Jerry and Paula created emotional systems. On the outside they looked OK, but inside each a quiet but steady resentment was building.

Many couples are like Jerry and Paula. They marry individuals who can carry the areas in themselves in which they are uncomfortable. The problem is that these issues are never discussed, but instead they are allowed to evolve into emotional systems that create roadblocks to intimacy.

When both spouses do not function as adults within their relationship, they will be robbed of intimacy. Many couples create emotion-based marriage systems without even knowing it. Use the following chart for self-improvement. You may notice the undeveloped areas in your spouse, but that is not the purpose for the chart.

You *cannot* change your spouse. Therefore, unless you use this information for individual prayer, in a loving and therapeutic manner or in an agreed-upon conversation with your spouse, it will be unproductive. Please don't use this information to attack, shame or otherwise injure the soul of your spouse. Use it only to improve *yourself*.

Developing Your Relationship

Area	Child	Adolescent	Adult
Spiritual	❏ Refuses to feed themselves by reading the Bible ❏ Wants others to feed them by attending church only ❏ Prayer is not really initiated on a regular basis ❏ Likes it if "you" pray ❏ States that the Bible is too difficult to understand ❏ Doesn't feel convicted of sin on any regular basis	❏ Feeds themselves ❏ Their interpretations of Scripture is "the" interpretation ❏ Prays but is inconsistent ❏ Will pray together "if you make them" ❏ Struggles with balancing biblical truths ❏ Convicted of sin but has struggles with authority issues	❏ Feeds themselves regularly ❏ Feeds others in their life by character and Word ❏ Prayer is consistent and desired ❏ Desires to pray with you anytime ❏ Convicted of even minor sin regularly
Social	❏ Does not initiate in relationships ❏ Only responds to those who want to initiate toward them ❏ Can't seem to find a person or group to connect to ❏ Most their friends do all the work in their relationship	❏ Will initiate in relationship if it serves a purpose ❏ Relationship based on activities ❏ Tends to have a rotating best friend ❏ Does some initiating in the relationship to set up activities	❏ Can initiate a relationship with those just because, with no need to serve a purpose ❏ Can create time just for relating, not requiring an activity ❏ Can have long-term friendships ❏ Accepts the seasons of friendships ❏ Tends to initiate equally in a relationship
Financial	❏ Refuses to have anything to do with money issues ❏ Money things are just overwhelming ❏ Has a naive status toward taxes and retirement ❏ As long as their needs are met there is no real need to talk about it ❏ Doesn't write checks or know the bills	❏ Financially selfish ❏ Thinks in short term, materialistic tendencies ❏ Toys are more important than future planning ❏ What they are, what the family looks like (house, cars, clothes) is really important ❏ Credit card debt is very common ❏ Will tithe when convenient	❏ Money has spiritual meaning ❏ Long-term planning is part of their thought process ❏ Short-term sacrifice is honorable for long term gain ❏ Tithing is consistent

INTIMACY

Area	Child	Adolescent	Adult
Sexual	❏ Does not accept or see themselves as sexual ❏ Will not initiate sex ❏ Talking about sex is always inappropriate	❏ Sex is for them mostly ❏ Unaware of spouse's sexual needs ❏ Angry when their needs don't get met ❏ Sex conversations seem to feel cheap and not about intimacy	❏ Accepts themselves sexually ❏ Accepts the sexuality of their spouse ❏ Has intimacy during sexuality ❏ Maintains sexual integrity
Feelings	❏ Doesn't know what you're talking about ❏ Becomes confused when emotions are addressed ❏ Feels you're asking too much of them to do feeling work	❏ Has feelings but limited ability to communicate them ❏ Has periods of emotional constipation then blows up or gets silent ❏ Really more concerned about their feelings and not yours	❏ Has feelings and the ability to communicate them ❏ Can be emotionally safe and keep confidences ❏ Values and hears the feelings of their spouses
Fun	❏ Can have some fun if others plan for it ❏ Loves to be invited but has little fun on their own ❏ Often unable to be silly at appropriate times	❏ Fun is what life is about ❏ Keeps self preoccupied by several hobbies ❏ Selfish with their time off and vacation ❏ Most of their friends revolve around hobbies	❏ Can plan fun for self and others ❏ Realizes the importance of fun in balance ❏ Will take some time for self but balances it with their spouse

In the columns in the next chart, indicate where you believe you may fit in the various areas. It is appropriate to do this portion on a separate sheet of paper if you feel more comfortable. Score yourself individually. I know you can't help but score your spouse, so if you do, don't tell them. They *may* disagree.

Individual Emotional System Development

Husband (check where appropriate)

Area	Child	Adolescent	Adult
Spiritual			
Social			
Financial			
Sexual			
Feelings			
Fun			

Wife (check where appropriate)

Area	Child	Adolescent	Adult
Spiritual			
Social			
Financial			
Sexual			
Feelings			
Fun			

Before you go further, if you agreed with your spouse to disclose your analysis to each other, talk over your responses now. If both have not agreed to do this, then please don't force the matter until you do agree.

These issues are emotionally based and often are hot buttons within a marriage. Resolving these issues will require work as individuals, not as a couple. Your work together as a couple begins when you move beyond these issues and can discuss them and see the impact that your personal development or lack of development is making on the marriage.

Discussing your emotional systems can move you toward creating the structural system that you both choose.

When you both want to discuss these emotional systems with each other you can. Check off the area of self-report that you feel ready to discuss with your spouse.

Self-reported Areas

Area	Spouse	Child	Adolescent	Adult
Spiritual	Him			
Spiritual	Her			
Social	Him			
Social	Her			
Financial	Him			
Financial	Her			
Sexual	Him			
Sexual	Her			
Feelings	Him			
Feelings	Her			
Fun	Him			
Fun	Her			

What were the apparent areas that each of you needs to address to have fewer roadblocks to future intimacy?

His Areas	Her Areas
1.	1.
2.	2.
3.	3.
4.	4.

As a couple, what areas seem to be impacted by the individual emotional systems?

Yes	No	Areas
		Spiritual
		Social
		Financial
		Sexual
		Feelings
		Fun

SOLUTIONS FOR EMOTION-BASED MARRIAGE SYSTEMS

Do you have roadblocks that you or your spouse has created? Unfortunately, each individual must take complete responsibility for the underdeveloped areas of his or her life.

I am responsible for my adulthood in these key areas of our relationship. My spouse is not responsible to guide me into adulthood.

You don't need your spouse to be your parent. Often a person is forced to carry or "parent" his or her spouse in an area where the spouse has chosen to remain a "child" or "adolescent." If this is the case, you may have heard these words: "If you stop acting like a child, I'll stop acting like your parent."

Couples can often correctly identify the area or areas of stress within their relationship. However, the solutions get interesting as a spouse who is an adult in one area tries to get the other spouse to be an adult, especially when this adult may be a child in another area of the relationship.

When we start attempting to change one another, we usually both end up acting like children when all is said and done. People change when they want to—and no sooner.

Your solution is not found in your spouse. The solution—

and the responsibility to find it—lies within each of you individually. Therefore, you must address these issues as individuals. For some, you may need to get some counseling with your pastor to create accountability. You must desire to change as an individual. Begin to set goals for change.

> When we start attempting to change one another, we usually both end up acting like children when all is said and done.

As an adult, you are responsible for yourself. You alone can decide to become more mature in these areas. Only you can stop your individual emotional systems from creating emotion-based marriage systems in your relationship.

You're not alone. You have the love, knowledge and support of counselors and of Christ and His Word, the Bible. You have a spouse who loves you. You can choose to take these roadblocks out of your way.

I realize that it's difficult work. I have had to grow up in every area that we have covered. It was hard work, and maintaining what you gain can be just as difficult at times. But in my life I have found that it is better to make a plan than to make excuses. I pray God's speed and wisdom for you as you love yourself and your marriage enough to strengthen the areas where you are lacking.

PART THREE

The 100 Days

NINE

Day by Day: Daily Exercises to Build Intimacy

Throughout my years of counseling, I have discovered that many marriages lack structures to encourage intimacy. We grow up believing that one day we will get married and live happily ever after. We enter marriage ill equipped for intimacy and are disappointed when our husband or wife doesn't possess the secret code to intimacy either.

At first marriage is fun as you begin to learn about your spouse, go to work or school, get your first apartment, pick out furniture, go to church and are physically intimate together without guilt. The sheer complexities of your new life together, along with the many new decisions you must make, can keep you talking and sharing regularly.

Slowly and subtly it happens. No one really knows when or where it happens, but something changes within the relationship. You don't seem to talk as much.

Decisions are not met with the same excitement as when

you were first married; instead, they are delegated, then discussed. Purchases become fewer, and sex and life take on a routine. You don't feel as close, but seem just to be living together. What happened? Where did the passion go for one another?

Roger and Constance are a classic example of a couple who lost their passion for each other. They are both intelligent and successful. Constance owns a small business, and Roger manages a large organization. They attend a large church and love God as individuals. To meet either of them is to love them. They have one little secret that nobody knows about—not even their pastor, whom they consider a good friend. Roger and Constance don't have sex. They haven't had sex in six years.

"What happened to us?" was their question for me. They told me their story, which included the history of their relationship. Constance said they dated for two years. Throughout those two years Roger called Constance frequently and wrote notes with scriptures inside. They prayed together, and their friends considered them inseparable. When they first married their sex life was good, fun and frequent. They traveled and did lots of fun things before their children came along.

Soon things changed. Schedules changed. Roger traveled some, and they prayed together less frequently. They seldom spoke to one another, and occasionally sex just happened, but it was no longer fun or exciting. The children started school, Constance started a business, and they drifted farther apart. Their interests grew apart, and their conversations focused on household management issues only.

Roger and Constance went to church every Sunday, but spiritually their lives revolved around a lot of religious activities. They remained disconnected. Communication stopped. Instead of talking, Roger read his financial and sports magazines, and Constance was too busy. Occasionally they reassured each other of their love for one another and would sometimes talk about sex, but neither of them really followed through anymore.

What happened to this couple has happened to many others. Roger and Constance lost their priorities. Passion—or loss of it—is a result of priorities. Americans believe that people are either passionate or they are not. But this kind of thinking is incorrect. Passion is a dividend of consistent investments made into a relationship.

Let's reflect back a minute to when you were dating. You were selling your spouse on the idea that being married to you was a great idea. Remember the passion you had for your future spouse? Of course you remember the passion, but what you may have forgotten is the foundation of that passion, the priority of the relationship.

Passion is a dividend of consistent investments made into a relationship.

Do you remember how you "made" time to be together? You planned your days and weeks around each other's work schedule, including your days off. Those of you who were attending school in another city away from your future spouse as I was had the phone bills to prove your passion and priority. In my case, those phone bills took a giant bite out of the little income I made just so I could tell her about my day.

If you were a Christian at the time, do you remember how spiritual you were? You prayed together as often as you could, and perhaps even read the Bible together. You desired to know God's will, and you wanted God to help you stay pure and still express your love to one another.

Do you remember the gratitude you had for the smallest things your spouse did for you? This was especially true for me when Lisa cooked for me. I was so grateful! I filled her life with a constant stream of praise. Do you remember when you thought she was so smart and attractive and had so much potential? You believed in her and regularly encouraged her.

Understand that passion is a result of setting priorities. Too many people attempt to get back the *passion* instead of getting back their *priorities*. Once you get the priorities back, the passion follows and grows naturally.

> I have seen genuine miracles of restoration in marriages when priorities were put back into the relationship.

What priorities? I will discuss priorities shortly, but before I do I want to share an analogy I often use in counseling sessions. Many couples come in for help with sprains or fractures in their relationships. I liken the repair of a marital relationship to fixing a broken bone. When your bone is broken, you can continue to function in a limited way, but you look and act unusual. Then you go to the doctor or emergency room.

The first thing the doctor does is order an x-ray of the bone. Sure enough, he looks at the structure. Regardless of how it happened, the x-ray shows a damaged structure (your bone is broken). The doctor and nurse apply a structural treatment to your structural problem in the form of a cast.

The cast is a structural treatment that allows the bone to heal. The cast itself is just plastic or plaster, and it has no healing properties. But when it is applied to a broken bone to hold the bone in place, surprise! Healing can and does happen.

The same thing happens when you place the priorities back into your marriage. No matter how sprained or broken a marriage is, healing can and does take place. I have seen genuine miracles of restoration in marriages when priorities were put back into the relationship. One of the structures I apply is what I call "the three dailies."

Roger and Constance incorporated the three dailies into their lives and are doing much better now. Not only are they still in love, but they are more in love with each other than before.

Constance said, "I know his heart now, and feel really special and close to him."

So what about the sex? According to both of them, not only is it very consistent, but also it's more fun and fulfilling than when they were younger.

Roger and Constance restored their priorities and practiced the three dailies in their relationship. It was difficult work at first, but it became easier over time, and now it is just part of their routine.

I want to add a personal note of testimony. As I have stated before, I would never ask you to do something that Lisa and I have not done or are not doing presently in our relationship. Lisa and I have done two of the three dailies every day for well over ten years, with only a few exceptions. When I developed the third exercise, we actively applied it to our marriage routine also.

These three exercises help Lisa and I maintain our relationship priorities. They are part of our bedtime routine. Neither of us expects to go to sleep without our relational ritual of the three dailies.

They are a major highlight of my day. I get to hear about my wife's day, hear her heart, and she gets to hear about my day and heart as well. This relational structure has richly developed our skill for intimacy to such a level that it can weather the day-to-day challenges of children, writing and media demands together with all of our other commitments.

When your marriage priorities are restored, your passion will be restored. Everyone who knows me is well aware of my passion for Lisa. I love her and really like her as well. This passion is the fruit of discipline that is born out of a heart of love.

Intimacy

THE THREE DAILIES

1. Prayer

Prayer is an absolute necessity in your marriage. I am constantly amazed when couples tell me that the last time they really prayed together, not including praying over food or a good night prayer with children, was years ago. Sometimes they say, "We both pray, just not together."

That's fine, but prayer as a couple is not optional. Earlier we discussed the importance of Psalm 127:1: "Unless the Lord builds the house, its builders labor in vain." The Lord must be part of building your house. Prayer is an active way to include the Lord as part of the building plan of your marriage.

> As we grow together spiritually, our intimacy in the other two areas will grow as well.

Matthew 18:19 says, "Again, I tell you that if two of you on earth agree about anything you ask for, it will be done for you by my Father in heaven." As we've previously noted, this verse discusses the importance of two or more agreeing in God's name. It doesn't say when *one* agrees—it says when *two* agree.

Since Christ's resurrection, He intercedes with and for His bride, which is the church. The Lord sees prayer as being extremely important. God's pleasure is for us to commune with Him, not just as individuals, but as a couple as well.

As we noted earlier, James 4:17 says, "Anyone, then, who knows the good he ought to do and doesn't do it, sins." I can tell you without a doubt in my mind that any man who has heard the Word of God and doesn't pray with his wife is sinning.

Men, leading prayer in your marriage is your job! (See Ephesians 5:25–28.) You serve a holy God, and I believe He will hold you accountable for the return on His investment: the precious gift of your spouse.

There will be no excuses when you meet her heavenly Father. I want that day to be a blessing to you. I want you to say, "Lord, I received Your daughter; she was young and insecure about herself, but I built her up and prayed her up. Now look at her; she is so much better than when I received her." I want God to smile on my responsibilities toward my wife.

Prayer is one of the priorities that must be set in place by a couple desiring more intimacy. Remember, intimacy is three dimensional, involving spirit, soul and body. As we grow together spiritually, our intimacy in the other two areas will grow as well.

Prayer is just talking aloud to God with your spouse, similar to talking with a friend. Prayer doesn't have to take long hours from any particular position. It is the principle of connecting with God that is essential.

As a couple, within your governing style in your marriage, process the decision of daily prayer. As a result of your decision as a couple, place a check by the statement you agree with below.

   _____   We have agreed to pray daily together to improve and maintain our intimacy for the next one hundred days.

   _____   We have agreed not to pray together daily for the next one hundred days knowing that it will negatively affect our intimacy.

The structure of prayer taking place within your marriage is one essential part of the three daily exercises. This structure will also be a part of your 100-day log at the very end of this book.

Hopefully by now you have agreed to daily prayer. I know better than most that each couple has many variables. Some of these differences include sleep preferences, work schedules, children's school and extracurricular activities, church and fellowshiping with family and friends.

Look at your schedules. When can you pray together? In the morning? At lunch? In the evening? Take the time to discuss this with your spouse, and see if you can agree on a time to pray together. In the space below, write your first and second option to pray together.

Option one is _____ A.M./P.M.

Option two is _____ A.M./P.M.

In your 100-day log, it's important to track your progress regarding this exercise to maintain the consistency that ignites the passion and intimacy you both desire.

Those who travel often ask how to maintain the 100-day program while out of town. In this day of modern technology, it is a nonissue for the creative person. You can use your calling card or mobile phone to pray with your spouse over the phone. This really demonstrates a commitment to maintain your spiritual intimacy. Even if you're in Hong Kong, you can send an e-mail with a prayer to your wife and chat with her. Remember that the *structure* first brings healing, then passion. As you walk together spiritually, your intimacy over the next one hundred days can flourish.

I love walking in the garden of my life with Lisa and coming with her into the presence of our loving Father. I really believe this has been instrumental in developing the strength and intimacy of our marriage.

2. FEELINGS

Emotional intimacy is the second very important aspect that couples need to develop and maintain throughout their relationship. Early in their dating relationship and then in marriage, they readily share with one another their feelings about life situations, people, God and their dreams. Often they can't remember exactly what happened to their feelings a little later on, but many couples appear to go into hiding. Life gets more complicated, and their conversations get more managerial. Discussions become limited to "Who does this? How will that get done?" or "That needs to get paid." There will be hundreds of details involving the children.

Your marriage can be managed and can function well and still not have the sense of connectedness that you once enjoyed. Eventually you can begin to feel alone, unsupported and misunderstood, and you can end up wondering why you are even going through the motions. These feelings are common for couples who lack a system that supports each other's emotions.

> I have seen husbands and wives move from emotional illiteracy to emotional communicative competence over the years.

Emotions are an important part of who both of you are. They encompass your spouse's personality and influence the way in which he or she processes life events. Many couples don't see each other for eight to ten hours a day. Your spouse has been out there in the big, bad world. People and situations have positively or negatively affected your spouse's heart all day long.

We seem to be more intuitive about talking to our children as we ask them about their day. We do not want just the facts—we want to know what their hearts have been through that day.

When I talk with couples about expressing feelings, I find that many have limited communication skills. I can totally empathize. Even though I had hundreds of feelings, I only had three major doors of communication. This can get really fun if you marry someone with the same three doors.

I'm sure you have been in a conversation in which the feelings being expressed didn't line up with the real feelings the other individual was experiencing. We come equipped with many feelings, all of which are standard operating equipment placed in us by our Maker. The problem isn't that we don't have feelings. The problem lies in the limitations we have in the skills to express them.

When I was first married I was emotionally illiterate. I had many feelings, but I lacked the skills to identify or communicate them to my beautiful bride, Lisa.

Even while getting my master's degree in marriage and family counseling I didn't learn how to identify or communicate my feelings. Therefore, I took it upon myself to learn these skills. I began to realize that most of life is about learning skills.

Let me give you an example. As a youth, I learned nothing about fixing cars. So even as an adult, lifting the hood of a car became shaming for me. No matter how many degrees or licenses I acquired, I still had no mechanical training or skills. But if I were to take a course in basic mechanics and learn these skills, I could become skilled at fixing a car.

That's what identifying and communicating feelings is—a *skill*. Skills can be learned by anyone. I can personally testify to that.

I have watched many couples grow in the skill of identifying and communicating their feelings. I have seen husbands and wives move from emotional illiteracy to emotional communicative competence over the years. I have countless memories of couples taking their first stab at practicing the feelings exercise that we will be discussing momentarily. They slowly attempt to communicate their first one or two feelings, and as they practice this daily for one hundred days, these couples end up freely expressing their feelings to each other.

Leaning to do this is critical for intimacy. If you can't share the feelings in your heart because you lack training and practice, how can you expect heart-to-heart intimacy to occur? If you have been able to skillfully tell your spouse what you feel and what is in your heart, then your spouse must also be able to clearly communicate his or her heart back to you.

Be warned that this communication exercise requires some effort to master it. Many adults have had to start from ground zero to learn the computer. The feelings exercises are much the same. At first, you may feel unfamiliar and awkward. Over time the learning curve speeds up a little. Before you know it, you have it figured out, and you begin to feel a little more confident. In the end you will wonder how you ever got along before you learned it.

Life is funny that way; many of the best things in life take effort to achieve. You may be familiar with the principle of sowing and reaping. If you plant corn, you get corn later during the harvest season. Likewise, as you sow emotional intimacy into your marriage, in time you will reap emotional intimacy.

Consider what a wonderful day it could be when you truly know that you are completely heard and accepted by your spouse. This truly gratifying experience can be yours after time and practice.

You can't enjoy the view from the top of a mountain without the climb. Living in Colorado, I personally know that the climb is part of the fun of the view. The following exercise is designed to increase your ability to share your feelings with others. Take the climb—you'll be glad you did.

The Feelings Exercise

The feelings exercise is relatively simple. Pick a feeling from the list of feelings in the appendix of this book. Place the feeling word within the following two sentences.

>I feel _____ (feeling word) when _____.
>
>I remember first feeling _____ (same feeling word) when _____.

Example 1:

>I feel *adventurous* when I take my wife and two children hiking up the mountains in Colorado Springs.
>
>I remember first feeling *adventurous* when I was about thirteen years old and my mom bought me a ten-speed bike, which I rode all over town.

Example 2:

>I feel *calm* when I can get alone in nature and sit really still for a short while.
>
>I remember first feeling *calm* when I was first taken out of foster homes and my mom gave me a stuffed animal that I could sleep with.

I think you get the idea. In the first sentence you pick whatever feeling you want and give a present-tense example of the feeling. In the second sentence you use the same feeling word but choose an early childhood or adolescent experience.

It is the earlier feeling that can be difficult. Do not cop out and try to give an example from a year or so ago. Think hard, and do the exercise correctly. Some men and women who have had difficulty trying to remember a feeling from the past have found it easier if they start with a past memory during childhood and attach a present feeling to that experience.

For example, someone having difficulty might go to a childhood experience in which their mother or father forgot to pick them up from school one day. One of the feelings they might have felt was *alone* because everyone else left on a bus or was already picked up. Now come up with an example of feeling alone in the present, such as "I feel alone when I am on hold on the phone for a long period of time."

I want to warn you about two things. The first thing you don't want to do with this exercise is use the same feeling word over and over again. This really serves no purpose and will not create the desired effect for developing intimacy over the next one hundred days.

The second thing you don't do in this feeling exercise is use one childhood example for twenty different feeling words. For instance, don't use the example of the child being left at the school every day with different feeling words such as *abandoned, helpless* and *confused*. Although these feelings may be legitimate for one example, you must not keep pumping one experience over and over again when your life is full of experiences from which to identify your feelings. It may be slow going at first, but even childhood experiences become easier to remember when you practice the feeling exercise.

I have developed some guidelines to be used while completing this exercise. The following guidelines will limit or remove some obstacles that you might otherwise experience within this exercise. Please follow these guidelines to make your experience much more positive.

1. *Don't use examples about each other.* You can talk about your feelings that include one another at any other time of day—but *not during the feelings exercise.* It is very important not to violate this guideline!

The feelings exercise is designed to be a safe place for both the husband and the wife to open their hearts to one another. If you start using the exercise to say, "I feel *frustrated* when *you* don't pick up your socks," the exercise will become unsafe and will dissolve. You can feel frustrated about traffic, your children, the dog or anyone other than your spouse during this exercise.

This guideline applies to positive feelings about your spouse, and not only negative ones. Suppose you use the word *cuddly*. Again, you can feel cuddly with the children or the dog, but don't use your spouse in the example during the feelings exercise.

This guideline is very important in order to keep the exercise alive and provide you both with a way to learn and maintain emotional intimacy. If your spouse inadvertently starts giving an example that involves you, kindly remind him or her that it doesn't count and ask for another example. If your spouse continues to violate this principle, I would question the intent. My experience is that those who sabotage this exercise don't want intimacy. They might say they want intimacy, which is similar to saying they would like to be a millionaire, but if they don't work for it, they truly don't desire it.

Couples working on their feelings exercise frequently ask me: "How should we choose our feeling word?" I warn couples against going down an alphabetical list, for it can be very difficult to start with words such as *abandoned*, *aching* and so on. It really doesn't matter how you or your spouse pick your individual feeling words.

Some couples just close their eyes and pick one from the list. Some pick one feeling word that starts with A, and the next day they pick a feeling word that begins with B, and so on. Others just pick a number, such as nine, and use every ninth feeling word. Some just choose a feeling from that particular day.

Another commonly asked question is: "How many feeling words should we do a day?" I recommend two feeling words a day per person. Therefore, the wife does a feeling, and then the husband does his. Then the wife does her second feeling, and the husband does his second feeling as well. Then you're finished with the feeling exercise.

Follow the next two guidelines to be sure to receive the optimal benefit from the exercise.

2. *Maintain eye contact.* Look each other in the eyes while sharing your feelings. Looking into each other's eyes is important for intimacy to take place. There is much truth in the old saying, "Eyes are the window of the soul." When we look into another person's eyes, we see them.

Many couples who have grown apart can't remember the last time they looked into each other's eyes for more than a few seconds. I have watched husbands and wives struggle to look into their spouse's eyes while doing the feelings exercise. They have become so accustomed to talking *at* each other instead of *to* each other that they look down at the floor, up at the ceiling or past their spouse. Jokingly, I often say, "It was great for you to share that feeling with your shoe, but now let's try and share it with your spouse this time." We all laugh, but some spouses have to do their feeling over and over again.

When a couple does their feelings exercise in my office, I watch their eye contact carefully throughout the exercise. After a few attempts, most couples can maintain eye contact throughout the exercise. Once again, this is an important part of the feelings exercise. If your spouse looks at his or her shoe or the ceiling, gently touch him and ask him to look into the eyes that love him.

As you and your spouse practice this exercise, eye contact will become increasingly natural. Many couples have experienced a significant breakthrough in their overall communication patterns simply by doing the exercise.

My wife, Lisa, has the biggest green eyes I have ever seen, and to look into them is to see her soul. Seeing her soul is what drives me crazy for her. As you practice this guideline to the feelings exercises, I pray that you experience this kind of intimacy—one that transcends words.

3. *Do not give feedback to your spouse.* The last of the guidelines for the feelings exercise is just as important as the first two guidelines. As your partner shares his or her feelings, do not comment about the feelings he or she shares.

This is critical to keeping the exercise safe for each spouse. When your spouse shares a feeling, pumping him or her for more information will not feel safe, and your spouse will be less likely to want to continue.

Another violation of the "no feedback" guideline would be suggesting that he or she "should not feel that way." Just accept what your spouse is saying. Don't interpret or comment verbally on what he or she has shared. Say thank you, and go ahead and share *your* feeling word next.

Follow the "seventy-two hour" rule. Whatever is shared during the exercise *cannot* be discussed for seventy-two hours. For example: Suppose your wife shares a feeling of being "betrayed." Her first memory example was when she was six and her nine-year-old sister took her favorite Barbie doll and gave it to the dog. At this point, you are not to give any feedback for at least seventy-two hours.

The reason for this rule is to give time for both of you to establish an emotional safety zone during this time. Intimacy, especially emotional intimacy, requires safety. If I am going to share my heart of hearts, I have to know, above all, that I am safe to do so. You see, the feelings exercise isn't just about identifying and communicating feelings. It's one hundred days of experiencing each other as emotionally safe people.

Over time, if these deeply personal feelings that your spouse shares get shoved back in his or her face when you are mad, your spouse will conclude that you are unsafe and will no longer want to share feelings with you. Or, if you get defensive as your spouse shares with you, he or she will conclude that you are not an emotionally safe person. If both of you respond to emotional intimacy in this way routinely, both will feel unsafe sharing.

In a marriage in which a spouse feels emotionally unsafe, over time the partner will choose to stop being emotionally intimate. The need for emotional intimacy doesn't just go away for the spouse who doesn't share. He or she will seek out another emotional outlet. It may be golf with the guys, lunch with the girls or a Bible study, but it won't be with the spouse. I feel truly sad for a couple whose primary emotional intimacy is experienced outside of their marriage. Over the long run, the emotionally vulnerable spouse can become receptive to emotional and sexual affairs.

Remember to follow the seventy-two hour rule. If you do this, your sense of emotional safety will increase tremendously. You will want to share your feelings with your spouse, and you will enjoy the emotional intimacy that God really desires for you. You will enjoy what I call the *abundant marriage*, where you can be intimate spirit, soul and body for a lifetime.

> In a marriage in which a spouse feels emotionally unsafe, over time the partner will choose to stop being emotionally intimate.

Lisa and I have done this exercise for over ten years. After one hundred days, you can adjust the feeling structure. But stick to this structure for one hundred days to gain the skills you need. I have experienced such safety with my wife, Lisa, in this area. Her acceptance of my feelings and heart without feedback during the exercise has given me the opportunity to conclude that she is the safest person on the planet. My soul is filled with feelings for my wife. They protect me from temptation and make my life fun.

Lisa and I often stop each other throughout the day to share what we are feeling at the moment or what we feel about an event. I know I can call Lisa anytime and share positive or negative feelings with her, and she can do the same with me. This is what emotional intimacy is all about. It's the feeling of not being alone in this world but connected spiritually and emotionally with your wife.

3. Praise and nurturing

This is the last of the three daily exercises you must practice with your husband or wife over the next one hundred days. This exercise addresses the God-given need for nurturing and praise that each one of us has.

As parents, we intuitively know our children need to hear, "I love you," "I'm proud of you," "You're smart," "Great choice" and so on. I don't know where we get the notion that as we become adults we no longer need nurturing. We need to be mature, but we never are without a need for nurturing.

My Bible clearly tells me to come to God as a child.

> And he said: "I tell you the truth, unless you change and become like little children, you will never enter the kingdom of heaven. Therefore, whoever humbles himself like this child is the greatest in the kingdom of heaven.
> —Matthew 18:3-4

Throughout God's Word we learn that we are God's sons and daughters. He is infinite, and we are terribly finite. I hope I never consider myself an adult in His presence. Actually, the older I become, the more childlike before God I am. I am a child of God, and I still need—not just want—praise and affirmation. When we see God talking to Jesus, He always affirms His love for Him and nurtures Him.

You are the primary voice in your spouse's life. A silent voice is cruel. The spouse who hears neither bad nor good from the husband or wife to whom they've committed their life feels hollow inside.

If we are to be as our Father in heaven, then nurturing and

praising others will be an expression of His goodness through us. I realize this better than most, for praise and nurturing is not something that I grew up with.

Praise and nurturing one another are essential ingredients for a vibrant, ongoing intimate relationship. As you practice praising and nurturing over the next one hundred days, you will become increasingly skilled and comfortable with giving and receiving it. It will be more difficult for some husbands and wives to give praise than others. For others, receiving or acknowledging the praise that is given will be hard. Still others will struggle with both aspects of giving and receiving praise.

Both the giving and receiving of praise require skill. Again, a skill can be learned by anyone. Anyone can praise and nurture a soul. As you practice the praise exercise in this section daily, the oil of intimacy will drip into your soul and heal areas of dryness that you didn't even know existed.

When I counsel couples, I ask them, "When was the last time you received a real praise, eye to eye, heart to heart? Something more than just the obligatory, 'Thanks, honey'?" They look at each other, then shrug their shoulders. This is sad because this is the icing on the cake for me. Lisa tells me something positive about myself almost every day, and my soul leaps. I feel affirmed, and I can take on another day of life events. I know in the deepest regions of my heart that at the end of even the worst day of my life, those big green eyes of hers are going to look right into my heart, and she's going to say something nice.

Now I ask you, how hard do you think it is to be around someone who affirms you every day? Not difficult at all! We love to be around people who think we're special or praiseworthy. It feels even greater from your spouse.

Imagine if you were going to take a very long journey, and you could choose between three spouses to travel with you. Spouse number one would be critical most of the time. This spouse would make you feel that you don't know enough, you don't do anything right and you can't please him or her no matter what you do. I call this *hell on earth*.

The second spouse would be silent most of the time. This person would never praise or compliment you, or really give you much of an opinion at all. His or her gifts would be locked up with fear, and he or she would think of himself or herself as too inferior to be a helpmate. You would get to do it all spiritually, emotionally, sexually and financially. This is what I call *purgatory on earth*; it isn't hell because at least you are in control, but it certainly is lonely.

Praise and nurturing one another are essential ingredients for a vibrant, ongoing intimate relationship.

The last spouse you could choose for your long journey knows how to compliment your qualities. He or she can stop on even the busiest day to offer a kind word and always sees the good in you. I call this *heaven on earth*, for this is a spouse who thinks and acts as the God who created and saved you.

So which spouse would you choose: spouse #1, spouse #2 or spouse #3? I am sure most of us would like spouse #3 for the journey of forty or fifty years if we could choose all over again.

I have great news for you—you do get to start all over again! Even greater, *you* get to choose to be spouse #3 to your husband or wife. Isn't it great that in a free society you can choose to be spouse #3 by bringing praise and nurturing to one of God's most special children, your spouse?

I have chosen to be spouse #3 to my wife, Lisa. Do you remember the principle of sowing and reaping we talked about earlier? If you sow praise, in time the harvest will come back to you.

The praise exercise is very similar to the feelings exercise. First, each of you individually must think of two things that you love, appreciate or value about the other person.

The praises can relate to something your spouse did during the day or can simply be a general statement of appreciation for your spouse. When you both have two praises in mind, you are ready to begin this exercise.

Let's suppose the husband goes first. The guidelines for maintaining eye contact apply here as well. The husband must look into his wife's eyes and state his praise. For example: "I really appreciate that you are such a thrifty person, as in the way you saved us money by checking into mortgage insurance today."

The wife continues to look at her husband until she has accepted the statement or let it sink into her heart.

I said *heart* and not *head* on purpose. This is not a *cognitive* exercise but a *heart* exercise. After the wife has let the praise into her heart, she says, "Thank you."

Saying thank you is an important part of this exercise, for it indicates that the praise has been received. I used the word *received* because you may not agree with your spouse's praise at first due to the lack of skill in saying it well or your own feelings of inferiority. Nevertheless, you must still acknowledge that you let the praise into your heart.

At this time the wife would give her husband his praise. When he lets it into his heart, he then says, "Thank you." Then he gives his wife a second praise, and she gives him a second praise with the follow-up words, "Thank you."

For example: I will use the following praises and statements of appreciation that a couple named Trent and Natalie offered to each other. Trent will go first.

Trent: I really appreciate the extra effort you made today in completing the decorating project.

Natalie: Thank you.

Natalie: What I really love about you is that you are sincere about working on our marriage.

Trent: Thank you.

Trent: I love the way you laugh. It brings me great happiness to hear your laughter.

Natalie: Thank you.

Natalie: I appreciate your making time for me at lunch today.

Trent: Thank you.

This is how the nurturing or praise exercise sounds. It may seem simple, but for some it is difficult work. This exercise is sweet. When it is combined with the other two daily exercises, it can make a profound shift in your intimacy over the next one hundred days. Track your progress over the next few months by using the 100-day guide at the end of this book. I am enjoying a lifestyle of both giving and receiving praise, and it has been great.

Take the time to process this exercise together. After discussing it as a couple, decide if this is something you would like to do daily over the next one hundred days. Record your answers below.

    ____   We are in agreement for one hundred days to do two praises each daily.

    ____   We are in agreement *not* to do praise on a daily basis.

These exercises will take time and work for each of you, but the work will get easier after ten days or so. Finding the time is going to be the most important part. As you both embark on the road to enhancing or maintaining your intimacy, you will need to set aside a time to practice these exercises.

In an earlier exercise you set a time aside to pray. Some couples do all three daily exercises at the same time to make it easier. When you become more skilled at them, all three exercises will take as little as ten to fifteen minutes each day. This is a very small amount of time to develop a vibrant, loving and intimate marriage.

In the space below, record the time you both agree to make available to complete your three daily exercises.

> We agree to pray, do two feeling exercises and two praises each day at _____ A.M./P.M.
>
> Our back up time is _____ A.M./P.M.

Wow! We've covered a great deal of ground in this chapter. I suggest that you become accountable over the next one hundred days to a safe couple, a cell group leader, a pastor or counselor. Adding accountability increases your motivation to make it through the next one hundred days successfully.

You can employ accountability by using something as simple as a telephone call to check in daily, or you can meet this person over lunch or at a check-in meeting every month. This person isn't supposed to give feedback or therapy. He or she is just there to hear about your daily progress on the three *pray*, *feel* and *praise* exercises. Decide together who the accountability person will be.

Are you willing to do this for the next one hundred days to intimacy? Record your findings below:

> _____ We agreed to meet with an outside accountability person for the three daily exercises over the next one hundred days.
>
> _____ We agree that if we miss more than three days of the three daily exercises, then we will implement an outside source of accountability.

_____ We agree *not* to have an outside accountability person for the daily exercises regardless of our progress over the next one hundred days.

If you agree to have accountability to maintain the three daily exercises over the next period of one hundred days, write down whom you choose. Also list a back-up person in case you need one.

Our person or persons for accountability on the three daily exercises is _____.

Our back-up person or persons is _____.

LET'S REVIEW

This was a lot of information. Therefore, I would like to follow up briefly with an illustration of the entire process.

1. Pray daily with your spouse
2. Do two feelings exercises, following the guidelines of no example about each other, maintaining eye contact and no feedback.
3. Do two praises daily with eye contact, and follow up with a thank you

This example of a couple actually going through all three exercises may help you to sense exactly what to expect. In our example, I will write out what David and Ellen would say during the exercises.

1. Exercise #1—Pray

David: Jesus, I thank You for a great day and for being with Ellen, the children and me. Thanks for the commission You gave me today at the job and for helping Ellen during her day. I love You, Jesus, and thanks for everything.

Ellen: I too want to praise You, Jesus. You have been so good to David and me. Thank You so much for providing all that we need and so much more. You are an awesome God. Thanks for little Tony's progress in school and for Darla's new friend Jennifer. We love You, Lord.

2. Exercise #2—Feelings

David: I feel *enthusiastic* when I close a deal as I did today at the office. I first remember feeling *enthusiastic* when Dad would wake me up early on Saturday when I was about six years old just to say we were going fishing.

Ellen: I feel *drained* after being stuck in traffic twice today. I first remember feeling *drained* when I was nine after being out in the snow until we were wet and cold from making snow angels.

David: I feel *safe* when I come home from work and I know the phone finally isn't for me. I first remember feeling *safe* when I was ten years old in a football league and I got to wear a real helmet and pads.

Ellen: I feel *appreciated* after Tony hugged me today and said, "You're the greatest mom." I first remember feeling *appreciated* when my mom made a big deal to my dad that I had cleaned my room without being told. I think I was about seven.

3. Exercise #3—Praise and nurturing

David: I really appreciate you being so patient with Darla's piano lessons every night.

Ellen: Thank you.

Ellen: I really appreciate your coming home thirty minutes early today and taking time to clean up the kitchen with me.

David: Thank you.

David: I love that you stay so attractive. Even in jeans and a T-shirt, you are still so beautiful.

Ellen: Thank you.

Ellen: I love the fact that you just trust my judgment in different areas of our relationship.

David: Thank you.

And that's it—the three dailies! I pray that for the next one hundred days you allow this structure to teach you many skills. And I pray that these skills will become a permanent, positive part of your marriage. May God truly bless all the sowing that you are investing into your marriage, and may your good harvest be a blessing in which all of your generations can share.

TEN

Date Your Spouse or Go to Therapy!

Few things are worse than being bored in your marriage. That's why dating your spouse is so powerful, for it can keep your relationship vibrant and freshly energized. Dating is an essential ingredient to a successful and intimate marriage relationship.

Imagine this scene of a wedding. The bride looks beautiful in her white gown and has spent countless hours and thousands of dollars to create a perfect event. She walks down the aisle as the organ plays "Here Comes the Bride." The pastor gives a great sermon about the man and woman becoming one flesh. He asks the groom to say the vows he has written.

The groom says: "I promise to be boring and to bore you all the days of our life. I promise to make you so poor and unimportant that we can never date or get away again."

The bride repeats: "I promise to be boring and to bore you all the days of our life. I promise to make you so poor and unimportant that we can never date or get away again."

Does this sound totally ridiculous? Of course it does. Nevertheless, I have counseled more married couples than I care to remember, and many of them lived lives together that reflected precisely this kind of commitment.

One of my standard questions for a couple is: "How often do you date each other without the children?"

The most common response I receive is, "What do you mean by date?" Some want to know if going to the bank, cleaners and Home Depot counts as a date.

> Dating provides an extremely important foundational part of a successfully intimate marriage.

The second most frequent response I am given is, "It's been a while." When I investigate a little further, I find that it really has been many weeks, months or sometimes years.

I'll never forget the response of one couple in the early years of my practice. When I asked them when the last time was that they dated, they both looked at each other (which is never a good sign) and agreed it had been at least twenty-two years since they went out together and had fun. I thought they were kidding, but they assured me that it was the honest truth. Of course, being the bright young therapist that I was, I encouraged them to start dating.

Tony and Laura were a smart, young couple in their late twenties. Both were college educated, and both had good careers and bright prospects for their future together. Tony finished law school and was in the beginning of his practice with a law firm. Laura was in the human resources department in a large company downtown. As a young married couple, they went out frequently to dinner, the theater, concerts and just about anything they could find to do. Time passed, and they had their first child. Laura opted to stay home to be with the baby. Eventually two additional children came along. Needless to say, money was tight as they expanded their family and their expenses. Tony and Laura found themselves in two different worlds.

Tony was busy at work, trying cases and studying to win one lawsuit after another, spending quite a bit of time at the office and bringing paperwork home to do in the evenings. Laura was changing diapers, losing sleep, trying to stay in shape, grocery shopping, going to the cleaners, going to the children's gym classes, taking children to preschool and active in church functions as well.

They came in for counseling because they were arguing frequently. They honestly didn't feel as if they liked each other very much anymore. He blamed her for being tired and grumpy all the time, and she began attacking him for not being supportive and for being insensitive toward her. As the session went on, I asked about their dating experiences. They both looked at each other and awkwardly laughed. "It's been a while."

This statement was true. After child number two came along, other than the Christmas party at the office and a few other events, they hadn't dated each other much. I told them that it sounded to me as if they were boring each other to death. Nobody was having fun anymore.

They agreed and started to date every other week while their parents watched the children. This, with a few other adjustments in their marriage, made a huge difference in the quality of their life and intimacy level. They were able to "be" together, not merely function together.

Dating provides an extremely important foundational part of a successfully intimate marriage. I cannot stress the importance enough. You must date if you plan to have a lifelong loving, intimate and fun relationship.

Friends and acquaintances sometimes ask me, "So how can I improve my marriage and not spend any money to come see you?" It's similar to having a stockbroker or medical doctor as a friend and asking, "Hey, what should I invest in this week?" Or, "Why do I have this pain in this area of my body when I do this, doc?"

I have a simple answer. I simply tell them, "Date your wife."

I am often quoted as saying, "You can either date your wife or go to therapy." Dating is a lot more fun, but if you don't date, you will be speaking to a therapist sooner or later.

Dating is a high priority for Lisa and me. As matter of fact, one of my real motivations for marrying Lisa was to date her permanently and exclusively. She is a fun date, and I love and enjoy the precious time we have together away from the distractions of work and family obligations.

Lisa and I had been married about nine years when our second child, Jubal, was born. After Jubal was born, Lisa asked if we could stop dating for a while to adapt to being parents to two children. Hadassah, our oldest, was eighteen months, and Jubal was one month old. I agreed, and life went on.

As you may know, having two infants can be stressful. After a few weeks you crave sleep and begin praying to God for just one good night's rest. You're fatigued, but you still have to make it through the day. Week after week went by like this: work, children, sleep, work, children, sleep. You get the picture. Life had no fun in it. Lisa and I were giving of ourselves all our waking hours.

The oil of dating and fun was no longer smoothing out the friction of a busy relationship. The normal stress of work and raising two precious infants were beginning to affect our marriage. I remember driving home one night and realizing that home wasn't fun any more. *What went wrong?* After some thought, I realized we hadn't dated for months.

So, we started dating again, and after two to three weeks our marriage was restored. We were both able to get refreshed, have some fun and just enjoy each other's company again without the other day-to-day distractions. Since that point we have dated nearly every week.

Let me tell you another story about dating. Many years ago a couple came into my office. Both were in their forties, and they had two teenaged sons. They came for counseling because they "just weren't getting along." They had been bickering, avoiding each other and displaying an intolerable level of disrespect for each other. They were considering a separation, but they thought they would try a marriage counselor first.

Typically, each spouse starts out by telling me how bad the other one is during the first few minutes. It's my custom then to ask for a "cease and desist decree" on the blaming. Afterward I take a system check on the marriage.

They both looked disappointed that they couldn't vent all their pent-up emotional poison, but I proceeded in a professional manner.

I asked my first question: "How often do you date each other?"

"Date?" they both asked. "What's that?"

"You know, when you leave the seventeen- and fifteen-year-olds at home, and you go have fun together," I explained.

When you're dating, restrain yourself from sensitive issues.

They both glared at me in amazed wonderment and confusion. In Texas, they would say, "They looked like a cow staring at a new gate." This couple truly had no reference point for fun or dating in their relationship. They had not gone on a date in nine years.

I explained to them that if you take any two people who love God, love each other and follow the rules of life in general, but you bore them for nine years and don't let them have a time alone together to rejuvenate, you're going to have two unhappy people. Their first homework assignment was to design two dates, one he would plan and the next one she would plan.

They came back a couple of weeks later. I asked them how it went on their dates. As they told me of the events, I asked them, "So did you have fun?"

They both looked at each other, then at me, and surprising themselves said, "Yes, actually we had a lot of fun!" They laughed because earlier they had convinced themselves that they couldn't be together and have fun.

Dating is important, and without it, you will be forfeiting much of the potential that your marriage holds. So let's define what a date is and what it is not.

Dating is simply planning to spend anywhere from three to five hours together—just you and your spouse. Occasionally you may select to do something with another couple, but let that comprise no more than 25 percent of the time. A date is to be a fun time with your spouse, and it is best to have some agreed-upon boundaries for dating.

SETTING YOUR BOUNDARIES FOR DATING

These boundaries will prove helpful as you develop a dating ritual in your marriage. Use them to protect your dating so that it can last a lifetime for you. Make sure that your dating is *safe* and fun for both of you, so it will have a much greater chance of becoming a fundamental part of your ongoing intimacy together.

1. No problem discussions

The first boundary for making dating successful is this: You may not discuss problems and personal issues that you are having with your spouse or children. In other words, never let this become a "gripe at your spouse" time about what he or she did or didn't do or how he or she is not meeting your needs. Remember, dating is supposed to be fun, and listening to your spouse whine and complain about you is not fun. You can discuss these issues during the other six and a half days of the week. But you must protect your date time from personal problems.

Countless couples tell me that the reason they stopped dating is because it became a gripe session at a restaurant, and they didn't feel like paying a babysitter to be griped at. When you're dating, restrain yourself from sensitive issues. If need be, set a separate night for those conversations, but not on the date.

I must warn you, some spouses will try to sabotage intimacy and dating. They think this relationship stuff is just too much work, so they make the other spouse pay for their displeasure when they go on a date. If your spouse follows these guidelines, there is less likelihood of either spouse being able to sabotage the experience.

If one spouse does continue to sabotage dating, then unresolved anger, relational plaque, intimacy anorexia or depression needs to be evaluated in the sabotaging spouse. If a couple can't date and have fun together, then professional help probably is in order to find out why.

2. No money discussions

The second boundary for couple dating: You may not discuss money.

Nothing can deflate an evening of fun quicker than saying, "We don't have the money for..." Keep your date evening as free as possible by avoiding any mention of money.

This boundary is particularly hard for the self-employed, especially if a couple works together for the company. Try to avoid talking about "the business" or financial issues related to the house or office. You have sixteen hours a day for six days a week to discuss these very important business issues. Don't do it at the time of the week that you get to celebrate your partner.

Some couples may need to schedule a business meeting during the week to discuss all the issues related to finances, children, house, car, future and financial plans and the business if applicable. This business meeting should be one to two hours long at a separate time from dating so that the issues don't bleed into your dating time.

3. No errands

The third boundary for a couple developing a successful dating ritual is this: Do not use this time to run errands. Dating is not a time to trap your spouse in a car and go to Target, Home Depot, the cleaners or the bank. Running errands is not dating.

Errands are an essential part of every busy family. If you need to divide and conquer during the week or on the weekends, ordain an errand evening in which the family does them together. But whatever you do, guard your valuable dating time from errands. It will pay off in the long run.

4. Limit shopping

The fourth boundary, and the last, involves shopping during dating. Ladies, most men don't like shopping, and not too many women want to spend a romantic evening in the power tool aisle at Home Depot. Shopping falls under the category of errands. Now, some couples may decide to use a date night to do some Christmas shopping, but I really caution couples against shopping dates in general.

Here is what sometimes happens. This is supposed to be a fun time together, but here we are in the dress department spending most of our time talking about what kind of dress you ought to purchase instead of talking with each other.

Shopping dates can also trigger one of those "if we only had the money" conversations. If you do agree to shop, really make sure that both of you are in 100 percent agreement that this is the way you want to spend your special night.

MAINTAINING YOUR BOUNDARIES

Maintaining these basic boundaries will insure positive dating experiences. Not every date will be perfect, but keeping these boundaries in place will help.

You will not only be paying for a movie or dinner, but you will also be paying a babysitter. With so much money invested, make sure it will be as positive an experience as possible.

HOW OFTEN?

How often should you date? As much as possible! I realize that with different schedules, work, children and babysitters that the details of dating must be worked out. Here are some options:

1. Weekly
2. Every other week
3. Monthly

I strongly encourage dating your husband or wife as much as possible. Personally, I could easily excuse myself from dating because of being busy with a practice, writing books and articles, speaking at conferences and other routine media activities. But for me, the choice of dating is like the choice of tithing. Once you have decided to do it, the "how to do it" will always follow.

In keeping with the principle of agreement, you both will need to agree about the details of dating. Honoring your governing style, circle your agreed-upon frequency in the space below.

Weekly   Two times a month   Once a month

You have just taken your first step in developing a dating ritual. Let's get even more specific.

Many couples agree to date but neglect to nail down their

commitment to the details, and therefore they don't follow through. Together as a couple, determine the best day for you to date considering both of your schedules. Please circle the day that works best for both of you.

Mon.   Tues.   Wed.   Thurs.   Fri.   Sat.   Sun.

The next issue to agree upon is the time. You can date in the morning, noon or night. It's totally up to both of you.

Lisa and I have had great dates in the middle of the day, such as Friday from 11 A.M. to 3 P.M. before we pick up the children from school. We have most of our dates in the evenings, but if the babysitter can't make it, we often select an afternoon date with regular success. The time isn't important, but the commitment to make it a consistent time is very important. As a couple, fill in the below space with the best time for you to date.

_____ A.M./P.M.

The last decision to make is agreeing to a start date. So in the space below write the date you would like to implement your dating ritual.

Our dating shall commence on _____.

Great! You have made real progress on this very important ritual. In the space below, write out your dating agreement for future reference.

Mr. and Mrs. _____ have agreed to date on a _____ basis, commencing on the day of our Lord Jesus Christ _____ in the year _____.
As often as humanly possible, this date shall begin at _____ A.M./P.M.

Agreeing to date *will* breathe a breath of fresh air into your marriage. Many of my most precious memories of my marriage are from our date nights. I really pray the Lord's richest blessings on this time of dating for you both, and may He confirm to you the blessedness of this tradition in your marriage.

WHO IS RESPONSIBLE?

Who will be responsible to decide what we do during our date?

I have heard countless horror stories about how dating gets destroyed for one spouse because the other one punishes him or her during the entire time they are on a date. You see, one partner didn't want to go to a certain event. Therefore, he or she spends the night withholding emotionally, punishing, criticizing or complaining.

This can happen because it wasn't clear who was responsible for the date.

A second scenario is more passive. This "martyr for a cause" just always does what the other spouse wants to do.

Both of these negative approaches can produce slow toxins that try to seep into this dating process.

The first toxin enters when one partner refuses to voice what he or she would rather do. This husband or wife eventually begins to feel resentful because the only kind of fun they get to experience is what the other spouse enjoys. He or she quietly endures, but often a slow, seething discontent in dating creeps in.

The other spouse experiences a toxic buildup, too. This spouse, who is making all the decisions, begins to resent shouldering 100 percent of the responsibility for dating. This spouse begins to feel that dating is unimportant to the other person. It feels unfair to this partner. It is similar to one spouse behaving as a dating *adult* and the other as a dating *child* with no responsibility.

Let me offer the single best solution that I have found from working with couples for applying dating responsibility. Even if your governing style is monarchical, I strongly suggest that you incorporate the following ideas to make dating last a lifetime.

Have you ever decided to date, lined up the babysitter and climbed into the car and sat in the driveway for fifteen to thirty minutes trying to decide what you are going to do? Perhaps you started driving around, and before long your positive feelings toward each other disintegrated into a low-grade frustration.

Your best shot at intimacy demands the behavior of two adults in the marriage. Each spouse must be 100 percent responsible 50 percent of the time.

Let me clarify what I mean by 100 percent responsible. On the night of the date, one person decides, without being influenced by the other partner, where they are going and what they will do. Now, the next time they date the other spouse will be 100 percent responsible to choose where they go and what they do.

I call this a rotating system. On the first date, the husband decides where to go and what to do. If he decides to go out to eat, he chooses where. The following week, the wife chooses where they go, and if eating is involved, she decides which restaurant they go to.

The expectations and benefits are clear in this system. You always know who is responsible, and you never have to play table tennis with the question, "What do you want to do?"

You probably have spent countless hours doing activities that were not fun. Remember your years in school? How much of that was fun for you? What about your first few jobs? Were they fun 100 percent of the time? Probably not! Most of us have done things that are not very much fun and survived to tell about them.

The responsibility of the person who chooses the date is to decide upon an outing that is fun for *himself* or *herself*. The objective is for the responsible person to have a really good time. In this arrangement, you are not trying to make the *other person* happy.

You can never make someone else happy. It is totally your spouse's responsibility to make himself or herself happy. Besides, your partner will get a chance to make himself or herself happy next week.

This is the fairest system of them all. You both get to choose your date. You have plenty of time to come up with something creative for yourself, and you need not feel any false guilt because your spouse gets a fair shot at it the following date.

Date designers, your only responsibility is to be sure that your spouse knows what to wear. You don't want your partner showing up at a ballet in shorts or wearing good slacks to go Rollerblading. You do not have to tell your spouse where you're going or what you're doing until you get there. Life is an adventure!

Before we go any further, let's discuss the role of the spouse who is *not* designing the date. You are the guest, and you simply are going along for the ride. You may or may not even know where you are going. The guest's role is to be *a happy camper* and to go through the date with grace. You are to love and celebrate your spouse during this event and to make it as positive as possible.

If you are a parent, you've had the opportunity to play the role of happy camper at your children's sporting events, recitals, school plays and other events. You chose to put on a happy face so that your approval and celebration blessed your child. If you can do this with your children, you can also do it for the one who committed never to leave you in sickness, in health, in wealth or in poverty.

Here's a quick example of a rotating dating system. First, let's outline a month of Jake and Tara's dating experiences.

Dating Responsibilities

Week	Responsible Person	Happy Camper	Activity
1	Jake	Tara	Dinner and Walk
2	Tara	Jake	Picnic
3	Jake	Tara	Workout at the gym and coffee shop
4	Tara	Jake	Movie and dessert

Jake has really wanted to try a new restaurant in town, so on week one he took Tara to dinner. Later, they went to a local park and walked and talked for an hour and even prayed together. Tara was the happy camper.

On week two, Tara picked up sandwiches, salads and drinks at a deli. She decided that she just wanted to lounge together, so she chose a secluded spot they had visited years ago and took Jake on a picnic. Jake was the happy camper.

You get the idea. Rotating the date clarifies who is responsible for the date. This system also sparks creativity, genuine romance and playfulness.

As a person accepts his or her responsibility to have fun, both spouses end up enjoying a great time. Personally, dating is the highlight of my week, regardless of what happens at work.

Dating isn't about how much money you spend.

Lisa is a creative lady, and she has come up with some great memorable dating experiences. More than once we've gone Rollerblading together. She took us to a nearby lake, and we waded in the water. Another time she told me to wear a nice suit. She surprised me with tickets to the Bass Performance Hall, one of the best of its kind in the world. But some of our fondest memories are of sitting on a beat-up couch in a coffee shop in Texas that Lisa loved.

To this day these are some of the fondest memories of our marriage, and all because of rotation dating. I encourage you to create your own rotation dating system so that you can increase and maintain your intimacy for a lifetime.

ANGEL-SITTERS

I have used the term *babysitters*. But it really does not adequately reflect the value of a good sitter to a married couple. Lisa and I have no family living nearby, so we've been forced to search diligently for just the right person, a conscientious individual who would make our children feel comfortable. The young people who have come alongside of us have been nothing less than a ministry to us.

Angels are seen ministering to Jesus after His forty-day fast. The Bible says that angels minister to the heirs of salvation. Hebrews 1:14 states, "Are not all angels ministering spirits sent to serve those who will inherit salvation?" The young ladies who have ministered to our children on a weekly basis have been angels to us. Our blessing of intimacy is a by-product of their service to our marriage and our children. Years later our children still talk about Britney, Erica, Liz and Corrie.

Angel-sitting is a ministry, which is why I use this term, not because my children were angels. I use the term because it elevates the service of these young people to the place of honor it should have.

Of course, the person you choose to watch your most precious gifts, your children, should be mature and responsible. Here is some practical advice:

1. *Always pay your angel-sitters well.* A minister is worth his or her wages according to 1 Timothy 5:18, which states, "The worker deserves his wages." These young ladies serve you, and the good ones are in high demand in every church and neighborhood.
2. *Always go the extra mile to communicate your expectations.* Be sure you have clearly instructed your sitters about such things as feeding times, playing crafts or games with your children, boundaries around answering the door, having friends stop by and what types of entertainment are acceptable. Clearly communicate these boundaries in writing. The clearer the communication, the more relaxed your date will be.
3. *Respect your angel-sitter's schedule.* If your sitter has to switch a day, be gracious to oblige when you can.
4. *Be overly responsible.* If your sitter is walking home or driving home, communicate with your sitter's parents and be sure she returns home safely after watching your children.
5. *If you are planning Christmas and New Year's Eve events, plan at least a month or two ahead and get a firm commitment.* Remember to pay more on holidays, because all other jobs get paid more on the holidays.
6. *Always verbally affirm to your sitters how important they are.* Personally, I go out of my way every single time to say how much I appreciate them. Their being able to sense that they mean a lot to you goes a long way in building loyalty.

Remembering that these young people, friends or family members are angels ministering to you and your children can help you to esteem them as highly as they deserve. Without angel-sitters, dating is impossible, so they are valuable people colaboring with you to have the utmost of intimacy in your marriage.

PLAN FINANCIALLY

Paying your angel-sitter as well as paying for your dating activities and meals can add up quickly. To make dating more relaxed, sit down with your spouse and briefly go over what you can currently afford to spend for a date. If you have a household budget already in place, include dating. In addition, discuss who will make the trip to the bank to prepare for the date. An easy method is having the person who is in charge of the date make sure the funds are available prior to the date.

Money spent on dating is money well invested, but it is still money spent. Using the principle of agreement within your governing style, discuss your financial boundaries for dating. In this way, both of you will be aware of the maximum amount you will spend on a date. Money talk will have less opportunity to place a damper on your date.

Dating isn't about how much money you spend. Some of my dates with Lisa cost absolutely nothing. Others have cost less than ten dollars. It is important, however, that you agree on what can be spent, excluding the angel-sitter.

The amount that you both believe you can agree on is:

$ _____ amount

minus $ _____ angel-sitter

equals $ _____

total to be spent on a date

ARE YOU COMMITTED?

Although dating is fun, it is also a real commitment. I want to encourage you both to keep your commitment to dating, for it is a very holy commitment. Our friends know that Lisa and I are not available on our date night. We are committed not to schedule anything on our date night. To reschedule, we both must fully agree to sacrifice a date for whatever reason. Neither husband nor wife solely has the authority to decide to disrupt a date night.

I want to illustrate my personal commitment to dating. There was a time when our only sitter lived thirty minutes away from our house. It took us a total of two hours in the car to pick her up and drop her off because she did not have a car. But I made this two-hour drive for more than a year so that we could date. That's a commitment!

I realized that if my wife and I didn't feel the children were safe, then dating would not be fun. But having Britney as our angel-sitter gave us a sense of assurance and peace so that we were free to enjoy our date.

Dating isn't only great for you, but it is also great for your children.

WHAT ABOUT THE CHILDREN?

Consistent dating sends a strong message to your children about the value of marriage. Our children will learn from what we do, not merely what we say. I want my son, Jubal, to celebrate and date his wife throughout his life. I also want my daughter to marry a man who will not bore her to death, but will celebrate her through dating.

If I don't want my children to end up in marriage counseling, I must consistently demonstrate the importance of dating.

I remember once when Hadassah was three years old and Lisa and I were leaving for a date. She said, "Daddy, I want to go with you." With that she gave one of these desperate little faces only a daughter can give.

I bent down, looked into her eyes and said, "Daddy loves Mommy with his whole heart, and I want to take her out tonight." Hadassah's big brown eyes lit up, and she smiled a big and happy grin as she walked up the stairs to be with our angel-sitter.

I don't know exactly what Hadassah was thinking, but she never asked again to go out on our date night. If you're just starting to date and your children are a little older, you may face some resistance because it is unfamiliar to them. Weather the storm, and they will soon accept your evenings out.

My daughter and son understand dating as a regular, normal part of marriage. Some day I hope to teach our grandchildren to maintain the tradition on a weekly basis. It's not what you believe about marriage that your children will repeat, it's what you *do* in your marriage.

Personally, I believe that our children desperately need a break from us just as much as we need a break from them. They need to experience different personalities. They need that time of eating pizza and popcorn and doing what they want without Mom and Dad hovering over them.

Our children love their angel-sitters. When we tell them Corrie is coming, they get so excited. All day long they will question us about her arrival. It has become a special time for them, too.

We have covered dating very thoroughly so that you can effectively implement this very important tradition into your relationship. Briefly, I would like to explore one more aspect of dating: discovering what you like to do on your date.

IDEAS FOR DATING

Although it is tempting to give you an exhaustive list of ideas for dating, I will resist. If you need some ideas, browse through your local bookstore. I am more interested in discovering what dates you as individuals would like to experience. Remember, dating is for you to have fun. It's not to try to guess what would make your spouse happy. So in the chart on the next page, I want both of you to record date ideas that you think would be fun.

Ideas for Dating

His Dates	Her Dates
1.	1.
2.	2.
3.	3.
4.	4.
5.	5.
6.	6.
7.	7.
8.	8.
9.	9.
10.	10.
11.	11.
12.	12.
13.	13.
14.	14.
15.	15.

Now that you have created a list on dating, two questions remain. Whose dating idea will be first, and when will you start? In my office, we simply flip a coin. The winner of the first toss starts the dating process. Record your winner by circling husband or wife on the following chart.

Dating Begins

Husband   Wife

Together, quickly decide when dating should start. Record that date: _____.

You are well on your way. I pray God's richest blessings upon you both as you invest in each other's hearts and interests. As you celebrate the spouse God has given to you, I pray that you experience a deeper sense of intimacy over the next one hundred days.

FUN TIMES AND GETAWAYS

Every couple needs to have fun to create a depth to intimacy throughout marriage. Before children arrive, having fun gives you something to do with all the extra energy you have, and it helps you to create new avenues of interest. As you move into the active child-raising years, the need for fun increases, because now you need to recharge yourself and escape the daily stress. As you mature, you need fun to maintain interest in the activities that will be essential for a stable retirement.

What I'm talking about is the one-, two- or three-day getaways that are not for the entire family, but only for you and your spouse. Where you go is not nearly as important as the fact that the two of you are together. Some couples choose a weekend at a hotel in the next city, a cabin in the woods or a cottage on the beach. This is unscheduled time together where the greatest decision is, *What's for lunch?* You can shop, eat, sleep or just relax together.

Soaking in fun, fellowship and refreshment can be one of the richest investments you can make in your marriage. Fun can revitalize a marriage like nothing else. Occasionally Lisa and I visit a very large hotel in Dallas. This hotel has three pools, a large gym and five restaurants. We park our car on

Friday and don't drive anywhere the entire time. Such long weekends can feel like a two-week vacation together. We come back replenished with more to give to our children and our work.

Fun must be scheduled. Some couples have a knack for regular fun, spontaneity and creativity. Most of us, however, really need to plan for it. Hopefully, your marriage will outlast your career and the days in which your children are at home. Therefore, have fun with your spouse. The returns on this investment are worth the money you spend, even if you have to save to do so.

PLANNING A GOOD TIME

What issues do you need to walk through to make fun a part of your marriage? How often do you want to plan for fun?

What is reasonable for you to do for fun in a year? You might choose to schedule a getaway annually, biannually or quarterly if you can afford it.

As a therapist, I encourage you to try to get away at least annually. It could keep you looking forward to something for a long time. Personally, I was able to get through some very tough work schedules because I knew our weekend together was coming up.

Using the principle of agreement within your governing style as a couple, discuss what you think your frequency of fun getaways could possibly be this year. After you have agreed upon the frequency for fun, please circle your decision for this below:

Annually   Biannually   Quarterly

As a couple, discuss your financial ability to plan for this expenditure. Saving twenty dollars a month over a year can pay for a weekend stay at a hotel in most cities. It's important that you both agree on this. It will be a lot less fun if you spend your entire time worrying how much all of it is costing.

Together, discuss the cost of what you circled above. Below, please fill out your agreed-upon spending per occurrence:

$ _____ per fun getaway

_____ times the number of fun getaways

$ _____ total of annual spending for fun getaways

If you have a budget, fun getaways together with dating could become line items. Having a strong, intimate marriage costs money, just as having a healthy body or increasing wealth takes money. So long as you remain in agreement, then fun can remain fun.

What would you like to do for fun? Each person in a relationship may consider different kinds of getaways to be fun. One person may want to go skiing, and the other desires a weekend in a cabin somewhere. Here again, be sure to honor both of you. If you only have fun in one manner, then only one person is being fulfilled.

Some couples have used the same system for fun that they use for dating. They create a rotating system. Each person takes a turn being responsible for planning the fun that they want to have. The other spouse's role is to be a happy camper. In this way, both of you get a fair shake at having fun. As you discuss this, if you would like to rotate fun times between the both of you, indicate it below:

Agree to rotate   Only one person decides

After deciding how often, how much and who will be responsible for the fun, there is only one thing left to decide. You must individually decide what you would like to do for fun.

Decide beforehand what you would like to do so you will be motivated to follow through.

Places to Go

Wife's list of places to go or things to do for fun:
1.
2.
3.
4.
5.
6.
7.
8.
9.
10.

Husband's list of places to go or things to do for fun:
1.
2.
3.
4.
5.
6.
7.
8.
9.
10.

Decide who should take the first turn. Flipping a coin works well for this, too. The winner is the first spouse to start the fun assignment. Record your decision.

Husband   Wife

The last phase of planning fun requires a calendar. Together I would like you to look at it and see what days are feasible for this fun event(s). Below record your agreed-upon date(s) for fun this coming year.

Mr. and Mrs. _____ commit to _____ days in the month(s) of _____ and _____, including the dates of _____, _____, _____.

Now, go have a great time! Discover that the spouse God gave to you is a blessing from Him. During your planned fun, I pray that you remember the reasons you first married. I pray that God refreshes your intimacy—spiritually, emotionally and physically. So enjoy yourselves, and make your friends jealous over the great relationship you have rediscovered with your spouse.

ELEVEN

Finding Sexual Agreement

You will probably have two- to five-thousand sexual encounters throughout the course of your life together as a married couple. You hold enormous power and potential to please each other through the absolute pleasure of sex.

Nevertheless, sex remains one of the primary reasons that people seek marriage counseling. It always amazes me how differently married couples view their sex lives. Many couples, regardless of how long they have been married, can't even agree on how often they have sex.

When a couple arrives for counseling I usually ask how often they are sexually active together. Inevitably one spouse will cite a low figure, such as once every ten to fourteen days. The other spouse will swear to having sex twice a week. I chuckle and tell them it is perfectly normal not to agree on the frequency of sex.

Another interesting issue is how much sex a couple says

they desire. I ask how often they would like to have sex. The answers are very similar. Often they look at each other and at me with amazement. They never realized that they agreed more than they disagreed about how often they desired sex.

They might even respond, "Then why aren't we doing it that often?" The answer is because they haven't found agreement regarding sexual frequency in any formal manner of discussion.

> Manipulation can go into multiple directions as the couple tries to deal with sexuality without talking about it.

An example of this is Amy and Fred who were married just seven years before they began to consider divorce. Fred was finishing his degree to become a chiropractor. Amy had been supporting the family financially and was feeling very neglected.

They were having sex once every six to eight weeks. Amy and Fred were in their thirties, and an average couple their age would typically be sexual about two to three times a week. They were way below the average. Amy and Fred loved each other and were active church members.

Amy and Fred said they argued about their sex life all the time. They wanted to stop arguing, and the only solution they could come up with was divorce. However, they had two children and didn't want to divorce. Except for the sexual issue, they got along fine.

I asked Amy and Fred to write down separately on a piece of paper how often each of them would like to be sexual. When Amy flipped her piece of paper over it read that she wanted to be sexual two or three times a week. Fred flipped his paper over, and as you may have guessed, it said two to three times a week! We all laughed and realized we could easily save this marriage.

"How is it that you both want sex the same amount of times and yet you're only having it once every six weeks?" I asked.

Amy and Fred answered very similarly. They said that when they have sex, it's great. But then a few days go by and he or she doesn't initiate. One of them ends up believing that other spouse doesn't want sex or he or she would have asked. Another week goes by, and they begin to feel unwanted and rejected. Neither of them talk about it, and they start to distance themselves from one another.

Eventually they both get irritable with these feelings building into angry outbursts over almost anything. By the next week they get so mad at each other that they finally apologize, make up and have sex again. Then the pattern starts all over again!

As we discussed this together, Amy and Fred realized a couple of things. The first thing they realized is they never really calmly talked through their desire for sexual frequency. Also, they never realized that both of them were 100 percent responsible for initiating sex. Both Amy and Fred regarded the other as 100 percent responsible to initiate sex. Thirdly, they realized that they could walk in agreement sexually and probably be really happy the rest of their life together.

SEXUAL CHAOS VS. SEXUAL ORDER

How do situations like this happen? How can a couple remain married, in love and still struggle so much in the area of sexuality? These are questions I want to address because many couples are just like Amy and Fred.

Here is what I believe happens as a normal young couple evolves sexually. A couple gets married, and in the first six months to a year sex is usually not an issue. They are having plenty of sex, and they feel relatively good about the quantity.

As a couple takes on more responsibilities such as school, work, children, two cars and a mortgage, life becomes more stressful and increasingly complicated.

During the next few years the couple doesn't talk about it, but a system of chaos and manipulation evolves. As the husband smartens up sexually, he realizes that sex is beginning to slow down, so he concludes, "If I ask for more, then I will get more, for if I ask twice and I am refused once, then I get sex half the time. If I ask four times, then I can at least get sex twice, and if I am lucky, maybe three times." So this brave young male pursues, and hence the dance of manipulation begins.

The wife begins to feel increasing pressure from her husband to be sexual, so she begins to make some generalizations about sex and her husband. She believes he starts with kissing and hugging in the kitchen, and if she lets him do that, then he thinks she wants to be sexual. So she concludes that she must not let him kiss and hug so he won't ask for sex. She then begins to manipulate how much affection she will participate in, in hopes of somehow managing the sexuality in her young marriage.

> This gift of sexuality and communion from her soul is as important to acknowledge as the husband's physiological sex drive.

Manipulation can go into multiple directions as the couple tries to deal with sexuality without talking about it. You may have heard the jokes about, "If the pillow is on the right side, you can ask. If it's on the left side, you better not."

When I was a teenager I remember seeing a plaque in a store that had two dials, one for him and one for her. The sayings around the dial were "Not tonight," "No way," "I'm tired," "If you hold me first," "Maybe," "Ask and take your chance," "OK, if I have to," "Tonight's your night." Back then I wondered why sex seemed so confusing. But it doesn't have to be that difficult, as we will see.

You can begin to see that over time every couple develops a sexual system. This system is a way in which a husband and wife figure out how to ask without asking and how to reject without communicating. However, these systems can be unclear, even to the couples participating in them.

Having a clear sexual communication system or sexual agreement is very important. Even the best spouses can injure each other in a marriage with a system of sex that has never been discussed or agreed upon, one that both partners co-created, yet neither is responsible for.

Responsibility is a big issue when it comes to sexuality. As we discussed earlier, just because a person is an adult physically does not mean that he or she is an adult sexually. Sexual adults are responsible for their own sexuality and can create an agreement together for sexual expression.

THE JOY OF SEXUAL ACCEPTANCE

A strong sex drive that doesn't quit until near death is a gift from God to men. A man's sexual drive forces him to push through his insecurities and self-doubts to start dating. It is also a large motivator for men to marry. This drive compels men to work through marital issues with their wives. This sexual gift from God is what glues a man to a woman spiritually, emotionally and neurologically.

The gift of sex is different for women. The woman's drive seems to come mostly from the communion on an emotional and spiritual realm. Generally speaking, when she feels close she wants to express herself physically. She is not looking for a sex act; she is looking for a love event during sexuality. I believe women intuitively desire spirit, soul and body sex for the majority of their sexual experiences. This gift of sexuality and communion from her soul is as important to acknowledge as the husband's physiological sex drive.

It is important that you never attempt to manipulate or change how your husband or wife is created. If you can learn to accept your spouse sexually, you will move much more quickly toward creating the best sex of your life.

There are no magic buttons on your wife that can get you more sex.

I vividly remember a conversation I was having with a man one day about his sexuality with his wife. He was a forty-seven-year-old blue collar worker with six boys and a wife who worked at a garment factory. They were having sex very infrequently. He and I started talking about the emotional needs of women. He said to me, "You're right!" Apparently about a year ago he read a book about women and what they need. He said the book told him to listen without trying to solve the problem. It said to ask questions about her feelings and to also share things about his life without being prompted. He told me, "I did everything the book told me to do for three months. That's when we were having the most and best sex of our marriage!" I asked him what happened. He said something that has stuck with me all these years: "I stopped doing my part."

For three months this husband accepted the fact that men are different from women. Women have needs that men don't necessarily have at the same level. Some men are pretty simple in their thought processes about sex. A major part of a woman's sexuality is wrapped up in her getting her spiritual and emotional needs met on a daily basis. When this happens, a man will see the transformation of his wife's spiritual, emotional and sexual demeanor. If you give your wife the oil of intimacy, you will find that sexuality is more comfortable for her to participate in and initiate.

NO MAGIC BUTTONS

There are no magic buttons on your wife that can get you more sex. Some women have not matured into sexual adults and still behave as sexual children. It's possible to be a prince of a guy for a year and still have no increased sexual expression from your wife. In cases like this, definitely pursue professional help.

Moving on toward the husband's side of the relationship, some men are sexual and most are very sexual. This will not change! They love to be touched and to touch. They love your beauty, your body and sexuality together. They think about sex almost as much as they think about food. Men are generally creatures of appetite, and most women were aware of this long before marriage.

> A sexual agreement occurs when a couple intelligently and calmly discusses how often they both desire to have sexual intimacy, and then fairly distribute the responsibility for initiating sex.

Imagine taking your husband to the mall early the day after Thanksgiving to go Christmas shopping. You know the sales are great, and you plan to accomplish a great deal because stores are open from 7 A.M. to 10 P.M. Your husband is running a little behind, so he forgets to eat breakfast.

Ten o'clock approaches, and he starts hinting about lunch. You continue to shop as 11 A.M. approaches, and your husband indicates more firmly that he's getting hungry. Again, you pacify him and assure him that you will eat soon. Twelve o'clock now goes by, and this fairly nice man you married is getting rude—you can tell food is increasingly occupying his thoughts. By 1 P.M. he's a monster. He won't say anything, and he is mad! He is totally fixated on food, and if you don't stop and eat soon, not only is shopping over, but it's going to be a bad day for everyone.

Ladies, you know what I am talking about. We call it male "food anxiety." We wake up wanting to know what's for breakfast. At 10:30 A.M. we want to know what's for lunch. When we come home from work, you know what the classic male greeting is: "Hi, honey. What's for dinner?" You would think we have little else on or minds. If men don't know when they are eating, they get food anxiety. If you don't think this is true, try not telling your husband when and what he is eating and see what happens.

I think we clearly illustrated that most men who are not depressed or sexually anorexic are appetite-driven. This will not change, for it is the gift of God. An appetite for life in general makes men work harder, create more and keep working, because if you don't work, you don't have money for food!

What does all this food talk have to do with sex? Food is a classic way to illustrate that, like food, men think a lot about sex. Most have heard the urban myths about how often men think about sex. Although I have never personally read these studies, I think the point is, we think about sex a lot.

Now, if a man is in a manipulation-based sexual system, then he must rely on his fine-tuned skills to manipulate his wife into sex. Living like this keeps most men in a constant state of "sexual anxiety." They don't know when they are having sex or if they are ever having sex again. This kind of system produces more sexual anxiety, which causes men to think about it even more.

Ladies, what I am telling you is the truth. I have counseled men for many years on sexual issues. When men know when sex will occur and who will initiate it, they will think about sex much less and experience almost no sexual anxiety.

Once two sexual adults in a marriage arrive at a place of sexual agreement, peace floods into the sexual system. We are talking about accepting men sexually where they are. You won't change his desire for sex, and if you try to manipulate him in this area, it can create passive or aggressive conflict in the marriage. Remember that male sexuality is a gift from God. It is to be celebrated by the couple, not tolerated. A man who is sexually tolerated by his wife will, over time, generate many negative feelings toward his wife. A man who generally feels sexual acceptance and is sexually celebrated will have an ongoing positive feeling and expression of love for his wife.

On the other hand a husband who ignores the spiritual and emotional aspects of his wife will also damage their sexuality over time. The man who is spiritually and emotionally lazy has a huge surprise down the road. The surprise is that she won't be interested, and it will be because you did not accept her sexually and emotionally.

If you want your wife to reject sex, don't pray with her, listen to her feelings or keep your word outside the bedroom. They laugh, but those who have refused to sexually accept their wife's intimacy needs know I am telling the truth.

WHAT IS SEXUAL AGREEMENT?

A sexual agreement occurs when a couple intelligently and calmly discusses how often they both desire to have sexual intimacy and then fairly distributes the responsibility for initiating sex. The husband and wife decide verbally and then record how they want to structure their sexuality so that both are reasonably happy.

Reasonably is a very important word. Life is about negotiation. This is especially true in a marriage. If a man is pestering his wife to have sex daily, or if the wife only wants sex once a month, they are both being sexually selfish and unreasonable.

In sexual agreement, we must apply the Amos 3:3 principle that says that two must agree to walk together. If you don't agree on a sexual system, you will still create one without really agreeing about it. Although unusual, some couples create a naturally evolved sexual system between them that works quite well.

CREATING A SEXUAL AGREEMENT

Sexual systems are an issue that many couples fight over for decades. As you walk through the process of creating a sexual agreement together, I will ask you to do three things.

1. Be open-minded to each other's sexual needs.
2. Be honest about your sexuality.
3. If you can't do this together, get professional help.

Agreements and management structures are used in almost every other area of your life. You organize, manage and oversee your financial system. You manage the raising of your children and their countless classes and activities. Your spiritual and emotional lives require many agreements and systems. Much of life involves effective management for optimal results. This is also true regarding sexual matters.

The first step toward creating a sexual agreement is the issue of frequency. First, both of you will need to write on a piece of paper your own personal preferences for frequency. The average couple enjoys sexual relations one, two, three or more times a week for couples up to the age of about fifty. After fifty, sexual intimacy usually decreases to about once a week. I'm providing this information as a reference point because I am asked this question so often.

Now you must share what you've written and begin negotiating. This is *your* marital sexual system, so you can be as creative as you desire. How can you handle differing desires? Here's one way: If he prefers two sexual experiences each week and she wants to be sexual three times a week, then on his week he can have his desired frequency and on her week she can choose hers.

Before you go any further, check off the box below saying that you have thus far agreed on the frequency of sex.

❐ We have agreed on sexual frequency.

Remember that this is *your* sexual agreement. I usually ask couples to stick to their agreements for a minimum of ninety days to see if the system works for both partners. If the system needs changing at that point, discuss it at a restaurant or in another public place. Don't discuss it in your bedroom or any other place in your house so that one spouse doesn't attempt to pressure the other into more or less sexual intimacy than they agreed to.

The following are several basic sexual systems for you to choose from. You may come up with your own version of a system, which is fine. As a couple has children, raises those children and then goes through the stage of the children leaving the home, the sexual systems will change. Nevertheless, both must continue to agree on the changes.

Lisa and I have had our sexual agreement for about a decade. Every year we review it to make changes as needed. This is not simply a good idea. Putting a system into place and practicing it brings great peace to many relationships. Over the years I've received many phone calls and letters from couples who are experiencing greater marital success because of walking in sexual agreement.

SYSTEM ONE

After you have agreed on your sexual frequency, you will now simply need to select the days that you want to be sexual. If you want to be sexual twice a week, then you can pick any two days of the week that work for your schedule. For example: Tuesday and Saturday or Wednesday and Sunday.

In this system, you can divide the responsibility to initiate sex by the day or by the week.

Here's an example of dividing by the day: Let's suppose Jason and Dana choose to be sexual two days a week on Tuesday and Saturday. Jason could be responsible to initiate on Tuesdays, and Dana could be responsible for initiating on Saturdays.

Here's an example of dividing responsibility by the week: On the first and third week of the month, Jason would initiate; on the second and fourth week, Dana would initiate the sexual encounters.

Many busy couples love this system because once it is in place they don't have to think about it. It easily fits into a busy schedule because they are both stress-free concerning sexuality. Other couples find this system too rigid and lacking in spontaneity.

SYSTEM TWO

System two is a little less rigid. In this system, you would split the week up between the two of you. If you agreed on having sex twice a week, then Jason could choose either Sunday, Monday and Tuesday for the day in which he wants to initiate sex. However, he would have to initiate sex one time during this three-day period.

Wednesday would be a day off for both of you in a two times a week system. Some couples make Wednesday a day that either can ask. If you chose to have sex two to three times a week, or simply three times a week, then try keeping Wednesday as a day that either can ask.

Dana would initiate sex once during the three-day period of Thursday, Friday and Saturday. So Jason has his part of the week to initiate, and Dana has her part of the week. They are both clear regarding what days to initiate and who is responsible to initiate.

This system allows flexibility for a person to choose when they want to be sexual. Again, some couples love this system, but for others this system would not work.

SYSTEM THREE

System three is a rotating system. In this system, if you decide to have sex twice a week, each person will have up to three days to initiate sex with the other spouse. You can initiate within any of your days.

Following the third day of the week, it becomes the other spouse's turn. This spouse now has up to three days to initiate sex.

In this system, Jason has three days to initiate. If he decides to wait until day two, then fine. Following day two, after they have sex then it immediately becomes Dana's turn.

Now it's Dana's turn. She can initiate sex on the very first day of her three-day period, or she can wait until day three.

Dana decides to initiate the very next day. Now Dana's turn is over, and the next day it is Jason's turn. He just had sex two days in a row, so he may wait to initiate.

> Most men find it very satisfying to know when sexual intimacy will occur.

This system provides both partners the most flexibility and is especially successful for those couples seeking spontaneity. It also accommodates couples who are seeking a greater frequency of sexuality in their relationship.

In this system, you can have sex as little as twice a week (when both partners wait for the third day to initiate), daily or anywhere in between. This system is ideal for some couples, but for others it is too fluid.

These are the three basic sexual agreement systems. Your coupleship is unique, so you can choose any of these three systems or come up with a sexual system of your own. The sexual system you choose—one, two, three or your own—isn't as important as the fact that you walk in agreement sexually.

Sexual agreement is a blessing. You will be married a long, long time, and it is better to agree about sex, negotiate and change systems over time than to have an unknown sexual system that neither one of you wants. Implementing this chapter can give you genuine sexual harmony and peace.

As a Christian marriage and family counselor, I know that where the Spirit of the Lord is, there can be peace. Too often Christian marriages do not reflect this peace in the bedroom. But it's not because of a lack of love or even a lack of sexual desire—it is often because of a lack of agreement.

ENJOYING THE BENEFITS OF AGREEMENT

The benefits of walking in sexual agreement are tremendous. In my own life, sexual agreement has brought clarity and peace into my marriage.

Sexual agreement reduces sexual anxiety. For the husband, he now knows he will be having sex on a regular basis, so his fear of rejection is gone. He is also less inclined to manipulate his partner sexually. Not only does he know he will be sexual regularly, but he also knows how often and when. Most men find it very satisfying to know when sexual intimacy will occur. Their need to be sexually fed has been heard, understood and agreed upon by the person whom they love the most.

Here's another benefit of this new system. In the past the husband may have been expected to be the primary, or sole, sexual initiator. Now he gets the opportunity to receive sexual initiation from his spouse. This is very important for some men. Years of being totally responsible for initiating sex can make a man feel as though his wife is merely tolerating him sexually. Some have even felt as if they had a disease.

The wife may or may not have actually felt that way, but the husband still projected that on her because she didn't initiate sex. A wife's age can have a great deal to do with her reluctance to initiate sex. Although attitudes have changed, years ago it was considered improper for a lady to express her desire for sex.

In an agreed-upon sexual system, a husband develops greater respect and appreciation for his wife. She becomes more precious and desirable in his heart. He feels, "She's in this with me." He no longer feels sexually alone.

Many men have pulled me aside to tell me that a sex system has changed their marriages. Some have remarked, "I've never been this in love with my wife." They were not just talking about sexual frequency. They were speaking of the unity and love they felt toward their spouse.

The benefit of being in sexual agreement greatly affects the wife as well. I can remember in counseling sessions where wives were very relieved finally to get this sexuality issue agreed upon. Many of them felt hopeless and frustrated trying to manage both their own and their husbands' sexuality.

Wives also express their gratitude. They often feel that their own sexuality had been submerged beneath their husbands. God made each woman sexual, but many have felt that they were always reacting to their husband's sexuality and couldn't express their own.

Forming a sexual agreement gives a woman a new sense of autonomy. She can say, "This is my sexuality, and this is how I want to express it." She can choose her time (within limits) when she will be sexual.

This sense of sexual choice is important for women. Too

often wives feel that they have no sexual choices, and they are just submitting sexually. Inevitably, she feels that her choice to be sexual was taken away or stifled. Sexual agreement is a real benefit to her because her husband also now respects her sexual choices and her right to be a sexual adult, equal to and not suppressed by him.

Women who have a sexual agreement in place are more free to relax, not only sexually, but also with physical affection. The wife becomes free to experience her husband's spontaneous hugs and kisses. When it's her turn, affection will become sexual only when she decides that's what she wants. She can let his affection into her heart instead of feeling as though she must defend herself.

They both know how much sexuality is going to take place in their marriage. Her sexual desires were heard and negotiated. She is an equal in the system, is respected and can respect herself. She is a sexual adult who doesn't need to be manipulated or coerced to be sexual.

She can relax because if she doesn't feel like having sex, and it's her turn to choose the day, she doesn't have to be sexual. The freedom not to be sexual for some women is just as important.

The couple as a unit also benefits from walking in sexual agreement. I have seen numerous couples significantly increase intimacy after they have been consistent with a sexual system. Sexual issues in the past drained both the husband and the wife. But when they no longer had to manipulate, argue, fuss or pout about sex anymore, they discovered a lot more energy to just enjoy one another.

Many couples experience a heightened sense of sexual esteem. Husbands and wives gain a new sense of sexual confidence as they grow increasingly aware that not only are they satisfying their own sexual needs, they are now satisfying their mate as well. Feeling good about your sexuality and your sexual expression plays an intricate part in your self-esteem.

Intimacy

A final benefit of sexual agreement is the removal of sexual authority from one person in the agreement. In a sense, the agreement now becomes the sexual authority, not the husband or wife. In the past one partner may have controlled or dominated the marriage sexually. Now no one person is to blame. It becomes easier to give authority to the agreement that you yourself created.

During the next one hundred days, I trust your own experience will be positive as you and your spouse learn to walk together in sexual agreement. Even though a sexual agreement may be challenging for some who have been living irresponsibly as sexual children or sexual adolescents, the journey to maturity is well worth it. In your 100-day log, you will be able to journal your progress as you learn to walk together.

GUIDELINES FOR A SUCCESSFUL AGREEMENT

Below are some guidelines for a successful sexual agreement. You can use these guidelines to answer any questions you may have.

1. ALWAYS SAY YES.

The first guideline relates to responding to sexual advances from your partner. Since we are sexual adults and not children or adolescents, here's my advice: *Always say yes* unless you have a doctor's excuse! This may seem extreme until you understand this agreement.

When it's the other person's turn, comply with his or her advances. When it's your turn, your partner should comply with yours as well. We all know when our spouse is truly too sick to be sexual, and we must be considerate of that. But I want to be clear, there are *no excuses!* "I'm tired" or "I have a headache" do not work in this arrangement.

Do not manipulate or withhold sex from each other. These behaviors are *enemies* of intimacy that will destroy the momentum and closeness of the relationship over the next one hundred days.

Realize that not everyone who says he or she wants intimacy really does. There is no greater way to create chaos and anger than for a spouse to break his or her word regarding sex.

2. IMPOSE CONSEQUENCES.

The second guideline involves consequences. I have worked with enough couples to know that change is difficult and can be intentionally resisted, especially in couples that have had lifelong struggles with sexual addiction, intimacy anorexia or sexual maturity issues.

What do you do when your spouse doesn't keep his or her word after you've set up a sexual agreement? Before you begin or after your spouse fails two times to either initiate sexually or respond appropriately to your sexual advances, consequences *must be implemented* for change. Setting up consequences generally works better *before* you start a sexual system.

A consequence is something negative that a person would prefer not to do rather than have sex. It is not enough to simply decide that one will have to do the dishes. To work, consequences must be much more painful than that. Let me provide some examples that have been effective for other couples. Each spouse must choose his or her own consequence.

- ❏ Hand wash and detail the spouse's automobile
- ❏ Volunteer for two to four hours at a nursing home
- ❏ Send $100 to the local political party to which you are most opposed
- ❏ Volunteer at the local political party to which you are most opposed
- ❏ Spend time with a relative you dislike

- ❏ Send money to a relative or organization you don't like
- ❏ Run two miles
- ❏ Give your spouse a sixty- to ninety-minute massage
- ❏ Watch the children for four hours while your spouse goes somewhere
- ❏ Give up watching sports for two weeks
- ❏ Give up going hunting or fishing
- ❏ Make a counseling appointment

Each person must decide what their own consequence would be for not fully participating in the sexual agreement. For example, John withholds sex from Mary when it was his turn to initiate by Tuesday bedtime. Regardless of the reason, since he wasn't dead and he definitely didn't have a doctor's excuse, he must face a consequence. Likewise, if John initiated during his time and Mary refused to participate, then Mary would do her agreed-upon consequence.

If a person refuses to do their consequence, or if one person is regularly not keeping their word sexually, then I would strongly suggest a counseling session.

3. Respect each other's sexual space.

Guideline number three, when it's *not* your turn, *you may not ask!* This is a simple guideline, but when someone consistently does not respect the sexual space of the other person, the sexual system can erode.

4. Determine how you will handle monthly cycles.

Guideline number four has to do with the menstrual cycles. It is important for a couple to make a clear communication about what is expected or accepted during this time of the month. The couple also needs to communicate about when

Finding Sexual Agreement

the wife needs to tell the spouse the news about the starting of the cycle.

Couples vary so much about sex and the cycle. For some couples, they just keep having intercourse, and for others, they wouldn't even consider sexual relations during this time. Options for couples seem to be one of the following:

1. Continue sexually as normal
2. Suspend sexual activity for a defined period (i.e., so many days or so many turns at initiating)
3. Be sexual but no intercourse

Any option is fine, but it is imperative that you both agree with the choice so that no misunderstandings occur.

Discuss and agree about how to communicate when a cycle begins. When it's the husband's turn, he may spend the day thinking about being sexual with his wife. He gets home, they eat, do the homework with children, take baths, put everyone to bed and he finally jumps into bed with his beloved. She turns over and announces that she can't, for she started her period that morning.

If he responds with anything less than "I hope you are feeling OK," he will be seen as insensitive and selfish.

What helps tremendously here is clear communication. A couple decides when she is to communicate the change in their normal sexual expression. Some couples have designed an agreement system for communicating this information:

- ❏ As soon as she finds out, she will let her husband know.
- ❏ She sends an e-mail with a catch phrase.
- ❏ She mentions it when he comes home before dinner.
- ❏ She mentions it after dinner but before homework.

Clear communication can save both spouses ill feelings due to a change in routine. Usually ill feelings are the result of the *change* in the sexual agreement. So for the sake of both of you, take a preventative measure as you go through the next one hundred days.

5. *Agree on sexual behaviors.*

Guideline number five is agreeing on what sexual behaviors are mutually satisfying and acceptable to *both* partners. As we stated earlier, people vary in their sexual personalities, preferences, histories and the amount of sexual behaviors they have participated in.

Since your sexuality is going to be the only garden of intimacy that you will both be eating from, it is helpful for you both to define what is acceptable. Some fruit, or types of expression, may be acceptable all the time, others may be acceptable on occasion, and some fruit is definitely forbidden. You also must determine who will initiate the sexual expression that is occasionally acceptable.

Again, this is your sexual garden. We are not addressing what is right or wrong, but rather what *both* of you want in your garden. On a separate sheet of paper, write out the various fruits of your sexual expression that each of you desires. Below you can indicate what is acceptable for each spouse or both.

Acceptable Sexual Behavior

Example (fill in)	He (circle one)	She (circle one)
Position 1	Yes No Only if I initiate	Yes No Only if I initiate
Position 2	Yes No Only if I initiate	Yes No Only if I initiate
Act A	Yes No Only if I initiate	Yes No Only if I initiate

Finding Sexual Agreement

Example (fill in)	He (circle one)	She (circle one)
Act B	Yes No Only if I initiate	Yes No Only if I initiate
Place 1	Yes No Only if I initiate	Yes No Only if I initiate
Place 2	Yes No Only if I initiate	Yes No Only if I initiate

After you write all this out, both of you circle the appropriate response: *Yes, No* or *Only if I initiate*. Everything you both circle *yes* is a fruit that you both agree on and can participate in with a clear conscious before God and each other.

The things you both circle no are forms of expression that would be defiling to your particular garden and would not even be requested by either spouse.

The forms of sexual expression for which one circled yes and the other *no* are areas of sexual disagreement. These are forms of sexual expression you would not participate in or request during sex because you *both* do not agree.

If you feel these areas need further discussion, you can seek out a counselor or see a pastor in your area. The purpose of counseling would be to hear the rationales and histories to determine if such a sexual behavior is negotiable. The goal of counseling is never to manipulate your spouse into doing what you want sexually.

The option that states *only if I initiate* can be used by a spouse who realizes a mate enjoys a particular form of sexual expression. Still, this spouse does not want to feel obliged to always participate in this expression, expect on occasion for the sake of the spouse.

Charles and Cindy are a middle-aged couple with two teenagers. Overall, Charles and Cindy had a good Christian marriage and had successfully worked through most of the difficult areas of their relationship. Nevertheless, one issue continued to surface again and again. They came to counseling to resolve the one issue of sexual behavior that Charles enjoyed but Cindy felt uncomfortable with.

Charles liked Cindy to wear fancy, sexy lingerie. Charles enjoyed his wife's body, and he liked the way she looked in sexy lingerie. Cindy, however, was more conservative in her sexual personality. She felt like a prostitute, not a Christian wife, when wearing the negligées.

If the only options Charles and Cindy had were yes or no, they would have remained polarized in disagreement. However, the issue wasn't the act itself but the feelings and perceptions related to the act. Cindy felt she was being coerced to be involved in this behavior. She felt that Charles didn't think she was sexy enough on her own and that by wearing the garments she was not being herself.

As we talked, she realized that she could do this once in a while but only if she picked out the clothes. She also would be the one to initiate the behavior when she wanted to express her sexuality in this way. Cindy felt free to choose and express herself. When she understood that she was loved regardless of whether or not she wore the clothes, then she felt more comfortable wearing them occasionally.

The option that states *only if I initiate* is designed for Cindy and Charles's type of situation. Agreement on what fruits are acceptable to both partners can add a greater sense of safety and trust in the area of sexuality. Agreement results in sexual freedom and fun.

6. BOTH MUST AGREE BEFORE CHANGING THE SYSTEM.

Guideline number six: The system stays in place for at least sixty to ninety days before changing any aspect of it. One person cannot make changes in sexual agreement. Both spouses must agree for a change to be made. If you feel you need a professional to navigate you through changes, please see one. Some couples agree to make changes in their sexual agreement only if their pastor or counselor also agrees. This minimizes any manipulation.

We have taken a lot of time on this area of sexual agreement. It is an area in which I find that couples need the most help. Walking through the complexities of the sexual issues is a mountain every couple must climb, and the view along the way is ever changing and growing.

You now have outlined how to create a sexual system. On a separate sheet of paper, both of you need to write down your sexual system. Below is a checklist for you to include the various ingredients of a successful sexual agreement.

Our Sexual Agreement

- ❑ Our sexual agreement is written down in a clear format that outlines how often sex will occur.
- ❑ Our sexual agreement is written down and is clear regarding who is responsible for initiating sex.
- ❑ Our agreement states that we will say *yes* unless we have a doctor's excuse.
- ❑ Our sexual agreement includes self-imposed consequences for both spouses if either does not keep the agreement.
- ❑ We have included the not-asking-when-it's-not-your-turn policy.
- ❑ We have an agreed-upon plan regarding menstrual cycles and the communication of their onset.
- ❑ We have a written agreement regarding what is *acceptable, not acceptable* and *only if I initiate* behavior.
- ❑ We have a clause as to when our agreement can be changed.

If you completed all eight steps, you only have one more step to go. When do you want to get started? You can write the date in the space below or put it on your agreement.

Date started: _____

Both of you have completed a lot of writing! In the 100-day log portion of this book, you will be asked to comment regularly about whether you are walking as sexual adults and maintaining your agreements.

Living in Colorado, I've learned that hiking is work. But it seems the higher you climb, the cleaner the air, the cooler the temperature and the more spectacular the view. I am very proud of you for taking the climb over the next one hundred days. I believe your intimacy will rise to a new level. I pray God's richest blessing on your marriage as you enjoy all the fruits you have agreed upon. The garden is a great place for a couple to be, naked, unashamed and in the presence of God.

> The man and his wife were both naked, *and they felt no shame.*
> —GENESIS 2:25, EMPHASIS ADDED

TWELVE

Blessed Are the Consistent

Consistency is the key to success in life and in relationships. Those who eat right, exercise and live by the principles of health typically are healthier than others who eat as they please and live like couch potatoes.

The principle of consistency also applies to matters of wealth. Those who work, save and invest will be wealthier than those with slothful work habits who waste their earnings. God rewards those who consistently seek Him. (See Hebrews 11:6.)

Consistency is especially beneficial in intimacy and marriage. Those who take the principles of relational health and practice them consistently enjoy relational success. Husbands and wives who ignore these principles end up harming relational intimacy. The Bible is filled with wisdom about living consistently.

Most of us start racing toward intimacy in our youth, but few of us successfully make it to the finish line. Some are dashed apart in divorces by temptations, sins and a long list of other obstacles. We must keep reaching for the principles that make intimacy work so we will win the race and obtain the prize.

In 2 Timothy 4:7 Paul speaks of finishing his course: "I have fought the good fight. I have finished the race, I have kept the faith."

> The anger that you do not conquer may be passed to your children to overcome.

Consistency was everything to Paul. Let's look at another powerful statement he made in Acts 20:24.

> However, I consider my life worth nothing to me, if only I may finish the race and complete the task the Lord Jesus has given me—the task of testifying to the gospel of God's grace.

Paul's life was full of focus and purpose. He yearned for the finish line. His goal was to run successfully to the end testifying of his Lord Jesus Christ. He longed to give God the glory in the end. Although Paul was referring to his personal mission, I believe the principle of running to the end strongly applies to many areas of your life—especially in marriage. I pray that God would help you to apply the principles of intimacy to successfully run the race for a lifetime.

Let's look at what Jesus Christ Himself had to say about finishing the course. In John 17:4, Jesus states, "I have brought you glory on earth by completing the work you gave me to do." In John 5:36, Jesus shared this about the issue of finishing:

> I have testimony weightier than that of John. For the very work that the Father has given me to finish, and which I am doing, testifies that the Father has sent me.

The Lord Himself was intent upon finishing what God had set before Him. This applies to husbands and wives. Finishing to the end was one of the things Jesus said we could observe about His life in order to truly know that God sent Him.

Wouldn't it be great to have this testimony to give to your spouse or children and grandchildren? What an exalted sense of purpose you would have if your spouse and children could look at your marriage and know that God has sent you.

I love this principle and aspire to having such a great testimony of intimacy unto the very end of my life. You see, the blessings of my consistency and yours will go down multiple generations.

As a therapist, I recognize that areas of personal and relational weaknesses are passed down from generation to generation. The anger that you do not conquer may be passed to your children to overcome. This is also true of addictions, emotional coldness, the lack of affection, the inability to praise another and fear.

How Dad treated Mom and how Mom treated Dad are huge issues in the field of counseling. Our emotional and spiritual heritage can be a roadblock we must overcome or a blessing that we pass along.

Your consistency with the principles of intimacy in your marriage will be passed down to your children and their children. I have talked with those who came from families that succeeded in establishing and living with these principles of intimacy. Such individuals naturally understand how a relationship should work.

Let me illustrate this just briefly. In Luke 14:28–30, Jesus taught on the principle of finishing. He said:

> Suppose one of you want to build a tower. Will he not first sit down and estimate the cost to see if he has enough money to complete it? For if he lays the foundation and is not able to finish it, everyone who sees it will ridicule him, saying, "This fellow began to build and was not able to finish."

What a tragedy this would be for the builder! It would be an even greater tragedy for the couple who could not finish the building of their God-given marriage. This is especially true when we can choose to ask God's help to do all things through Christ Jesus who strengthens us (Phil. 4:13).

How is it that God's power is available to us through prayer, and yet we see skyrocketing divorce rates, even in Christian marriages? Could it be that we are not looking toward finishing the race of marriage with our spouse?

We must look at our marriages as long term and consider the effect our marriages will have on future generations. Looking at your marriage as a long-distance marathon runner can be helpful.

Lisa and I settled this issue early in our marriage. Murder might be an option, but divorce—never! We laugh when we tell our friends this, but we are committed to the end. Sometimes Lisa and I will kid each other about being committed to the end, and tell each other, "May the best man win!" We enjoy joking about it, but deep down both of us have guts of steel in regard to our long-term marriage commitment.

Lisa and I expect storms. We know life isn't always rosy, and change in life is the only constant. We've learned that in the seasons of our life new changes come with new friends and lots of new lessons. We accept that not every single day of marriage is bliss, but that has nothing to do with our commitment toward one another. For we have vowed, "Till death do us part."

Even the marathon runner who charts his or her way and trains consistently to get in shape has an occasional cramp.

When we go on vacations, we know something will not work out exactly as planned. You know what I mean. We may encounter a problem with the car, our airline tickets may be incorrect, the hotel might be all booked up, or the restaurant we expected to enjoy left us disappointed. That's life! When such things happen, we don't pack our bags and go home. We stay on vacation and accept life on it's own terms.

I tell my single clients and friends that if they find someone they love and are considering marrying them, if they can find five or fewer things that bother them about their intended, then the person is perfect. Inevitably they start counting on their fingers: "One, two, three... He only has three."

I say, "That's great! You better marry him (or her)."

This is all done in fun. But the point is this, when you look at a long-term relationship, you and your spouse will have differences and imperfections! That's life in the real world!

I have learned that the quickest way to deal with the imperfections I see in Lisa (both of them) is to get on my face and pray to God and ask Him to deal with it. I am not called to change or fix Lisa's imperfections. Therefore, I ask God to change her or to change me—either is fine. I have witnessed real miracles in Lisa and in myself when I get with God about it.

I pray that as you read this you will understand that intimacy is a lifelong journey. On your journey, you will encounter all kinds of stuff along the way. Nevertheless, the commitment you have to stay in it till the end will help you to get from marriage what God truly intended.

HOLIEST OF COMPETITIONS

As you go through the next one hundred days of exercises, you will be working hard on building and maintaining intimacy. I want to share with you something that can make it fun for you as well.

This part is an individual choice, not a couple choice. I call it the holiest of competitions. Let's look at Hebrews 12:1–3.

> Therefore, since we are surrounded by such a great cloud of witnesses, let us throw off everything that hinders and the sin that so easily entangles, and let us run with perseverance the race marked out for us. Let us fix our eyes on Jesus, the author and perfector of our faith, who for the joy set before him endured the cross, scorning its shame, and sat down at the right hand of the throne of God. Consider him who endured such opposition from sinful men, so that you will not grow weary and lose heart.

In this scripture, the writer of Hebrews is giving us a lot of how-to on running the race toward the finish line. For me, I am in daily competition to love Lisa. I commit myself to win the race by loving her. I am committed to be patient, kind, loving and gentle to her. When I start my day with this attitude, everything changes for me.

I am a relatively competitive person, so winning is important. When Lisa gets fussy, I can win by loving her more. When I see such situations as a competition, then they become opportunities to give love. When I give love as a response, then I win that round. If I stay in the spirit and consistently respond in a loving manner, then I can win for the entire day. I love to win, so competing in this way makes my day much more fun.

Now you must understand this is your own competition. There is no need to tell your spouse that you're engaging in the holiest of competitions. Just start.

Lisa never knew about my holiest of competitions until I conducted a couple's seminar at a local church in Texas. Lisa was at the conference as I explained my strategy of holy competition. I think there are days when she competes as well.

I don't win all the time, but I play to win. This makes the

day a lot more fun for me. If Lisa is in a mode of frustration, I get a kick out of looking her in the eye and saying, "I love you so much today. I am going to love you until my love for you feels greater than this mood, and I am going to love you all day for the rest of your life." I score a point in the holiest of competition.

Having a paradigm of competition really helps me to run the race consistently to the finish line.

HOW TO WIN THE HOLIEST OF COMPETITION

1. BE AWARE THAT YOU ARE BEING WATCHED.

The writer of Hebrews tells us that a "cloud of witnesses" is watching our behavior toward our spouse. Theologians differ on whether these witnesses are those who have died before us, the angels or those people who surround us each day. Regardless of who these witnesses are, your behavior is being watched.

God Himself watches our behavior. This understanding of being watched by God is what the Old Testament calls "the fear of the Lord." When you are truly aware that the Almighty is watching you, it will help you to stay on the up and up with your spouse.

We never get away with sarcasm, yelling or injuring the soul of our spouse through selfishness.

The awareness of being watched can bring accountability into your life as you pursue the holiest of competitions by loving your spouse. The best part of having a heavenly Father who is always watching along with a cloud of witnesses is that when you are doing what's right, you can almost hear them clapping. Sometimes when God gives me the grace to love Lisa in a moment of need, I just want to say aloud to them, "Did you see that one? Did ya? Did ya?"

It's similar to being in a big baseball stadium surrounded

by crowds of onlookers while you play the game of marriage. You give your spouse hugs, a nudge, you ignore a mood and choose to minister grace and love, and the crowd goes nuts! The cloud of witnesses shout, scream and give you the wave as your home run of love racks up the score. As children of God we are graced and anointed to hit the ball of love right out of the park while the crowd of witnesses goes wild.

Imaging being in heaven and having Abraham, Jacob or Paul come up to you and say, "Do you remember the day your spouse was in a funk and you blessed her? What a party we had up here! You really encouraged us." I want those conversations. I want the crowd to go wild. Throw me the ball; I want to play and win every day.

> There is great joy in knowing that your succeeding generation is blessed because of you.

If you alone commit to the holiest of competitions, you will hit more balls out of the park than if you are not in the holiest of competitions. It is more fun than humans should be allowed to have!

So, the first principle of winning the holiest of competition is to know that there is an audience, and they are pulling for you. You can make their day by loving your spouse on a daily basis.

2. *STAY FOCUSED.*

In Hebrews 12:1–2, the author of Hebrews gives principles to win in the holiest of competitions. He states, "Let us run with perseverance the race marked out for us. Let us fix our eyes on Jesus, the author and perfector of our faith."

Running a race requires a process of enduring. I know that when I run I must keep my mind focused on something to keep me going, especially when it gets tough. The same is true regarding the intimacy race with your spouse. When you're running the marathon of intimacy, you need to stay focused. I am glad that the writers of Hebrews tell us what to focus on during the race.

Focus on Jesus during the race. Don't focus on your husband or wife. Don't focus on how fair things are for you or how bad you have it. Focus on Jesus. This great wisdom solidly applies to the holiest of competitions.

If I run the race looking at myself, I will get selfish and lose. I can look at Lisa on some days and be ungrateful for God's wisdom in her and lose the competition that day. I hate to lose, and so to be sure I will win, I must look to Jesus.

It is difficult to complain, gripe or whine in the presence of the Lord who was whipped, beaten, humiliated and who died for my sins.

If I focus on Lisa alone, I might be tempted to justify an action or response that is less than Christlike. But when I am focused on Jesus, I won't give up. Nothing Lisa does or doesn't do can move me. That's the fun. I get the thrill of victory when I focus on Him.

3. Do it for the joy set before you.

The writer of Hebrews provides insight regarding why our Lord Jesus Christ persevered in the race. "For the joy set before Him [He] endured the cross." The last principle of winning the holiest of competitions is the joy that is set before you.

There is the joy at the end of the day when you know you have sown love into your spouse that day. That joy is the short-term taste of victory.

The second kind of joy set before you is the legacy of love you leave in the soul of your husband or wife. This legacy of love prepares your children to create marriages that glorify God and are intimately satisfying.

There is great joy in knowing that your succeeding

generation is blessed because of you. I want to leave my generations blessed because I was willing to discipline myself to love Lisa and to be intimate. I want life without the regret of my failures in marriage and parenting. Don't you?

Don't you want your children's children to talk about the blessings that were passed along to them? Our generation knows little of legacy building. We should leave a legacy of love and intimacy to our children so that they can give it to their children and so on.

When you choose the holiest of competitions, you will find that being consistent to the end is easier. I encourage you and your spouse to join the race as a couple. Remember, you don't have to compete against each other. You already have an audience watching your race toward intimacy.

Never forget that you are being watched, so keep the joy that's ahead of you as your focus. If you do this, you can win more days than you lose. Everyone who plays the holiest competition wins.

To those who run consistently, the blessings are too numerous to write. The moment you face confrontation, you receive understanding and spiritual, emotional and physical acceptance of who you are. The blessing of peace that enters your life as you keep your financial and sexual agreements is wonderful.

I truly hope that I have thoroughly enticed you to desire greater intimacy. As you run your forty-year or longer marathon with your lifelong mate, enjoy going the distance. You only get one journey together, so make it the best for both of you!

PART FOUR

The 100-Day Log

THIRTEEN

Beginning Your One Hundred Days

On the following pages is a 100-day log to help you monitor the progress of intimacy in your marriage. Similar to Christian growth, those who pray, soak themselves in the Scripture, have regular fellowship and obey the Holy Spirit of God will enjoy intimacy with the Father. Disciplines are the structures of life breathed into us. This truth applies to intimacy in marriage, too.

As you and your spouse take the next one hundred days to commit to behaviors that support intimacy, your marriage can be completely transformed—no matter what state it is in right now.

This 100-day log is designed for the long haul. Remember, you are developing a marathon runner's mentality, not a sprinter's. So please take your 100-day guide seriously and discipline yourselves for the long haul. Happy training as you begin the happiest journey of your life—intimacy with your spouse.

The 100-day guide has two sections. The first six days will provide a place for you to record your daily progress and make notes along the way. On the seventh day of each week there will be a place to assess your progress for the week.

In the weekly section, space is provided for notes on three evaluation areas. You may write about your progress, such as whose date it was and the progress you are making on your financial structure. You may also make notes regarding your budget. In the second month, you may write out your savings and debt-reduction plans, and in the final month you can include your retirement plans.

The third area of progress that you will be recording in your log is sexual agreement. Are you both behaving as sexual adults, and are you both maintaining your agreement? As you keep track of your progress, change will take place.

When your one hundred days are completed, this journal will be an enduring tool for developing and maintaining intimacy for a lifetime.

Happy trails,
Douglas Weiss

Day 1

Three Daily Exercises

PRAY TOGETHER?	_____ YES	_____ NO
FEELINGS EXERCISE?	_____ YES	_____ NO
PRAISE/NURTURE TOGETHER?	_____ YES	_____ NO

HE SHARED _____
        (FEELING #1)

   AND _____
        (FEELING #2)

SHE SHARED _____
        (FEELING #1)

   AND _____
        (FEELING #2)

HE SHARED _____
        (PRAISE #1)

SHE SHARED _____
        (PRAISE #1)

HE SHARED _____
        (PRAISE #2)

SHE SHARED _____
        (PRAISE #2)

SEXUALITY: SPOUSE'S TURN TODAY IS

        HUSBAND'S _____ WIFE'S _____

Day 2

Three Daily Exercises

PRAY TOGETHER?	_____ YES	_____ NO
FEELINGS EXERCISE?	_____ YES	_____ NO
PRAISE/NURTURE TOGETHER?	_____ YES	_____ NO

HE SHARED _____
        (FEELING #1)

AND   _____
        (FEELING #2)

SHE SHARED _____
        (FEELING #1)

AND   _____
        (FEELING #2)

HE SHARED _____
        (PRAISE #1)

SHE SHARED _____
        (PRAISE #1)

HE SHARED _____
        (PRAISE #2)

SHE SHARED _____
        (PRAISE #2)

SEXUALITY: SPOUSE'S TURN TODAY IS

        HUSBAND'S _____ WIFE'S _____

Day 3

Three Daily Exercises

PRAY TOGETHER?	_____ YES	_____ NO
FEELINGS EXERCISE?	_____ YES	_____ NO
PRAISE/NURTURE TOGETHER?	_____ YES	_____ NO

HE SHARED _____
    (FEELING #1)

AND _____
    (FEELING #2)

SHE SHARED _____
    (FEELING #1)

AND _____
    (FEELING #2)

HE SHARED _____
    (PRAISE #1)

SHE SHARED _____
    (PRAISE #1)

HE SHARED _____
    (PRAISE #2)

SHE SHARED _____
    (PRAISE #2)

SEXUALITY: SPOUSE'S TURN TODAY IS

    HUSBAND'S _____ WIFE'S _____

Day 4

Three Daily Exercises

PRAY TOGETHER?	_____ YES	_____ NO
FEELINGS EXERCISE?	_____ YES	_____ NO
PRAISE/NURTURE TOGETHER?	_____ YES	_____ NO

HE SHARED _____
        (FEELING #1)

  AND _____
        (FEELING #2)

SHE SHARED _____
        (FEELING #1)

  AND _____
        (FEELING #2)

HE SHARED _____
        (PRAISE #1)

SHE SHARED _____
        (PRAISE #1)

HE SHARED _____
        (PRAISE #2)

SHE SHARED _____
        (PRAISE #2)

SEXUALITY: SPOUSE'S TURN TODAY IS

        HUSBAND'S _____ WIFE'S _____

Day 5

Three Daily Exercises

Pray together?	_____ Yes	_____ No
Feelings exercise?	_____ Yes	_____ No
Praise/nurture together?	_____ Yes	_____ No

He shared _____
      (feeling #1)

and _____
      (feeling #2)

She shared _____
      (feeling #1)

and _____
      (feeling #2)

He shared _____
      (praise #1)

She shared _____
      (praise #1)

He shared _____
      (praise #2)

She shared _____
      (praise #2)

Sexuality: Spouse's turn today is

husband's _____ wife's _____

Day 6

Three Daily Exercises

PRAY TOGETHER?	_____ YES	_____ NO
FEELINGS EXERCISE?	_____ YES	_____ NO
PRAISE/NURTURE TOGETHER?	_____ YES	_____ NO

HE SHARED _____
        (FEELING #1)

AND _____
        (FEELING #2)

SHE SHARED _____
        (FEELING #1)

AND _____
        (FEELING #2)

HE SHARED _____
        (PRAISE #1)

SHE SHARED _____
        (PRAISE #1)

HE SHARED _____
        (PRAISE #2)

SHE SHARED _____
        (PRAISE #2)

SEXUALITY: SPOUSE'S TURN TODAY IS

        HUSBAND'S _____ WIFE'S _____

Weekly Progress Notes

Week 1

Whose responsibility was it to plan a *date* this week?
❏ His ❏ Hers

Rate your date (the spouse who planned it).
1 2 3 4 5 6 7 8 9 10

Did you stick to the guidelines on dating?
He ❏ Yes ❏ No
She ❏ Yes ❏ No

Record your progress for the week on your spiritual exercise of *prayer.*
Husband: 1 2 3 4 5 6 7
Wife: 1 2 3 4 5 6 7

Record your progress on your *feelings* exercise.
Husband: 1 2 3 4 5 6 7
Wife: 1 2 3 4 5 6 7

Record your progress on the *praise and nurturing* exercise.
Husband: 1 2 3 4 5 6 7
Wife: 1 2 3 4 5 6 7

Have you both kept your *sexual agreement?*
He ❏ Yes ❏ No
She ❏ Yes ❏ No

If no, did that person complete their consequences?
❏ Yes ❏ No

This week did you work on your *financial goals?* Record your individual progress.
Husband: 1 2 3 4 5 6 7
Wife: 1 2 3 4 5 6 7

Day 8

Three Daily Exercises

PRAY TOGETHER?	_____ YES	_____ NO
FEELINGS EXERCISE?	_____ YES	_____ NO
PRAISE/NURTURE TOGETHER?	_____ YES	_____ NO

HE SHARED _____
        (FEELING #1)

AND _____
        (FEELING #2)

SHE SHARED _____
        (FEELING #1)

AND _____
        (FEELING #2)

HE SHARED _____
        (PRAISE #1)

SHE SHARED _____
        (PRAISE #1)

HE SHARED _____
        (PRAISE #2)

SHE SHARED _____
        (PRAISE #2)

SEXUALITY: SPOUSE'S TURN TODAY IS

        HUSBAND'S _____ WIFE'S _____

Day 9

Three Daily Exercises

Pray together?	_____ Yes	_____ No
Feelings exercise?	_____ Yes	_____ No
Praise/nurture together?	_____ Yes	_____ No

He shared _____
  (feeling #1)

  and _____
  (feeling #2)

She shared _____
  (feeling #1)

  and _____
  (feeling #2)

He shared _____
  (praise #1)

She shared _____
  (praise #1)

He shared _____
  (praise #2)

She shared _____
  (praise #2)

Sexuality: Spouse's turn today is

  husband's _____ wife's _____

Day 10

Three Daily Exercises

PRAY TOGETHER?	_____ YES	_____ NO
FEELINGS EXERCISE?	_____ YES	_____ NO
PRAISE/NURTURE TOGETHER?	_____ YES	_____ NO

HE SHARED _____
       (FEELING #1)

AND _____
       (FEELING #2)

SHE SHARED _____
       (FEELING #1)

AND _____
       (FEELING #2)

HE SHARED _____
       (PRAISE #1)

SHE SHARED _____
       (PRAISE #1)

HE SHARED _____
       (PRAISE #2)

SHE SHARED _____
       (PRAISE #2)

SEXUALITY: SPOUSE'S TURN TODAY IS

       HUSBAND'S _____ WIFE'S _____

Day 11

Three Daily Exercises

PRAY TOGETHER?	_____ YES	_____ NO
FEELINGS EXERCISE?	_____ YES	_____ NO
PRAISE/NURTURE TOGETHER?	_____ YES	_____ NO

HE SHARED _____
      (FEELING #1)

AND _____
      (FEELING #2)

SHE SHARED _____
      (FEELING #1)

AND _____
      (FEELING #2)

HE SHARED _____
      (PRAISE #1)

SHE SHARED _____
      (PRAISE #1)

HE SHARED _____
      (PRAISE #2)

SHE SHARED _____
      (PRAISE #2)

SEXUALITY: SPOUSE'S TURN TODAY IS

      HUSBAND'S _____ WIFE'S _____

Day 12

Three Daily Exercises

Pray together?	_____ Yes	_____ No
Feelings exercise?	_____ Yes	_____ No
Praise/nurture together?	_____ Yes	_____ No

He shared _____
        (feeling #1)

  and _____
        (feeling #2)

She shared _____
        (feeling #1)

  and _____
        (feeling #2)

He shared _____
        (praise #1)

She shared _____
        (praise #1)

He shared _____
        (praise #2)

She shared _____
        (praise #2)

Sexuality: Spouse's turn today is

    husband's _____ wife's _____

Day 13

Three Daily Exercises

Pray together?	_____ Yes	_____ No
Feelings exercise?	_____ Yes	_____ No
Praise/nurture together?	_____ Yes	_____ No

He shared _____
(feeling #1)

and _____
(feeling #2)

She shared _____
(feeling #1)

and _____
(feeling #2)

He shared _____
(praise #1)

She shared _____
(praise #1)

He shared _____
(praise #2)

She shared _____
(praise #2)

Sexuality: Spouse's turn today is

husband's _____ wife's _____

Weekly Progress Notes

Week 2

Whose responsibility was it to plan a *date* this week?
  ❏ His ❏ Hers

Rate your date (the spouse who planned it).
  1 2 3 4 5 6 7 8 9 10

Did you stick to the guidelines on dating?
  He ❏ Yes ❏ No
  She ❏ Yes ❏ No

Record your progress for the week on your spiritual exercise of *prayer*.
  Husband: 1 2 3 4 5 6 7
  Wife: 1 2 3 4 5 6 7

Record your progress on your *feelings* exercise.
  Husband: 1 2 3 4 5 6 7
  Wife: 1 2 3 4 5 6 7

Record your progress on the *praise and nurturing* exercise.
  Husband: 1 2 3 4 5 6 7
  Wife: 1 2 3 4 5 6 7

Have you both kept your *sexual agreement*?
  He ❏ Yes ❏ No
  She ❏ Yes ❏ No

If no, did that person complete their consequences?
  ❏ Yes ❏ No

This week did you work on your *financial goals*? Record your individual progress.
  Husband: 1 2 3 4 5 6 7
  Wife: 1 2 3 4 5 6 7

Day 15

Three Daily Exercises

PRAY TOGETHER?	_____ YES	_____ NO
FEELINGS EXERCISE?	_____ YES	_____ NO
PRAISE/NURTURE TOGETHER?	_____ YES	_____ NO

HE SHARED _____
        (FEELING #1)

   AND _____
        (FEELING #2)

SHE SHARED _____
        (FEELING #1)

   AND _____
        (FEELING #2)

HE SHARED _____
        (PRAISE #1)

SHE SHARED _____
        (PRAISE #1)

HE SHARED _____
        (PRAISE #2)

SHE SHARED _____
        (PRAISE #2)

SEXUALITY: SPOUSE'S TURN TODAY IS

        HUSBAND'S _____ WIFE'S _____

Day 16

Three Daily Exercises

PRAY TOGETHER?	_____ YES	_____ NO
FEELINGS EXERCISE?	_____ YES	_____ NO
PRAISE/NURTURE TOGETHER?	_____ YES	_____ NO

HE SHARED _____
            (FEELING #1)

AND _____
            (FEELING #2)

SHE SHARED _____
            (FEELING #1)

AND _____
            (FEELING #2)

HE SHARED _____
            (PRAISE #1)

SHE SHARED _____
            (PRAISE #1)

HE SHARED _____
            (PRAISE #2)

SHE SHARED _____
            (PRAISE #2)

SEXUALITY: SPOUSE'S TURN TODAY IS

HUSBAND'S _____ WIFE'S _____

Day 17

Three Daily Exercises

PRAY TOGETHER?	_____ YES	_____ NO
FEELINGS EXERCISE?	_____ YES	_____ NO
PRAISE/NURTURE TOGETHER?	_____ YES	_____ NO

HE SHARED _____
(FEELING #1)

AND _____
(FEELING #2)

SHE SHARED _____
(FEELING #1)

AND _____
(FEELING #2)

HE SHARED _____
(PRAISE #1)

SHE SHARED _____
(PRAISE #1)

HE SHARED _____
(PRAISE #2)

SHE SHARED _____
(PRAISE #2)

SEXUALITY: SPOUSE'S TURN TODAY IS

HUSBAND'S _____ WIFE'S _____

Day 18

Three Daily Exercises

PRAY TOGETHER?	_____ YES	_____ NO
FEELINGS EXERCISE?	_____ YES	_____ NO
PRAISE/NURTURE TOGETHER?	_____ YES	_____ NO

HE SHARED _____

    (FEELING #1)

AND _____

    (FEELING #2)

SHE SHARED _____

    (FEELING #1)

AND _____

    (FEELING #2)

HE SHARED _____

    (PRAISE #1)

SHE SHARED _____

    (PRAISE #1)

HE SHARED _____

    (PRAISE #2)

SHE SHARED _____

    (PRAISE #2)

SEXUALITY: SPOUSE'S TURN TODAY IS

HUSBAND'S _____ WIFE'S _____

Day 19

Three Daily Exercises

PRAY TOGETHER?	_____ YES	_____ NO
FEELINGS EXERCISE?	_____ YES	_____ NO
PRAISE/NURTURE TOGETHER?	_____ YES	_____ NO

HE SHARED _____
 (FEELING #1)

AND _____
 (FEELING #2)

SHE SHARED _____
 (FEELING #1)

AND _____
 (FEELING #2)

HE SHARED _____
 (PRAISE #1)

SHE SHARED _____
 (PRAISE #1)

HE SHARED _____
 (PRAISE #2)

SHE SHARED _____
 (PRAISE #2)

SEXUALITY: SPOUSE'S TURN TODAY IS

HUSBAND'S _____ WIFE'S _____

Day 20

Three Daily Exercises

PRAY TOGETHER?	_____ YES	_____ NO
FEELINGS EXERCISE?	_____ YES	_____ NO
PRAISE/NURTURE TOGETHER?	_____ YES	_____ NO

HE SHARED _____
          (FEELING #1)

   AND   _____
          (FEELING #2)

SHE SHARED _____
          (FEELING #1)

   AND   _____
          (FEELING #2)

HE SHARED _____
          (PRAISE #1)

SHE SHARED _____
          (PRAISE #1)

HE SHARED _____
          (PRAISE #2)

SHE SHARED _____
          (PRAISE #2)

SEXUALITY: SPOUSE'S TURN TODAY IS

           HUSBAND'S _____ WIFE'S _____

Weekly Progress Notes

Week 3

Whose responsibility was it to plan a *date* this week?
❑ His ❑ Hers

Rate your date (the spouse who planned it).
1 2 3 4 5 6 7 8 9 10

Did you stick to the guidelines on dating?
He ❑ Yes ❑ No
She ❑ Yes ❑ No

Record your progress for the week on your spiritual exercise of *prayer*.
Husband: 1 2 3 4 5 6 7
Wife: 1 2 3 4 5 6 7

Record your progress on your *feelings* exercise.
Husband: 1 2 3 4 5 6 7
Wife: 1 2 3 4 5 6 7

Record your progress on the *praise and nurturing* exercise.
Husband: 1 2 3 4 5 6 7
Wife: 1 2 3 4 5 6 7

Have you both kept your *sexual agreement*?
He ❑ Yes ❑ No
She ❑ Yes ❑ No

If no, did that person complete their consequences?
❑ Yes ❑ No

This week did you work on your *financial goals?* Record your individual progress.
Husband: 1 2 3 4 5 6 7
Wife: 1 2 3 4 5 6 7

Day 22

Three Daily Exercises

PRAY TOGETHER?	_____ YES	_____ NO
FEELINGS EXERCISE?	_____ YES	_____ NO
PRAISE/NURTURE TOGETHER?	_____ YES	_____ NO

HE SHARED _____
        (FEELING #1)

AND _____
        (FEELING #2)

SHE SHARED _____
        (FEELING #1)

AND _____
        (FEELING #2)

HE SHARED _____
        (PRAISE #1)

SHE SHARED _____
        (PRAISE #1)

HE SHARED _____
        (PRAISE #2)

SHE SHARED _____
        (PRAISE #2)

SEXUALITY: SPOUSE'S TURN TODAY IS

        HUSBAND'S _____ WIFE'S _____

Day 23

Three Daily Exercises

PRAY TOGETHER?	_____ YES	_____ NO
FEELINGS EXERCISE?	_____ YES	_____ NO
PRAISE/NURTURE TOGETHER?	_____ YES	_____ NO

HE SHARED _____
(FEELING #1)

AND _____
(FEELING #2)

SHE SHARED _____
(FEELING #1)

AND _____
(FEELING #2)

HE SHARED _____
(PRAISE #1)

SHE SHARED _____
(PRAISE #1)

HE SHARED _____
(PRAISE #2)

SHE SHARED _____
(PRAISE #2)

SEXUALITY: SPOUSE'S TURN TODAY IS

HUSBAND'S _____ WIFE'S _____

Day 24

Three Daily Exercises

PRAY TOGETHER?	_____ YES	_____ NO
FEELINGS EXERCISE?	_____ YES	_____ NO
PRAISE/NURTURE TOGETHER?	_____ YES	_____ NO

HE SHARED _____

        (FEELING #1)

AND _____

        (FEELING #2)

SHE SHARED _____

        (FEELING #1)

AND _____

        (FEELING #2)

HE SHARED _____

        (PRAISE #1)

SHE SHARED _____

        (PRAISE #1)

HE SHARED _____

        (PRAISE #2)

SHE SHARED _____

        (PRAISE #2)

SEXUALITY: SPOUSE'S TURN TODAY IS

        HUSBAND'S _____ WIFE'S _____

Day 25

Three Daily Exercises

PRAY TOGETHER?	_____ YES	_____ NO
FEELINGS EXERCISE?	_____ YES	_____ NO
PRAISE/NURTURE TOGETHER?	_____ YES	_____ NO

HE SHARED _____
      (FEELING #1)

AND _____
      (FEELING #2)

SHE SHARED _____
      (FEELING #1)

AND _____
      (FEELING #2)

HE SHARED _____
      (PRAISE #1)

SHE SHARED _____
      (PRAISE #1)

HE SHARED _____
      (PRAISE #2)

SHE SHARED _____
      (PRAISE #2)

SEXUALITY: SPOUSE'S TURN TODAY IS

      HUSBAND'S _____ WIFE'S _____

Day 26

Three Daily Exercises

PRAY TOGETHER? _____ YES _____ NO
FEELINGS EXERCISE? _____ YES _____ NO
PRAISE/NURTURE TOGETHER? _____ YES _____ NO

HE SHARED _____
(FEELING #1)

AND _____
(FEELING #2)

SHE SHARED _____
(FEELING #1)

AND _____
(FEELING #2)

HE SHARED _____
(PRAISE #1)

SHE SHARED _____
(PRAISE #1)

HE SHARED _____
(PRAISE #2)

SHE SHARED _____
(PRAISE #2)

SEXUALITY: SPOUSE'S TURN TODAY IS

HUSBAND'S _____ WIFE'S _____

Day 27

Three Daily Exercises

PRAY TOGETHER?	_____ YES	_____ NO
FEELINGS EXERCISE?	_____ YES	_____ NO
PRAISE/NURTURE TOGETHER?	_____ YES	_____ NO

HE SHARED _____
        (FEELING #1)

AND _____
        (FEELING #2)

SHE SHARED _____
        (FEELING #1)

AND _____
        (FEELING #2)

HE SHARED _____
        (PRAISE #1)

SHE SHARED _____
        (PRAISE #1)

HE SHARED _____
        (PRAISE #2)

SHE SHARED _____
        (PRAISE #2)

SEXUALITY: SPOUSE'S TURN TODAY IS

HUSBAND'S _____ WIFE'S _____

Weekly Progress Notes

Week 4

Whose responsibility was it to plan a *date* this week?
❑ His ❑ Hers

Rate your date (the spouse who planned it).
1 2 3 4 5 6 7 8 9 10

Did you stick to the guidelines on dating?
He ❑ Yes ❑ No
She ❑ Yes ❑ No

Record your progress for the week on your spiritual exercise of *prayer.*
Husband: 1 2 3 4 5 6 7
Wife: 1 2 3 4 5 6 7

Record your progress on your *feelings* exercise.
Husband: 1 2 3 4 5 6 7
Wife: 1 2 3 4 5 6 7

Record your progress on the *praise and nurturing* exercise.
Husband: 1 2 3 4 5 6 7
Wife: 1 2 3 4 5 6 7

Have you both kept your *sexual agreement?*
He ❑ Yes ❑ No
She ❑ Yes ❑ No

If no, did that person complete their consequences?
❑ Yes ❑ No

This week did you work on your *financial goals?* Record your individual progress.
Husband: 1 2 3 4 5 6 7
Wife: 1 2 3 4 5 6 7

Day 29

Three Daily Exercises

PRAY TOGETHER?	_____ YES	_____ NO
FEELINGS EXERCISE?	_____ YES	_____ NO
PRAISE/NURTURE TOGETHER?	_____ YES	_____ NO

HE SHARED _____
        (FEELING #1)

    AND _____
        (FEELING #2)

SHE SHARED _____
        (FEELING #1)

    AND _____
        (FEELING #2)

HE SHARED _____
        (PRAISE #1)

SHE SHARED _____
        (PRAISE #1)

HE SHARED _____
        (PRAISE #2)

SHE SHARED _____
        (PRAISE #2)

SEXUALITY: SPOUSE'S TURN TODAY IS

        HUSBAND'S _____ WIFE'S _____

Day 30

Three Daily Exercises

PRAY TOGETHER?	_____ YES	_____ NO
FEELINGS EXERCISE?	_____ YES	_____ NO
PRAISE/NURTURE TOGETHER?	_____ YES	_____ NO

HE SHARED _____
        (FEELING #1)

  AND _____
        (FEELING #2)

SHE SHARED _____
        (FEELING #1)

  AND _____
        (FEELING #2)

HE SHARED _____
        (PRAISE #1)

SHE SHARED _____
        (PRAISE #1)

HE SHARED _____
        (PRAISE #2)

SHE SHARED _____
        (PRAISE #2)

SEXUALITY: SPOUSE'S TURN TODAY IS

    HUSBAND'S _____ WIFE'S _____

Day 31

Three Daily Exercises

PRAY TOGETHER?	_____ YES	_____ NO
FEELINGS EXERCISE?	_____ YES	_____ NO
PRAISE/NURTURE TOGETHER?	_____ YES	_____ NO

HE SHARED _____
      (FEELING #1)

AND _____
      (FEELING #2)

SHE SHARED _____
      (FEELING #1)

AND _____
      (FEELING #2)

HE SHARED _____
      (PRAISE #1)

SHE SHARED _____
      (PRAISE #1)

HE SHARED _____
      (PRAISE #2)

SHE SHARED _____
      (PRAISE #2)

SEXUALITY: SPOUSE'S TURN TODAY IS

      HUSBAND'S _____ WIFE'S _____

Day 32

Three Daily Exercises

PRAY TOGETHER?	_____ YES	_____ NO
FEELINGS EXERCISE?	_____ YES	_____ NO
PRAISE/NURTURE TOGETHER?	_____ YES	_____ NO

HE SHARED _____
(FEELING #1)

AND _____
(FEELING #2)

SHE SHARED _____
(FEELING #1)

AND _____
(FEELING #2)

HE SHARED _____
(PRAISE #1)

SHE SHARED _____
(PRAISE #1)

HE SHARED _____
(PRAISE #2)

SHE SHARED _____
(PRAISE #2)

SEXUALITY: SPOUSE'S TURN TODAY IS

HUSBAND'S _____ WIFE'S _____

Day 33

Three Daily Exercises

PRAY TOGETHER?	_____ YES	_____ NO
FEELINGS EXERCISE?	_____ YES	_____ NO
PRAISE/NURTURE TOGETHER?	_____ YES	_____ NO

HE SHARED _____
(FEELING #1)

AND _____
(FEELING #2)

SHE SHARED _____
(FEELING #1)

AND _____
(FEELING #2)

HE SHARED _____
(PRAISE #1)

SHE SHARED _____
(PRAISE #1)

HE SHARED _____
(PRAISE #2)

SHE SHARED _____
(PRAISE #2)

SEXUALITY: SPOUSE'S TURN TODAY IS

HUSBAND'S _____ WIFE'S _____

Day 34

Three Daily Exercises

PRAY TOGETHER?	_____ YES	_____ NO
FEELINGS EXERCISE?	_____ YES	_____ NO
PRAISE/NURTURE TOGETHER?	_____ YES	_____ NO

HE SHARED _____
        (FEELING #1)

AND _____
        (FEELING #2)

SHE SHARED _____
        (FEELING #1)

AND _____
        (FEELING #2)

HE SHARED _____
        (PRAISE #1)

SHE SHARED _____
        (PRAISE #1)

HE SHARED _____
        (PRAISE #2)

SHE SHARED _____
        (PRAISE #2)

SEXUALITY: SPOUSE'S TURN TODAY IS

HUSBAND'S _____ WIFE'S _____

Weekly Progress Notes

Week 5

Whose responsibility was it to plan a *date* this week?
❏ His ❏ Hers

Rate your date (the spouse who planned it).
1 2 3 4 5 6 7 8 9 10

Did you stick to the guidelines on dating?
He ❏ Yes ❏ No
She ❏ Yes ❏ No

Record your progress for the week on your spiritual exercise of *prayer*.
Husband: 1 2 3 4 5 6 7
Wife: 1 2 3 4 5 6 7

Record your progress on your *feelings* exercise.
Husband: 1 2 3 4 5 6 7
Wife: 1 2 3 4 5 6 7

Record your progress on the *praise and nurturing* exercise.
Husband: 1 2 3 4 5 6 7
Wife: 1 2 3 4 5 6 7

Have you both kept your *sexual agreement*?
He ❏ Yes ❏ No
She ❏ Yes ❏ No

If no, did that person complete their consequences?
❏ Yes ❏ No

This week did you work on your *financial goals?* Record your individual progress.
Husband: 1 2 3 4 5 6 7
Wife: 1 2 3 4 5 6 7

Day 36

Three Daily Exercises

Pray together?	_____ Yes	_____ No
Feelings exercise?	_____ Yes	_____ No
Praise/nurture together?	_____ Yes	_____ No

He shared _____
(feeling #1)

and _____
(feeling #2)

She shared _____
(feeling #1)

and _____
(feeling #2)

He shared _____
(praise #1)

She shared _____
(praise #1)

He shared _____
(praise #2)

She shared _____
(praise #2)

Sexuality: Spouse's turn today is

husband's _____ wife's _____

Day 37

Three Daily Exercises

Pray together?	_____ Yes	_____ No
Feelings exercise?	_____ Yes	_____ No
Praise/nurture together?	_____ Yes	_____ No

He shared _____
        (feeling #1)

and _____
        (feeling #2)

She shared _____
        (feeling #1)

and _____
        (feeling #2)

He shared _____
        (praise #1)

She shared _____
        (praise #1)

He shared _____
        (praise #2)

She shared _____
        (praise #2)

Sexuality: Spouse's turn today is

        husband's _____ wife's _____

Day 38

Three Daily Exercises

PRAY TOGETHER? _____ YES _____ NO
FEELINGS EXERCISE? _____ YES _____ NO
PRAISE/NURTURE TOGETHER? _____ YES _____ NO

HE SHARED _____
(FEELING #1)

AND _____
(FEELING #2)

SHE SHARED _____
(FEELING #1)

AND _____
(FEELING #2)

HE SHARED _____
(PRAISE #1)

SHE SHARED _____
(PRAISE #1)

HE SHARED _____
(PRAISE #2)

SHE SHARED _____
(PRAISE #2)

SEXUALITY: SPOUSE'S TURN TODAY IS

HUSBAND'S _____ WIFE'S _____

Day 39

Three Daily Exercises

PRAY TOGETHER?	_____ YES	_____ NO
FEELINGS EXERCISE?	_____ YES	_____ NO
PRAISE/NURTURE TOGETHER?	_____ YES	_____ NO

HE SHARED _____
           (FEELING #1)

    AND   _____
           (FEELING #2)

SHE SHARED _____
           (FEELING #1)

    AND   _____
           (FEELING #2)

HE SHARED _____
          (PRAISE #1)

SHE SHARED _____
           (PRAISE #1)

HE SHARED _____
          (PRAISE #2)

SHE SHARED _____
           (PRAISE #2)

SEXUALITY: SPOUSE'S TURN TODAY IS

           HUSBAND'S _____ WIFE'S _____

Day 40

Three Daily Exercises

PRAY TOGETHER?	_____ YES	_____ NO
FEELINGS EXERCISE?	_____ YES	_____ NO
PRAISE/NURTURE TOGETHER?	_____ YES	_____ NO

HE SHARED _____
        (FEELING #1)

AND _____
        (FEELING #2)

SHE SHARED _____
        (FEELING #1)

AND _____
        (FEELING #2)

HE SHARED _____
        (PRAISE #1)

SHE SHARED _____
        (PRAISE #1)

HE SHARED _____
        (PRAISE #2)

SHE SHARED _____
        (PRAISE #2)

SEXUALITY: SPOUSE'S TURN TODAY IS

HUSBAND'S _____ WIFE'S _____

Day 41

Three Daily Exercises

PRAY TOGETHER?	_____ YES	_____ NO
FEELINGS EXERCISE?	_____ YES	_____ NO
PRAISE/NURTURE TOGETHER?	_____ YES	_____ NO

HE SHARED _____
  (FEELING #1)

AND _____
  (FEELING #2)

SHE SHARED _____
  (FEELING #1)

AND _____
  (FEELING #2)

HE SHARED _____
  (PRAISE #1)

SHE SHARED _____
  (PRAISE #1)

HE SHARED _____
  (PRAISE #2)

SHE SHARED _____
  (PRAISE #2)

SEXUALITY: SPOUSE'S TURN TODAY IS

  HUSBAND'S _____ WIFE'S _____

Weekly Progress Notes

Week 6

Whose responsibility was it to plan a *date* this week?
❑ His ❑ Hers

Rate your date (the spouse who planned it).
1 2 3 4 5 6 7 8 9 10

Did you stick to the guidelines on dating?
He ❑ Yes ❑ No
She ❑ Yes ❑ No

Record your progress for the week on your spiritual exercise of *prayer.*
Husband: 1 2 3 4 5 6 7
Wife: 1 2 3 4 5 6 7

Record your progress on your *feelings* exercise.
Husband: 1 2 3 4 5 6 7
Wife: 1 2 3 4 5 6 7

Record your progress on the *praise and nurturing* exercise.
Husband: 1 2 3 4 5 6 7
Wife: 1 2 3 4 5 6 7

Have you both kept your *sexual agreement?*
He ❑ Yes ❑ No
She ❑ Yes ❑ No

If no, did that person complete their consequences?
❑ Yes ❑ No

This week did you work on your *financial goals?* Record your individual progress.
Husband: 1 2 3 4 5 6 7
Wife: 1 2 3 4 5 6 7

Day 43

Three Daily Exercises

Pray together? _____ Yes _____ No

Feelings exercise? _____ Yes _____ No

Praise/nurture together? _____ Yes _____ No

He shared _____
(feeling #1)

and _____
(feeling #2)

She shared _____
(feeling #1)

and _____
(feeling #2)

He shared _____
(praise #1)

She shared _____
(praise #1)

He shared _____
(praise #2)

She shared _____
(praise #2)

Sexuality: Spouse's turn today is

husband's _____ wife's _____

Day 44

Three Daily Exercises

PRAY TOGETHER?	_____ YES	_____ NO
FEELINGS EXERCISE?	_____ YES	_____ NO
PRAISE/NURTURE TOGETHER?	_____ YES	_____ NO

HE SHARED _____
      (FEELING #1)

AND _____
      (FEELING #2)

SHE SHARED _____
      (FEELING #1)

AND _____
      (FEELING #2)

HE SHARED _____
      (PRAISE #1)

SHE SHARED _____
      (PRAISE #1)

HE SHARED _____
      (PRAISE #2)

SHE SHARED _____
      (PRAISE #2)

SEXUALITY: SPOUSE'S TURN TODAY IS

      HUSBAND'S _____ WIFE'S _____

Day 45

Three Daily Exercises

PRAY TOGETHER?	_____ YES	_____ NO
FEELINGS EXERCISE?	_____ YES	_____ NO
PRAISE/NURTURE TOGETHER?	_____ YES	_____ NO

HE SHARED _____
    (FEELING #1)

AND _____
    (FEELING #2)

SHE SHARED _____
    (FEELING #1)

AND _____
    (FEELING #2)

HE SHARED _____
    (PRAISE #1)

SHE SHARED _____
    (PRAISE #1)

HE SHARED _____
    (PRAISE #2)

SHE SHARED _____
    (PRAISE #2)

SEXUALITY: SPOUSE'S TURN TODAY IS

    HUSBAND'S _____ WIFE'S _____

Day 46

Three Daily Exercises

PRAY TOGETHER?	_____ YES	_____ NO
FEELINGS EXERCISE?	_____ YES	_____ NO
PRAISE/NURTURE TOGETHER?	_____ YES	_____ NO

HE SHARED _____
        (FEELING #1)

AND _____
        (FEELING #2)

SHE SHARED _____
        (FEELING #1)

AND _____
        (FEELING #2)

HE SHARED _____
        (PRAISE #1)

SHE SHARED _____
        (PRAISE #1)

HE SHARED _____
        (PRAISE #2)

SHE SHARED _____
        (PRAISE #2)

SEXUALITY: SPOUSE'S TURN TODAY IS

HUSBAND'S _____ WIFE'S _____

Day 47

Three Daily Exercises

PRAY TOGETHER?	_____ YES	_____ NO
FEELINGS EXERCISE?	_____ YES	_____ NO
PRAISE/NURTURE TOGETHER?	_____ YES	_____ NO

HE SHARED _____
        (FEELING #1)

AND _____
        (FEELING #2)

SHE SHARED _____
        (FEELING #1)

AND _____
        (FEELING #2)

HE SHARED _____
        (PRAISE #1)

SHE SHARED _____
        (PRAISE #1)

HE SHARED _____
        (PRAISE #2)

SHE SHARED _____
        (PRAISE #2)

SEXUALITY: SPOUSE'S TURN TODAY IS

        HUSBAND'S _____ WIFE'S _____

Day 48

Three Daily Exercises

PRAY TOGETHER?	_____ YES	_____ NO
FEELINGS EXERCISE?	_____ YES	_____ NO
PRAISE/NURTURE TOGETHER?	_____ YES	_____ NO

HE SHARED _____
        (FEELING #1)

AND _____
        (FEELING #2)

SHE SHARED _____
        (FEELING #1)

AND _____
        (FEELING #2)

HE SHARED _____
        (PRAISE #1)

SHE SHARED _____
        (PRAISE #1)

HE SHARED _____
        (PRAISE #2)

SHE SHARED _____
        (PRAISE #2)

SEXUALITY: SPOUSE'S TURN TODAY IS

        HUSBAND'S _____ WIFE'S _____

Weekly Progress Notes

Week 7

Whose responsibility was it to plan a *date* this week?
 ❏ His ❏ Hers

Rate your date (the spouse who planned it).
 1 2 3 4 5 6 7 8 9 10

Did you stick to the guidelines on dating?
 He ❏ Yes ❏ No
 She ❏ Yes ❏ No

Record your progress for the week on your spiritual exercise of *prayer*.
 Husband: 1 2 3 4 5 6 7
 Wife: 1 2 3 4 5 6 7

Record your progress on your *feelings* exercise.
 Husband: 1 2 3 4 5 6 7
 Wife: 1 2 3 4 5 6 7

Record your progress on the *praise and nurturing* exercise.
 Husband: 1 2 3 4 5 6 7
 Wife: 1 2 3 4 5 6 7

Have you both kept your *sexual agreement*?
 He ❏ Yes ❏ No
 She ❏ Yes ❏ No

If no, did that person complete their consequences?
 ❏ Yes ❏ No

This week did you work on your *financial goals?* Record your individual progress.
 Husband: 1 2 3 4 5 6 7
 Wife: 1 2 3 4 5 6 7

Day 50

Three Daily Exercises

P<small>RAY TOGETHER</small>?	_____ Y<small>ES</small>	_____ N<small>O</small>
F<small>EELINGS EXERCISE</small>?	_____ Y<small>ES</small>	_____ N<small>O</small>
P<small>RAISE</small>/<small>NURTURE TOGETHER</small>?	_____ Y<small>ES</small>	_____ N<small>O</small>

H<small>E SHARED</small> _____

        (<small>FEELING</small> #1)

<small>AND</small> _____

        (<small>FEELING</small> #2)

S<small>HE SHARED</small> _____

        (<small>FEELING</small> #1)

<small>AND</small> _____

        (<small>FEELING</small> #2)

H<small>E SHARED</small> _____

        (<small>PRAISE</small> #1)

S<small>HE SHARED</small> _____

        (<small>PRAISE</small> #1)

H<small>E SHARED</small> _____

        (<small>PRAISE</small> #2)

S<small>HE SHARED</small> _____

        (<small>PRAISE</small> #2)

S<small>EXUALITY</small>: S<small>POUSE'S TURN TODAY IS</small>

        <small>HUSBAND'S</small> _____ <small>WIFE'S</small> _____

Day 51

Three Daily Exercises

Pray together?	_____ Yes	_____ No
Feelings exercise?	_____ Yes	_____ No
Praise/nurture together?	_____ Yes	_____ No

He shared _____
(feeling #1)

and _____
(feeling #2)

She shared _____
(feeling #1)

and _____
(feeling #2)

He shared _____
(praise #1)

She shared _____
(praise #1)

He shared _____
(praise #2)

She shared _____
(praise #2)

Sexuality: Spouse's turn today is

husband's _____ wife's _____

Day 52

Three Daily Exercises

PRAY TOGETHER?	_____ YES	_____ NO
FEELINGS EXERCISE?	_____ YES	_____ NO
PRAISE/NURTURE TOGETHER?	_____ YES	_____ NO

HE SHARED _____
      (FEELING #1)

AND _____
      (FEELING #2)

SHE SHARED _____
      (FEELING #1)

AND _____
      (FEELING #2)

HE SHARED _____
      (PRAISE #1)

SHE SHARED _____
      (PRAISE #1)

HE SHARED _____
      (PRAISE #2)

SHE SHARED _____
      (PRAISE #2)

SEXUALITY: SPOUSE'S TURN TODAY IS

      HUSBAND'S _____ WIFE'S _____

Day 53

Three Daily Exercises

PRAY TOGETHER?	_____ YES	_____ NO
FEELINGS EXERCISE?	_____ YES	_____ NO
PRAISE/NURTURE TOGETHER?	_____ YES	_____ NO

HE SHARED _____
             (FEELING #1)

AND   _____
             (FEELING #2)

SHE SHARED _____
             (FEELING #1)

AND   _____
             (FEELING #2)

HE SHARED _____
             (PRAISE #1)

SHE SHARED _____
             (PRAISE #1)

HE SHARED _____
             (PRAISE #2)

SHE SHARED _____
             (PRAISE #2)

SEXUALITY: SPOUSE'S TURN TODAY IS

HUSBAND'S _____ WIFE'S _____

Day 54

Three Daily Exercises

PRAY TOGETHER?	_____ YES	_____ NO
FEELINGS EXERCISE?	_____ YES	_____ NO
PRAISE/NURTURE TOGETHER?	_____ YES	_____ NO

HE SHARED _____
 (FEELING #1)

AND _____
 (FEELING #2)

SHE SHARED _____
 (FEELING #1)

AND _____
 (FEELING #2)

HE SHARED _____
 (PRAISE #1)

SHE SHARED _____
 (PRAISE #1)

HE SHARED _____
 (PRAISE #2)

SHE SHARED _____
 (PRAISE #2)

SEXUALITY: SPOUSE'S TURN TODAY IS

 HUSBAND'S _____ WIFE'S _____

Day 55

Three Daily Exercises

PRAY TOGETHER?	_____ YES	_____ NO
FEELINGS EXERCISE?	_____ YES	_____ NO
PRAISE/NURTURE TOGETHER?	_____ YES	_____ NO

HE SHARED _____
   (FEELING #1)

AND _____
   (FEELING #2)

SHE SHARED _____
   (FEELING #1)

AND _____
   (FEELING #2)

HE SHARED _____
   (PRAISE #1)

SHE SHARED _____
   (PRAISE #1)

HE SHARED _____
   (PRAISE #2)

SHE SHARED _____
   (PRAISE #2)

SEXUALITY: SPOUSE'S TURN TODAY IS

   HUSBAND'S _____ WIFE'S _____

Weekly Progress Notes

Week 8

Whose responsibility was it to plan a *date* this week?
 ❏ His ❏ Hers

Rate your date (the spouse who planned it).
 1 2 3 4 5 6 7 8 9 10

Did you stick to the guidelines on dating?
 He ❏ Yes ❏ No
 She ❏ Yes ❏ No

Record your progress for the week on your spiritual exercise of *prayer*.
 Husband: 1 2 3 4 5 6 7
 Wife: 1 2 3 4 5 6 7

Record your progress on your *feelings* exercise.
 Husband: 1 2 3 4 5 6 7
 Wife: 1 2 3 4 5 6 7

Record your progress on the *praise and nurturing* exercise.
 Husband: 1 2 3 4 5 6 7
 Wife: 1 2 3 4 5 6 7

Have you both kept your *sexual agreement*?
 He ❏ Yes ❏ No
 She ❏ Yes ❏ No

If no, did that person complete their consequences?
 ❏ Yes ❏ No

This week did you work on your *financial goals?* Record your individual progress.
 Husband: 1 2 3 4 5 6 7
 Wife: 1 2 3 4 5 6 7

Day 57

Three Daily Exercises

PRAY TOGETHER?	_____ YES	_____ NO
FEELINGS EXERCISE?	_____ YES	_____ NO
PRAISE/NURTURE TOGETHER?	_____ YES	_____ NO

HE SHARED _____
          (FEELING #1)

   AND   _____
          (FEELING #2)

SHE SHARED _____
          (FEELING #1)

   AND   _____
          (FEELING #2)

HE SHARED _____
          (PRAISE #1)

SHE SHARED _____
          (PRAISE #1)

HE SHARED _____
          (PRAISE #2)

SHE SHARED _____
          (PRAISE #2)

SEXUALITY: SPOUSE'S TURN TODAY IS

           HUSBAND'S _____ WIFE'S _____

Day 58

Three Daily Exercises

PRAY TOGETHER?	_____ YES	_____ NO
FEELINGS EXERCISE?	_____ YES	_____ NO
PRAISE/NURTURE TOGETHER?	_____ YES	_____ NO

HE SHARED _____
    (FEELING #1)

    AND _____
    (FEELING #2)

SHE SHARED _____
    (FEELING #1)

    AND _____
    (FEELING #2)

HE SHARED _____
    (PRAISE #1)

SHE SHARED _____
    (PRAISE #1)

HE SHARED _____
    (PRAISE #2)

SHE SHARED _____
    (PRAISE #2)

SEXUALITY: SPOUSE'S TURN TODAY IS

    HUSBAND'S _____ WIFE'S _____

Day 59

Three Daily Exercises

PRAY TOGETHER?	_____ YES	_____ NO
FEELINGS EXERCISE?	_____ YES	_____ NO
PRAISE/NURTURE TOGETHER?	_____ YES	_____ NO

HE SHARED _____
        (FEELING #1)

AND _____
        (FEELING #2)

SHE SHARED _____
        (FEELING #1)

AND _____
        (FEELING #2)

HE SHARED _____
        (PRAISE #1)

SHE SHARED _____
        (PRAISE #1)

HE SHARED _____
        (PRAISE #2)

SHE SHARED _____
        (PRAISE #2)

SEXUALITY: SPOUSE'S TURN TODAY IS

        HUSBAND'S _____ WIFE'S _____

Day 60

Three Daily Exercises

Pray together?	_____ Yes	_____ No
Feelings exercise?	_____ Yes	_____ No
Praise/nurture together?	_____ Yes	_____ No

He shared _____
(feeling #1)

and _____
(feeling #2)

She shared _____
(feeling #1)

and _____
(feeling #2)

He shared _____
(praise #1)

She shared _____
(praise #1)

He shared _____
(praise #2)

She shared _____
(praise #2)

Sexuality: Spouse's turn today is

husband's _____ wife's _____

Day 61

Three Daily Exercises

Pray together?	_____ Yes	_____ No
Feelings exercise?	_____ Yes	_____ No
Praise/nurture together?	_____ Yes	_____ No

He shared _____
          (feeling #1)

and _____
          (feeling #2)

She shared _____
          (feeling #1)

and _____
          (feeling #2)

He shared _____
          (praise #1)

She shared _____
          (praise #1)

He shared _____
          (praise #2)

She shared _____
          (praise #2)

Sexuality: Spouse's turn today is

husband's _____ wife's _____

Day 62

Three Daily Exercises

PRAY TOGETHER?	_____ YES	_____ NO
FEELINGS EXERCISE?	_____ YES	_____ NO
PRAISE/NURTURE TOGETHER?	_____ YES	_____ NO

HE SHARED _____
  (FEELING #1)

AND _____
  (FEELING #2)

SHE SHARED _____
  (FEELING #1)

AND _____
  (FEELING #2)

HE SHARED _____
  (PRAISE #1)

SHE SHARED _____
  (PRAISE #1)

HE SHARED _____
  (PRAISE #2)

SHE SHARED _____
  (PRAISE #2)

SEXUALITY: SPOUSE'S TURN TODAY IS

HUSBAND'S _____ WIFE'S _____

Weekly Progress Notes

Week 9

Whose responsibility was it to plan a *date* this week?
❏ His ❏ Hers

Rate your date (the spouse who planned it).
1 2 3 4 5 6 7 8 9 10

Did you stick to the guidelines on dating?
He ❏ Yes ❏ No
She ❏ Yes ❏ No

Record your progress for the week on your spiritual exercise of *prayer.*
Husband: 1 2 3 4 5 6 7
Wife: 1 2 3 4 5 6 7

Record your progress on your *feelings* exercise.
Husband: 1 2 3 4 5 6 7
Wife: 1 2 3 4 5 6 7

Record your progress on the *praise and nurturing* exercise.
Husband: 1 2 3 4 5 6 7
Wife: 1 2 3 4 5 6 7

Have you both kept your *sexual agreement?*
He ❏ Yes ❏ No
She ❏ Yes ❏ No

If no, did that person complete their consequences?
❏ Yes ❏ No

This week did you work on your *financial goals?* Record your individual progress.
Husband: 1 2 3 4 5 6 7
Wife: 1 2 3 4 5 6 7

Day 64

Three Daily Exercises

Pray together?	_____ Yes	_____ No
Feelings exercise?	_____ Yes	_____ No
Praise/nurture together?	_____ Yes	_____ No

He shared _____
       (feeling #1)

and _____
       (feeling #2)

She shared _____
       (feeling #1)

and _____
       (feeling #2)

He shared _____
       (praise #1)

She shared _____
       (praise #1)

He shared _____
       (praise #2)

She shared _____
       (praise #2)

Sexuality: Spouse's turn today is

husband's _____ wife's _____

Day 65

Three Daily Exercises

PRAY TOGETHER?	___ YES	___ NO
FEELINGS EXERCISE?	___ YES	___ NO
PRAISE/NURTURE TOGETHER?	___ YES	___ NO

HE SHARED _____
      (FEELING #1)

AND _____
      (FEELING #2)

SHE SHARED _____
      (FEELING #1)

AND _____
      (FEELING #2)

HE SHARED _____
      (PRAISE #1)

SHE SHARED _____
      (PRAISE #1)

HE SHARED _____
      (PRAISE #2)

SHE SHARED _____
      (PRAISE #2)

SEXUALITY: SPOUSE'S TURN TODAY IS

      HUSBAND'S _____ WIFE'S _____

Day 66

Three Daily Exercises

PRAY TOGETHER?	_____ YES	_____ NO
FEELINGS EXERCISE?	_____ YES	_____ NO
PRAISE/NURTURE TOGETHER?	_____ YES	_____ NO

HE SHARED _____
    (FEELING #1)

AND _____
    (FEELING #2)

SHE SHARED _____
    (FEELING #1)

AND _____
    (FEELING #2)

HE SHARED _____
    (PRAISE #1)

SHE SHARED _____
    (PRAISE #1)

HE SHARED _____
    (PRAISE #2)

SHE SHARED _____
    (PRAISE #2)

SEXUALITY: SPOUSE'S TURN TODAY IS

    HUSBAND'S _____ WIFE'S _____

Day 67

Three Daily Exercises

PRAY TOGETHER?	_____ YES	_____ NO
FEELINGS EXERCISE?	_____ YES	_____ NO
PRAISE/NURTURE TOGETHER?	_____ YES	_____ NO

HE SHARED _____
      (FEELING #1)

AND _____
      (FEELING #2)

SHE SHARED _____
      (FEELING #1)

AND _____
      (FEELING #2)

HE SHARED _____
      (PRAISE #1)

SHE SHARED _____
      (PRAISE #1)

HE SHARED _____
      (PRAISE #2)

SHE SHARED _____
      (PRAISE #2)

SEXUALITY: SPOUSE'S TURN TODAY IS

HUSBAND'S _____ WIFE'S _____

Day 68

Three Daily Exercises

Pray together?	_____ Yes	_____ No
Feelings exercise?	_____ Yes	_____ No
Praise/nurture together?	_____ Yes	_____ No

He shared _____
      (feeling #1)

  and _____
      (feeling #2)

She shared _____
      (feeling #1)

  and _____
      (feeling #2)

He shared _____
      (praise #1)

She shared _____
      (praise #1)

He shared _____
      (praise #2)

She shared _____
      (praise #2)

Sexuality: Spouse's turn today is

    husband's _____ wife's _____

Day 69

Three Daily Exercises

PRAY TOGETHER?	_____ YES	_____ NO
FEELINGS EXERCISE?	_____ YES	_____ NO
PRAISE/NURTURE TOGETHER?	_____ YES	_____ NO

HE SHARED _____
   (FEELING #1)

AND _____
   (FEELING #2)

SHE SHARED _____
   (FEELING #1)

AND _____
   (FEELING #2)

HE SHARED _____
   (PRAISE #1)

SHE SHARED _____
   (PRAISE #1)

HE SHARED _____
   (PRAISE #2)

SHE SHARED _____
   (PRAISE #2)

SEXUALITY: SPOUSE'S TURN TODAY IS

   HUSBAND'S _____ WIFE'S _____

Weekly Progress Notes

Week 10

Whose responsibility was it to plan a *date* this week?
❑ His ❑ Hers

Rate your date (the spouse who planned it).
1 2 3 4 5 6 7 8 9 10

Did you stick to the guidelines on dating?
He ❑ Yes ❑ No
She ❑ Yes ❑ No

Record your progress for the week on your spiritual exercise of *prayer.*
Husband: 1 2 3 4 5 6 7
Wife: 1 2 3 4 5 6 7

Record your progress on your *feelings* exercise.
Husband: 1 2 3 4 5 6 7
Wife: 1 2 3 4 5 6 7

Record your progress on the *praise and nurturing* exercise.
Husband: 1 2 3 4 5 6 7
Wife: 1 2 3 4 5 6 7

Have you both kept your *sexual agreement?*
He ❑ Yes ❑ No
She ❑ Yes ❑ No

If no, did that person complete their consequences?
❑ Yes ❑ No

This week did you work on your *financial goals?* Record your individual progress.
Husband: 1 2 3 4 5 6 7
Wife: 1 2 3 4 5 6 7

Day 71

Three Daily Exercises

PRAY TOGETHER?	_____ YES	_____ NO
FEELINGS EXERCISE?	_____ YES	_____ NO
PRAISE/NURTURE TOGETHER?	_____ YES	_____ NO

HE SHARED _____
        (FEELING #1)

AND _____
        (FEELING #2)

SHE SHARED _____
        (FEELING #1)

AND _____
        (FEELING #2)

HE SHARED _____
        (PRAISE #1)

SHE SHARED _____
        (PRAISE #1)

HE SHARED _____
        (PRAISE #2)

SHE SHARED _____
        (PRAISE #2)

SEXUALITY: SPOUSE'S TURN TODAY IS

    HUSBAND'S _____ WIFE'S _____

Day 72

Three Daily Exercises

PRAY TOGETHER?	_____ YES	_____ NO
FEELINGS EXERCISE?	_____ YES	_____ NO
PRAISE/NURTURE TOGETHER?	_____ YES	_____ NO

HE SHARED _____
   (FEELING #1)

   AND _____
   (FEELING #2)

SHE SHARED _____
   (FEELING #1)

   AND _____
   (FEELING #2)

HE SHARED _____
   (PRAISE #1)

SHE SHARED _____
   (PRAISE #1)

HE SHARED _____
   (PRAISE #2)

SHE SHARED _____
   (PRAISE #2)

SEXUALITY: SPOUSE'S TURN TODAY IS

   HUSBAND'S _____ WIFE'S _____

Day 73

Three Daily Exercises

PRAY TOGETHER?	_____ YES	_____ NO
FEELINGS EXERCISE?	_____ YES	_____ NO
PRAISE/NURTURE TOGETHER?	_____ YES	_____ NO

HE SHARED _____
        (FEELING #1)

AND _____
        (FEELING #2)

SHE SHARED _____
        (FEELING #1)

AND _____
        (FEELING #2)

HE SHARED _____
        (PRAISE #1)

SHE SHARED _____
        (PRAISE #1)

HE SHARED _____
        (PRAISE #2)

SHE SHARED _____
        (PRAISE #2)

SEXUALITY: SPOUSE'S TURN TODAY IS

        HUSBAND'S _____ WIFE'S _____

Day 74

Three Daily Exercises

PRAY TOGETHER?	_____ YES	_____ NO
FEELINGS EXERCISE?	_____ YES	_____ NO
PRAISE/NURTURE TOGETHER?	_____ YES	_____ NO

HE SHARED _____
        (FEELING #1)

AND _____
        (FEELING #2)

SHE SHARED _____
        (FEELING #1)

AND _____
        (FEELING #2)

HE SHARED _____
        (PRAISE #1)

SHE SHARED _____
        (PRAISE #1)

HE SHARED _____
        (PRAISE #2)

SHE SHARED _____
        (PRAISE #2)

SEXUALITY: SPOUSE'S TURN TODAY IS

HUSBAND'S _____ WIFE'S _____

Day 75

Three Daily Exercises

PRAY TOGETHER?	_____ YES	_____ NO
FEELINGS EXERCISE?	_____ YES	_____ NO
PRAISE/NURTURE TOGETHER?	_____ YES	_____ NO

HE SHARED _____
        (FEELING #1)

AND _____
        (FEELING #2)

SHE SHARED _____
        (FEELING #1)

AND _____
        (FEELING #2)

HE SHARED _____
        (PRAISE #1)

SHE SHARED _____
        (PRAISE #1)

HE SHARED _____
        (PRAISE #2)

SHE SHARED _____
        (PRAISE #2)

SEXUALITY: SPOUSE'S TURN TODAY IS

        HUSBAND'S _____ WIFE'S _____

Day 76

Three Daily Exercises

PRAY TOGETHER?	_____ YES	_____ NO
FEELINGS EXERCISE?	_____ YES	_____ NO
PRAISE/NURTURE TOGETHER?	_____ YES	_____ NO

HE SHARED _____
       (FEELING #1)

  AND _____
       (FEELING #2)

SHE SHARED _____
       (FEELING #1)

  AND _____
       (FEELING #2)

HE SHARED _____
       (PRAISE #1)

SHE SHARED _____
       (PRAISE #1)

HE SHARED _____
       (PRAISE #2)

SHE SHARED _____
       (PRAISE #2)

SEXUALITY: SPOUSE'S TURN TODAY IS

       HUSBAND'S _____ WIFE'S _____

Weekly Progress Notes

Week 11

Whose responsibility was it to plan a *date* this week?
❑ His ❑ Hers

Rate your date (the spouse who planned it).
1 2 3 4 5 6 7 8 9 10

Did you stick to the guidelines on dating?
He ❑ Yes ❑ No
She ❑ Yes ❑ No

Record your progress for the week on your spiritual exercise of *prayer.*
Husband: 1 2 3 4 5 6 7
Wife: 1 2 3 4 5 6 7

Record your progress on your *feelings* exercise.
Husband: 1 2 3 4 5 6 7
Wife: 1 2 3 4 5 6 7

Record your progress on the *praise and nurturing* exercise.
Husband: 1 2 3 4 5 6 7
Wife: 1 2 3 4 5 6 7

Have you both kept your *sexual agreement?*
He ❑ Yes ❑ No
She ❑ Yes ❑ No

If no, did that person complete their consequences?
❑ Yes ❑ No

This week did you work on your *financial goals?* Record your individual progress.
Husband: 1 2 3 4 5 6 7
Wife: 1 2 3 4 5 6 7

Day 78

Three Daily Exercises

Pray together?	_____ Yes	_____ No
Feelings exercise?	_____ Yes	_____ No
Praise/nurture together?	_____ Yes	_____ No

He shared _____
   (feeling #1)

   and _____
   (feeling #2)

She shared _____
   (feeling #1)

   and _____
   (feeling #2)

He shared _____
   (praise #1)

She shared _____
   (praise #1)

He shared _____
   (praise #2)

She shared _____
   (praise #2)

Sexuality: Spouse's turn today is

   husband's _____ wife's _____

Day 79

Three Daily Exercises

PRAY TOGETHER?	_____ YES	_____ NO
FEELINGS EXERCISE?	_____ YES	_____ NO
PRAISE/NURTURE TOGETHER?	_____ YES	_____ NO

HE SHARED _____
  (FEELING #1)

AND _____
  (FEELING #2)

SHE SHARED _____
  (FEELING #1)

AND _____
  (FEELING #2)

HE SHARED _____
  (PRAISE #1)

SHE SHARED _____
  (PRAISE #1)

HE SHARED _____
  (PRAISE #2)

SHE SHARED _____
  (PRAISE #2)

SEXUALITY: SPOUSE'S TURN TODAY IS

  HUSBAND'S _____ WIFE'S _____

Day 80

Three Daily Exercises

PRAY TOGETHER?	_____ YES	_____ NO
FEELINGS EXERCISE?	_____ YES	_____ NO
PRAISE/NURTURE TOGETHER?	_____ YES	_____ NO

HE SHARED _____
        (FEELING #1)

AND _____
        (FEELING #2)

SHE SHARED _____
        (FEELING #1)

AND _____
        (FEELING #2)

HE SHARED _____
        (PRAISE #1)

SHE SHARED _____
        (PRAISE #1)

HE SHARED _____
        (PRAISE #2)

SHE SHARED _____
        (PRAISE #2)

SEXUALITY: SPOUSE'S TURN TODAY IS

HUSBAND'S _____ WIFE'S _____

Day 81

Three Daily Exercises

PRAY TOGETHER?	_____ YES	_____ NO
FEELINGS EXERCISE?	_____ YES	_____ NO
PRAISE/NURTURE TOGETHER?	_____ YES	_____ NO

HE SHARED _____
        (FEELING #1)

AND _____
        (FEELING #2)

SHE SHARED _____
        (FEELING #1)

AND _____
        (FEELING #2)

HE SHARED _____
        (PRAISE #1)

SHE SHARED _____
        (PRAISE #1)

HE SHARED _____
        (PRAISE #2)

SHE SHARED _____
        (PRAISE #2)

SEXUALITY: SPOUSE'S TURN TODAY IS

        HUSBAND'S _____ WIFE'S _____

Day 82

Three Daily Exercises

PRAY TOGETHER? _____ YES _____ NO
FEELINGS EXERCISE? _____ YES _____ NO
PRAISE/NURTURE TOGETHER? _____ YES _____ NO

HE SHARED _____
　　　　　(FEELING #1)

AND _____
　　　(FEELING #2)

SHE SHARED _____
　　　　　(FEELING #1)

AND _____
　　　(FEELING #2)

HE SHARED _____
　　　　　(PRAISE #1)

SHE SHARED _____
　　　　　(PRAISE #1)

HE SHARED _____
　　　　　(PRAISE #2)

SHE SHARED _____
　　　　　(PRAISE #2)

SEXUALITY: SPOUSE'S TURN TODAY IS

　　　HUSBAND'S _____ WIFE'S _____

Day 83

Three Daily Exercises

PRAY TOGETHER?	_____ YES	_____ NO
FEELINGS EXERCISE?	_____ YES	_____ NO
PRAISE/NURTURE TOGETHER?	_____ YES	_____ NO

HE SHARED _____
        (FEELING #1)

AND _____
        (FEELING #2)

SHE SHARED _____
        (FEELING #1)

AND _____
        (FEELING #2)

HE SHARED _____
        (PRAISE #1)

SHE SHARED _____
        (PRAISE #1)

HE SHARED _____
        (PRAISE #2)

SHE SHARED _____
        (PRAISE #2)

SEXUALITY: SPOUSE'S TURN TODAY IS

HUSBAND'S _____ WIFE'S _____

Weekly Progress Notes

Week 12

Whose responsibility was it to plan a *date* this week?
❏ His ❏ Hers

Rate your date (the spouse who planned it).
1 2 3 4 5 6 7 8 9 10

Did you stick to the guidelines on dating?
He ❏ Yes ❏ No
She ❏ Yes ❏ No

Record your progress for the week on your spiritual exercise of *prayer.*
Husband: 1 2 3 4 5 6 7
Wife: 1 2 3 4 5 6 7

Record your progress on your *feelings* exercise.
Husband: 1 2 3 4 5 6 7
Wife: 1 2 3 4 5 6 7

Record your progress on the *praise and nurturing* exercise.
Husband: 1 2 3 4 5 6 7
Wife: 1 2 3 4 5 6 7

Have you both kept your *sexual agreement?*
He ❏ Yes ❏ No
She ❏ Yes ❏ No

If no, did that person complete their consequences?
❏ Yes ❏ No

This week did you work on your *financial goals?* Record your individual progress.
Husband: 1 2 3 4 5 6 7
Wife: 1 2 3 4 5 6 7

Day 85

Three Daily Exercises

PRAY TOGETHER?	_____ YES	_____ NO
FEELINGS EXERCISE?	_____ YES	_____ NO
PRAISE/NURTURE TOGETHER?	_____ YES	_____ NO

HE SHARED _____
  (FEELING #1)

AND _____
  (FEELING #2)

SHE SHARED _____
  (FEELING #1)

AND _____
  (FEELING #2)

HE SHARED _____
  (PRAISE #1)

SHE SHARED _____
  (PRAISE #1)

HE SHARED _____
  (PRAISE #2)

SHE SHARED _____
  (PRAISE #2)

SEXUALITY: SPOUSE'S TURN TODAY IS

  HUSBAND'S _____ WIFE'S _____

Day 86

Three Daily Exercises

PRAY TOGETHER?	_____ YES	_____ NO
FEELINGS EXERCISE?	_____ YES	_____ NO
PRAISE/NURTURE TOGETHER?	_____ YES	_____ NO

HE SHARED _____
(FEELING #1)

AND _____
(FEELING #2)

SHE SHARED _____
(FEELING #1)

AND _____
(FEELING #2)

HE SHARED _____
(PRAISE #1)

SHE SHARED _____
(PRAISE #1)

HE SHARED _____
(PRAISE #2)

SHE SHARED _____
(PRAISE #2)

SEXUALITY: SPOUSE'S TURN TODAY IS

HUSBAND'S _____ WIFE'S _____

Day 87

Three Daily Exercises

PRAY TOGETHER?	_____ YES	_____ NO
FEELINGS EXERCISE?	_____ YES	_____ NO
PRAISE/NURTURE TOGETHER?	_____ YES	_____ NO

HE SHARED _____
       (FEELING #1)

AND _____
       (FEELING #2)

SHE SHARED _____
       (FEELING #1)

AND _____
       (FEELING #2)

HE SHARED _____
       (PRAISE #1)

SHE SHARED _____
       (PRAISE #1)

HE SHARED _____
       (PRAISE #2)

SHE SHARED _____
       (PRAISE #2)

SEXUALITY: SPOUSE'S TURN TODAY IS

       HUSBAND'S _____ WIFE'S _____

Day 88

Three Daily Exercises

PRAY TOGETHER?	_____ YES	_____ NO
FEELINGS EXERCISE?	_____ YES	_____ NO
PRAISE/NURTURE TOGETHER?	_____ YES	_____ NO

HE SHARED _____
        (FEELING #1)

AND _____
        (FEELING #2)

SHE SHARED _____
        (FEELING #1)

AND _____
        (FEELING #2)

HE SHARED _____
        (PRAISE #1)

SHE SHARED _____
        (PRAISE #1)

HE SHARED _____
        (PRAISE #2)

SHE SHARED _____
        (PRAISE #2)

SEXUALITY: SPOUSE'S TURN TODAY IS

HUSBAND'S _____ WIFE'S _____

Day 89

Three Daily Exercises

PRAY TOGETHER?	_____ YES	_____ NO
FEELINGS EXERCISE?	_____ YES	_____ NO
PRAISE/NURTURE TOGETHER?	_____ YES	_____ NO

HE SHARED _____
        (FEELING #1)

AND _____
        (FEELING #2)

SHE SHARED _____
        (FEELING #1)

AND _____
        (FEELING #2)

HE SHARED _____
        (PRAISE #1)

SHE SHARED _____
        (PRAISE #1)

HE SHARED _____
        (PRAISE #2)

SHE SHARED _____
        (PRAISE #2)

SEXUALITY: SPOUSE'S TURN TODAY IS

        HUSBAND'S _____ WIFE'S _____

Day 90

Three Daily Exercises

PRAY TOGETHER?	_____ YES	_____ NO
FEELINGS EXERCISE?	_____ YES	_____ NO
PRAISE/NURTURE TOGETHER?	_____ YES	_____ NO

HE SHARED _____
　　　　　　　(FEELING #1)

AND _____
　　　(FEELING #2)

SHE SHARED _____
　　　　　　　　(FEELING #1)

AND _____
　　　(FEELING #2)

HE SHARED _____
　　　　　　　(PRAISE #1)

SHE SHARED _____
　　　　　　　　(PRAISE #1)

HE SHARED _____
　　　　　　　(PRAISE #2)

SHE SHARED _____
　　　　　　　　(PRAISE #2)

SEXUALITY: SPOUSE'S TURN TODAY IS

　　　　　HUSBAND'S _____ WIFE'S _____

Weekly Progress Notes

Week 13

Whose responsibility was it to plan a *date* this week?
❏ His ❏ Hers

Rate your date (the spouse who planned it).
1 2 3 4 5 6 7 8 9 10

Did you stick to the guidelines on dating?
He ❏ Yes ❏ No
She ❏ Yes ❏ No

Record your progress for the week on your spiritual exercise of *prayer*.
Husband: 1 2 3 4 5 6 7
Wife: 1 2 3 4 5 6 7

Record your progress on your *feelings* exercise.
Husband: 1 2 3 4 5 6 7
Wife: 1 2 3 4 5 6 7

Record your progress on the *praise and nurturing* exercise.
Husband: 1 2 3 4 5 6 7
Wife: 1 2 3 4 5 6 7

Have you both kept your *sexual agreement*?
He ❏ Yes ❏ No
She ❏ Yes ❏ No

If no, did that person complete their consequences?
❏ Yes ❏ No

This week did you work on your *financial goals*? Record your individual progress.
Husband: 1 2 3 4 5 6 7
Wife: 1 2 3 4 5 6 7

Day 92

Three Daily Exercises

PRAY TOGETHER?	_____ YES	_____ NO
FEELINGS EXERCISE?	_____ YES	_____ NO
PRAISE/NURTURE TOGETHER?	_____ YES	_____ NO

HE SHARED _____
 (FEELING #1)

AND _____
 (FEELING #2)

SHE SHARED _____
 (FEELING #1)

AND _____
 (FEELING #2)

HE SHARED _____
 (PRAISE #1)

SHE SHARED _____
 (PRAISE #1)

HE SHARED _____
 (PRAISE #2)

SHE SHARED _____
 (PRAISE #2)

SEXUALITY: SPOUSE'S TURN TODAY IS

 HUSBAND'S _____ WIFE'S _____

Day 93

Three Daily Exercises

P<small>RAY TOGETHER</small>?	_____ Y<small>ES</small>	_____ N<small>O</small>
F<small>EELINGS EXERCISE</small>?	_____ Y<small>ES</small>	_____ N<small>O</small>
P<small>RAISE</small>/<small>NURTURE TOGETHER</small>?	_____ Y<small>ES</small>	_____ N<small>O</small>

H<small>E SHARED</small> _____
              (<small>FEELING</small> #1)

    <small>AND</small> _____
              (<small>FEELING</small> #2)

S<small>HE SHARED</small> _____
              (<small>FEELING</small> #1)

    <small>AND</small> _____
              (<small>FEELING</small> #2)

H<small>E SHARED</small> _____
              (<small>PRAISE</small> #1)

S<small>HE SHARED</small> _____
              (<small>PRAISE</small> #1)

H<small>E SHARED</small> _____
              (<small>PRAISE</small> #2)

S<small>HE SHARED</small> _____
              (<small>PRAISE</small> #2)

S<small>EXUALITY</small>: S<small>POUSE'S TURN TODAY IS</small>

        <small>HUSBAND'S</small> _____ <small>WIFE'S</small> _____

Day 94

Three Daily Exercises

PRAY TOGETHER?	_____ YES	_____ NO
FEELINGS EXERCISE?	_____ YES	_____ NO
PRAISE/NURTURE TOGETHER?	_____ YES	_____ NO

HE SHARED _____
        (FEELING #1)

AND _____
        (FEELING #2)

SHE SHARED _____
        (FEELING #1)

AND _____
        (FEELING #2)

HE SHARED _____
        (PRAISE #1)

SHE SHARED _____
        (PRAISE #1)

HE SHARED _____
        (PRAISE #2)

SHE SHARED _____
        (PRAISE #2)

SEXUALITY: SPOUSE'S TURN TODAY IS

        HUSBAND'S _____ WIFE'S _____

Day 95

Three Daily Exercises

PRAY TOGETHER?	_____ YES	_____ NO
FEELINGS EXERCISE?	_____ YES	_____ NO
PRAISE/NURTURE TOGETHER?	_____ YES	_____ NO

HE SHARED _____
      (FEELING #1)

AND _____
      (FEELING #2)

SHE SHARED _____
      (FEELING #1)

AND _____
      (FEELING #2)

HE SHARED _____
      (PRAISE #1)

SHE SHARED _____
      (PRAISE #1)

HE SHARED _____
      (PRAISE #2)

SHE SHARED _____
      (PRAISE #2)

SEXUALITY: SPOUSE'S TURN TODAY IS

HUSBAND'S _____ WIFE'S _____

Day 96

Three Daily Exercises

PRAY TOGETHER?	_____ YES	_____ NO
FEELINGS EXERCISE?	_____ YES	_____ NO
PRAISE/NURTURE TOGETHER?	_____ YES	_____ NO

HE SHARED _____
      (FEELING #1)

AND _____
      (FEELING #2)

SHE SHARED _____
      (FEELING #1)

AND _____
      (FEELING #2)

HE SHARED _____
      (PRAISE #1)

SHE SHARED _____
      (PRAISE #1)

HE SHARED _____
      (PRAISE #2)

SHE SHARED _____
      (PRAISE #2)

SEXUALITY: SPOUSE'S TURN TODAY IS

      HUSBAND'S _____ WIFE'S _____

Day 97

Three Daily Exercises

PRAY TOGETHER?	_____ YES	_____ NO
FEELINGS EXERCISE?	_____ YES	_____ NO
PRAISE/NURTURE TOGETHER?	_____ YES	_____ NO

HE SHARED _____
        (FEELING #1)

AND _____
        (FEELING #2)

SHE SHARED _____
        (FEELING #1)

AND _____
        (FEELING #2)

HE SHARED _____
        (PRAISE #1)

SHE SHARED _____
        (PRAISE #1)

HE SHARED _____
        (PRAISE #2)

SHE SHARED _____
        (PRAISE #2)

SEXUALITY: SPOUSE'S TURN TODAY IS

        HUSBAND'S _____ WIFE'S _____

Weekly Progress Notes

Week 14

Whose responsibility was it to plan a *date* this week?
❑ His ❑ Hers

Rate your date (the spouse who planned it).
1   2   3   4   5   6   7   8   9   10

Did you stick to the guidelines on dating?
He ❑ Yes ❑ No
She ❑ Yes ❑ No

Record your progress for the week on your spiritual exercise of *prayer*.
Husband: 1   2   3   4   5   6   7
Wife: 1   2   3   4   5   6   7

Record your progress on your *feelings* exercise.
Husband: 1   2   3   4   5   6   7
Wife: 1   2   3   4   5   6   7

Record your progress on the *praise and nurturing* exercise.
Husband: 1   2   3   4   5   6   7
Wife: 1   2   3   4   5   6   7

Have you both kept your *sexual agreement*?
He ❑ Yes ❑ No
She ❑ Yes ❑ No

If no, did that person complete their consequences?
❑ Yes ❑ No

This week did you work on your *financial goals?* Record your individual progress.
Husband: 1   2   3   4   5   6   7
Wife: 1   2   3   4   5   6   7

Day 99

Three Daily Exercises

Pray together?	_____ Yes	_____ No
Feelings exercise?	_____ Yes	_____ No
Praise/nurture together?	_____ Yes	_____ No

He shared _____
　　　　(feeling #1)

　　and _____
　　　　(feeling #2)

She shared _____
　　　　(feeling #1)

　　and _____
　　　　(feeling #2)

He shared _____
　　　　(praise #1)

She shared _____
　　　　(praise #1)

He shared _____
　　　　(praise #2)

She shared _____
　　　　(praise #2)

Sexuality: Spouse's turn today is

　　　　husband's _____ wife's _____

Day 100

Three Daily Exercises

PRAY TOGETHER?	_____ YES	_____ NO
FEELINGS EXERCISE?	_____ YES	_____ NO
PRAISE/NURTURE TOGETHER?	_____ YES	_____ NO

HE SHARED _____
(FEELING #1)

AND _____
(FEELING #2)

SHE SHARED _____
(FEELING #1)

AND _____
(FEELING #2)

HE SHARED _____
(PRAISE #1)

SHE SHARED _____
(PRAISE #1)

HE SHARED _____
(PRAISE #2)

SHE SHARED _____
(PRAISE #2)

SEXUALITY: SPOUSE'S TURN TODAY IS

HUSBAND'S _____ WIFE'S _____

APPENDIX

Feelings Exercise

1. I feel _____ when _____.
   (put word here)   (put a present situation when you feel this)

2. I first remember feeling _____.
                            (put the same feeling word here)

   when _____.
        (explain earliest occurrence of this feeling).

Choose your feeling words from the following list (or select your own word).

Abandoned	Anxious	Battered	Callous
Abused	Apart	Beaten	Calm
Aching	Apathetic	Beautiful	Capable
Accepted	Apologetic	Belligerent	Captivated
Accepting	Appreciated	Belittled	Carefree
Accused	Appreciative	Bereaved	Careful
Admired	Appropriate	Betrayed	Careless
Adored	Approved	Bewildered	Caring
Adventurous	Argumentative	Blamed	Cautious
Affectionate	Aroused	Blaming	Certain
Agony	Astonished	Bonded	Chased
Alienated	Assertive	Bored	Cheated
Aloof	Attached	Bothered	Cheerful
Aggravated	Attacked	Brave	Childlike
Agreeable	Attentive	Breathless	Choked up
Aggressive	Attractive	Bristling	Close
Amazed	Aware	Broken up	Cold
Amused	Awestruck	Bruised	Comfortable
Angry	Badgered	Bubbly	Comforted
Anguished	Baited	Burdened	Competent
Annoyed	Bashful	Burned	Competitive

Intimacy

Complacent	Disgusted	Gay	Isolated
Complete	Disinterested	Generous	Inspired
Confident	Dispirited	Gentle	Insulted
Confused	Distressed	Genuine	Interested
Considerate	Distrustful	Giddy	Intimate
Consumed	Distrusted	Giving	Intolerant
Content	Disturbed	Goofy	Involved
Cool	Dominated	Grateful	Irate
Courageous	Domineering	Greedy	Irrational
Courteous	Doomed	Grief	Irked
Coy	Doubtful	Grim	Irresponsible
Crabby	Dreadful	Grimy	Irritable
Cranky	Eager	Grouchy	Irritated
Crazy	Ecstatic	Grumpy	Isolated
Creative	Edgy	Hard	Jealous
Critical	Edified	Harried	Jittery
Criticized	Elated	Healthy	Joyous
Cross	Embarrassed	Helpful	Lively
Crushed	Empowered	Helpless	Lonely
Cuddly	Empty	Hesitant	Loose
Curious	Enraged	High	Lost
Cut	Enraptured	Hollow	Loving
Damned	Enthusiastic	Honest	Low
Dangerous	Enticed	Hopeful	Lucky
Daring	Esteemed	Hopeless	Lustful
Dead	Exasperated	Horrified	Mad
Deceived	Excited	Hostile	Maudlin
Deceptive	Exhilarated	Humiliated	Malicious
Defensive	Exposed	Hurried	Mean
Delicate	Fake	Hurt	Miserable
Delighted	Fascinated	Hyper	Misunderstood
Demeaned	Feisty	Ignorant	Moody
Demoralized	Ferocious	Ignored	Morose
Dependent	Foolish	Immature	Mournful
Depressed	Forced	Impatient	Mystified
Deprived	Forceful	Important	Nasty
Deserted	Forgiven	Impotent	Nervous
Desirable	Forgotten	Impressed	Nice
Desired	Free	Incompetent	Numb
Despair	Friendly	Incomplete	Nurtured
Despondent	Frightened	Independent	Nuts
Destroyed	Frustrated	Insecure	Obsessed
Different	Full	Innocent	Offended
Dirty	Funny	Insignificant	Open
Disenchanted	Furious	Insincere	Ornery

342

APPENDIX

Out of control
Overcome
Overjoyed
Overpowered
Overwhelmed
Pampered
Panicked
Paralyzed
Paranoid
Patient
Peaceful
Pensive
Perceptive
Perturbed
Phony
Pleasant
Pleased
Positive
Powerless
Present
Precious
Pressured
Pretty
Proud
Pulled apart
Put down
Puzzled
Quarrelsome
Queer
Quiet
Raped
Ravished
Ravishing
Real
Refreshed
Regretful
Rejected
Rejuvenated
Rejecting
Relaxed
Relieved
Remarkable
Remembered
Removed
Repulsed

Repulsive
Resentful
Resistant
Responsible
Repressed
Respected
Restless
Revolved
Riled
Rotten
Ruined
Sad
Safe
Satiated
Satisfied
Scared
Scolded
Scorned
Scrutinized
Secure
Seduced
Seductive
Self-centered
Self-conscious
Selfish
Separated
Sensuous
Sexy
Shattered
Shocked
Shot down
Shy
Sickened
Silly
Sincere
Sinking
Smart
Smothered
Smug
Sneaky
Snowed
Soft
Solid
Solitary
Sorry

Spacey
Special
Spiteful
Spontaneous
Squelched
Starved
Stiff
Stimulated
Stifled
Strangled
Strong
Stubborn
Stuck
Stunned
Stupid
Subdued
Submissive
Successful
Suffocated
Sure
Sweet
Sympathy
Tainted
Tearful
Tender
Tense
Terrific
Terrified
Thrilled
Ticked
Tickled
Tight
Timid
Tired
Tolerant
Torn
Tortured
Touched
Trapped
Tremendous
Tricked
Trusted
Trustful
Trusting
Ugly

Unacceptable
Unapproachable
Unaware
Uncertain
Uncomfortable
Under control
Understanding
Understood
Undesirable
Unfriendly
Ungrateful
Unified
Unhappy
Unimpressed
Unsafe
Unstable
Upset
Uptight
Used
Useful
Useless
Unworthy
Validated
Valuable
Valued
Victorious
Violated
Violent
Voluptuous
Vulnerable
Warm
Wary
Weak
Whipped
Whole
Wicked
Wild
Willing
Wiped out
Wishful
Withdrawn
Wonderful
Worried
Worthy

NOTES

Chapter 6
Dealing With Sexuality

1. Source obtained from the Internet: "Prevalence of child sexual abuse," http://home.t-online.de/home/B.Herrmann/preval.htm. B. Herrmann, M.D., "Medical diagnosis in child abuse," Children's Hospital, Kassel/Germany, www.kindesmisshandlung.de.

2. For more information on the effects of sexual abuse, see: David Finkelhor, *Child Sexual Abuse: New Theory and Research* (New York: Free Press, 1984).

3. Statistics taken from an Internet study conducted by Doug Weiss in 1995 with pastors of six denominations and Christian counselors.

4. Douglas Weiss, *Partners: Healing From His Addiction* (Colorado Springs, CO: Discovery Press, 2001).

Chapter 7
Money Matters

1. Source obtained from the Internet: Dr. Mark Smutny, "Cleansed on the Way," sermon preached March 26, 2000 at Pasadena Presbyterian Church; www.ppc.net/sermons/text/03–26.00.html.

PRODUCTS FOR INTIMACY ANOREXIA

Helping My Spouse Heal from My Intimacy Anorexia Video Course
$99.00

Are you struggling to validate your spouse's pain from Intimacy Anorexia and help them begin to heal? For the spouse of an intimacy anorexic, the pain is excruciating and sometimes even debilitating. This course is for the intimacy anorexic who is aware of their behaviors and wants to transition into a connected, intimate relationship with their spouse.

Intimacy Anorexia
BOOK:$22.95/DVD:$69.95

This hidden addiction is destroying so many marriages today. In your hands is the first antidote for someone with intimacy anorexia to turn the pages on this addiction process. Excerpts from intimacy anorexics and their spouses help this book become clinically helpful and personal in its impact to communicate hope and healing for the intimacy anorexic and the marriage.

Intimacy Anorexia: The Workbook
$39.95

Intimacy Anorexia is a hidden addiction that is destryoing many marriages today. Within the pages of this workbook you will find more than 100 practical and empowering exercises to guide you through your personal recovery towards intimacy. Douglas Weiss has been successfully counseling intimacy anorexics for many years in his practice.

Intimacy Anorexia: The Steps
$14.95

This workbook follows in the tradition of the Twelve-Steps breaking down the various principles for readers so that they can experience freedom from intimacy anorexia. It is our hope that you will join the millions who have received help in their personal recovery using these Twelve-Steps.

Pain for Love
$29.95

This DVD describes in detail one of the most insidious strategies of an intimacy anorexic with their spouse. This dynamic is experienced by many who are married to an intimacy anorexic. This paradigm can empower the spouse and help them stop participating in a pain for love dynamic in their marriage.

Sin of Withholding
$49.95

This DVD is the first to address the Biblical foundation of the sin of withholding in believers' hearts. The practical application in marriage addressing Intimacy Anorexia is also interwoven in this revelational teaching on the Sin of Withholding. Once a believer is free of this sin, their walk with the Lord and their fruit towards others can increase expediently.

Narcissism Sex Addiction & Intimacy Anorexia
$29.95

The profound information that you will learn in this DVD will help you fairly evaluate your specific situation for narcissism, which will help you develop a treatment plan to address the issue you are dealing with at its core. Having this clarity can help expedite the healing process for the sex addict, intimacy anorexic, and the spouse, as they are able to tackle the real issue at hand.

Married and Alone
BOOK:$14.95/DVD:$49.95

The impact of being married and alone is very real. Dr. Weiss explains why and will help you to start a journey of recovery from living with a spouse with intimacy or sexual anorexia. My hope is that whatever reason you are watching this DVD you realize that you are worthy of being loved, whether your spouse has decided to pursue recovery or has chosen his or her anorexia over you.

Married and Alone: Healing Exercises for Spouses
$39.95

This workbook is designed to help the spouse heal from the impact of their relationship with an intimacy anorexic which may have been experienced over years or decades. The addiction patterns of an alcoholic, gambler, overeater, sex addict or intimacy anorexic have a direct impact on their spouse's life in so many ways.

Married and Alone: The Twelve Step Guide
$14.95

This book follows in the tradition of the Twelve-Steps by breaking down the various principles for each reader so that they can experience the discovery of the Twelve-Step promises. It is our hope that you will join the millions who have received help in their recovery by using these Twelve-Steps. These Steps can further your healing and recovery from your spouse's Intimacy Anorexia.

PRODUCTS FOR PARTNER'S RECOVERY

Partners: Healing From His Addiction
$14.95

Partners: Healing from His Addiction offers real hope that you can heal from his sexual addictions. After presenting statistics and personal stories, it will walk you down the path to reclaim your life, your voice, and your power, to be who you are without the impact of his addiction.

Partners Recovery Guide: 100 Empowering Exercises
$39.95

The *Partners Recovery Guide: 100 Empowering Exercises* guide was borne out of the latest in Christian self help books research on the effects on a woman who has lived with a sexual addict. This workbook will take you down the clear path of healing from the devastating impact of his sex addiction and accompany you along your entire journey.

Beyond Love: A 12 Step Guide for Partners
$14.95

Beyond Love is an interactive workbook that allows the partners of sex addicts to gain insight and strength through working the Twelve Steps. This book can be used for individual purposes or as a group study workbook.

Partner Betrayal Trauma
BOOK: $22.95/DVD: $65.95

Partner Betrayal Trauma will help you unlock that power by providing an outstanding guide on how to become stronger every day and get past the trauma of betrayal. The pain and experience of betrayal impacts all of your being and relationships. Fix your broken heart, help your relationships, and reclaim your marriage with the necessary strategies for your personal recovery.

Partner Betrayal Trauma: The Workbook
$39.95

In this workbook by Dr. Weiss, you will gain the insight and support you need to understand what betrayal trauma is and how to overcome it to be the strongest version of yourself. This is an excellent guide for those struggling to overcome the past trauma of a betrayal in their relationship.

Partner Betrayal Trauma: Step Guide
$14.95

This is an excellent step-by-step guide for those struggling to overcome the past trauma of a betrayal in their relationship. You will gain insight from a therapist who has worked with countless patients and families for over 30 years to provide them with the support they need to come out the other side whole and better versions of themselves.

He Needs To Change, Dr. Weiss
$29.95

He Needs To Change, Dr. Weiss DVD addresses the pain, trauma, and betrayal women experience because of their partner's sex addiction, betrayal, and/or intimacy anorexia. In this DVD, Dr. Weiss addresses the issue of change that he has explained to thousands of women in his office.

Unstuck for Partners
$29.95

The *Unstuck* DVD is for every woman who has experienced the pain of their partner's sex addiction or intimacy anorexia and feels stuck, confused, frustrated and unable to move on. You didn't sign up for this and honestly, you don't get it! This DVD helps you "get it" so you can process the painful reality you are in and start to live again.

Why Do I Stay, When it Doesn't make Sense
$39.95

In this video, Dr. Doug Weiss utilizes his several decades of experience to give you information and tools that can help you make your decision with mental clarity and confidence. Whether you decide to stay, separate, or divorce, your future can be filled with new opportunities and a life that you genuinely enjoy.

Triggered
$49.00

In the Triggered DVD, Dr. Weiss gives women a repertoire of tools to be successful when a trigger occurs. Triggers are normal for partners of sex addicts, but each woman's triggers are unique and must be navigated in different ways. This DVD can be a life-changing message which will validate your struggles to heal and help you face the challenges of being triggered after partner betrayal trauma.

PRODUCTS FOR MEN'S RECOVERY

The Final Freedom
BOOK: $22.95/$35.00

The Final Freedom gives more current information than many professional counselors have today. In addition to informing sex addicts and their partners about sex addiction, it gives hope for recovery. The information provided in this book would cost hundreds of dollars in counseling hours to receive. Many have attested to successful recovery from this information alone.

101 Freedom Exercises
$39.95

This workbook provides tips, principles, survival techniques and therapeutic homework that has been tested and proven on many recovering sex addicts from all walks of life who have practiced these principles and have maintained their sobriety for many years. Jesus promised us a life of freedom, this book makes this promise a practical journey.

Steps to Freedom
$14.95

The Twelve Steps of recovery have become a major influence in the restoration of this country from the age old problem of alcohol and substance abuse. This book follows in the tradition of the Twelve Steps from a Christian perspective breaking down the various principles for each reader so that they can experience the freedom from sexual addiction.

Partner Betrayal Trauma
DVD:$69.95/COMPANION GUIDE:$11.95

The *Helping Her Heal* DVD paired with this companion guide are both vital tools for the man who has struggled with sexual addiction, exposed his marriage to the fallout of betrayal by acting on his urges, and is now seeking how to help his wife heal from the trauma of this devastating discovery.

Disclosure: Preparing and Completing
$39.95

This information can help the addict and the spouse navigate these often uncharted and misguided waters, saving the addict and the spouse from unnecessary pain or trauma. This DVD can expedite the understanding of each of the significant processes of disclosure for the addict, the spouse, and the marriage.

Healing Her Heart After Relapse
$29.95

This DVD is way more than, "He relapses, he does a consequence and moves on." The addict is given real tools to address the emotional damage and repair of her heart as a result of a relapse. Every couple in recovery would do well to have these tools before a potential relapse.

Boundaries: His. Hers.Ours
$49.95

Boundaries are a healthy, normal, and necessary part of the recovery process for sex addicts, intimacy anorexics, and their spouses. Implementing boundaries in a relationship may seem difficult, but with the proper tools and guidance you can successfully introduce and implement boundaries in your relationship. In this DVD set, Dr. Doug Weiss provides an answer to the clarion call on boundaries by educating and guiding you through this process.

Marriage After Addiction
$29.95

Addiction can have devastating effects on even good marriages. In this DVD you are intelligently guided through the journey you will experience if addiction is part of your marriage story. You will learn important information about the early and later stages of recovery for your marriage.

Shattering Sexualization
$29.95

Dr. Doug Weiss, a Licensed Psychologist who has worked with thousands of men and women struggling with sexualization, will walk you step-by-step as you heal from sexualization and the impact it has had on your life. Start living a life free of sexualization and objectification today!

Series For Men

Clean: A Proven Plan For Men Committed to Sexual Integrity
BOOK: $16.95/DVD:$29.95/JOURNAL:$14.95

Clean is a priceless, no-nonsense resource for every husband, father, brother, son, friend, pastor, and Christian leader on the front lines of this war. It is a soldier's handbook for those ready to reclaim their homes, churches, and nations for the God who has built them to succeed.

Lust Free Living
BOOK:$13.95/DVD:$23.95

Every man can fight for and obtain a lust free lifestyle. Once you know how to stop lust, you will realize how weak lust really can be. God gace you the power to protect those you love from the ravages of lust for the rest of your life! It's time to take it back!

Men Make Men
DVD:$29.95/GUIDEBOOK:$11.95

Dr. Weiss takes the listeners by the hand and step-by-step walks through the creative process God used to make every man into a man of God. This practical teaching on DVD combined with the Men Make Guidebook can revitalize the men in any home or local church.

Addiction Recovery

Recovery for Everyone
BOOK: $22.95/DVD:$99.00/WORKBOOK:$39.95/STEPBOOK: $14.95

Recovery for Everyone helps addicts fight and recover from any addiction they are facing. Learn truths and gain a biblical understanding to break the strongholds in your life.

You will also find an explanation as to how an addiction may have become a part of your life and details as to how you can walk the path to recovery. You will find a roadmap to help you begin and navigate an incredible journey toward freedom. Then you can become part of the solution and even help others get free as well.

Secret Solutions: More Than 100 Ways to End the Secret
$39.95

Female sexual addiction is real and impacting many women's lives today. This Workbook is a practical step-by-step guide for recovery from this growing issue in our culture. The *Secret Solutions*, can be used in conjunction with therapy or as part of Twelve Step relationships or groups you may be a part of. My hope is that you receive the precious gift of recovery as many others have, and that you maintain it the rest of your life, for your benefit and for the benefit of those you love.

OTHER RESOURCES

Worthy
WORKBOOK: $29.95/DVD$29.95

The Worthy Workbook and DVD, is designed for a 12 week study. Here is a path that anyone can take to get and stay worthy. Follow this path, and you too will make the journey from worthless to worthy just as others have.

Emotional Fitness
$16.95

Everyone has an unlimited number of emotions, but few have been trained to identify, choose, communicate, and master them. More than a guide for gaining emotional fitness and mastery, in these pages you will find a pathway to a much more fulfilling life.

Letters to My Daughter
$14.95

A gift for your daughter as she enters college. Letters to my Daughter includes my daily letters to my daughter during her first year of college. The letters are about life, God, boys, relationships and being successful in college and life in general.

Born for War
$29.95

Born for War teaches practical tools to defeat these sexual landmines and offers scriptural truths that empower young men to desire successfulness in the war thrust upon them. In this DVD, he equips this generation to win the war for their destiny. It also includes one session for parents to support their son through this battle.

Princes Take Longer Than Frogs
$29.95

This 2 hour DVD helps single women ages 15-30, to successfully navigate through the season of dating. Dr. Weiss' *Princes Take Longer Than Frogs* is a faith-based discussion broken up into several segments including Characteristics of Princes and Frogs, lies women Believe, Dating, Accountability, Boundaries, Sex and the Brain and so much more.

Indestructible
$29.95

The Indestructible series gives you a foundational understanding about your innate design as God's child. Addiction, betrayal, and abuse or neglected can all cause trials in our lives that can trigger feelings of worthlessness and defeat. God's Word reveals that your soul is not capable of being destroyed. Once you recognize and embrace your indestructible nature, you can change how you think, feel, and believe about your past, present, and future!

Sex after Recovery
$59.95

Sex after Recovery will help you navigate a variety of issues including how to reclaim a healthy sexual life together. This DVD set will help you to reclaim and recover your sexuality both individually and with each other.

Sexual Templates
$29.95

Dr. Doug Weiss, a Licensed Psychologist who has worked with thousands of men and women who are sexually addicted, have experienced trauma, or have had negative sexual experiences which have impacted their sexual template, will use his thirty years experience to help you rewire your brain and recreate a new, relational sexual template with your spouse.

I Need to Feel Safe
$29.95

This DVD provides a clear path to processing your desire for safety and creates a roadmap to reclaim safety regardless of your partner or spouse's choices. Dr. Weiss has helped thousands of women rebuild their fractured safety, heal the betrayal, and find hope for themselves. If your heart has cried out to feel safe, this DVD is a response to that heart cry.

Intrigue Addiction
$29.95

The intrigue addict is constantly on the hunt for a look or gesture from another person that insinuates they are attracted to or interested in them. The intrigue addiction can go unnoticed, but it can create just as much pain for the spouse as other sexually addictive behaviors.

PRODIGAL PARENT PROCESS RESOURCES

Prodigal Parent Process
BOOK: $19.95/DVD $59.95

Dr. Weiss, drawing upon his thirty-plus years of experience working with prodigals and parents of prodigals, delivers biblical and practical tools to aid you in your journey to hope and healing. You can't change the fact that you have a prodigal but you can set your mind upon how you will go through this journey with your prodigal.

Prodigal Parent Process Workbook
$16.95

In conjunction with the Parent Prodigal Process videos and book, this workbook helps you therapeutically work through deep-rooted struggles related to being a parent of a prodigal. Working through this series and workbook will prompt serious internal dialogue with yourself as it relates to your prodigal child.

MARRIAGE RESOURCES

Lover Spouse
$13.95

This book provides guidelines to lead a prosperous married life and is helpful for anyone wanting to know more about what the Lord Almighty desires for your love and marriage. Featured with practical tips and foundational relationship skills, the information offered in this book will guide couples through the process of creating an intimate Christian marriage based on a solid biblical worldview.

Upgrade Your Sex Life
BOOK:$16.95/DVD:$29.95

Upgrade Your Sex Life actually teaches you own unique sexual expression that you and your partner are pre-wired to enjoy. Once you learn what your type is, you can communicate and have sex on a more satisfying level.

Servant Marriage
$13.95

Servant Marriage book is a Revelation on God's Masterpiece of marriage. In these pages, you will walk with God as He creates the man, the woman and his masterpiece called marriage.

Marriage Mondays
$59.95

This is an eight week marriage training that actually gives you the skills to have a healthy, more vibrant marriage. Each week Dr. Weiss tackles major aspects of marriage from a biblical perspective. Apply these techniques and it will transform your marriage. This course provides couples to grow their marriages either in a small group setting or as their very own private marriage retreat.

Intimacy: 100 Day Guide to a Lasting Relationship
$11.95

The *Intimacy: A 100 Day Guide to Lasting Relationships* book gives you a game plan to improve your relationships. Intimacy doesn't need to be illusive! It's time to recognize intimacy for what it is – a loving and lifelong process that you can learn and develop.

Counseling Services

"Without the intensive, my marriage would have ended and I would not have known why. Now I am happier than ever and my marriage is bonded permanently."

Counseling Sessions

Couples are helped through critical phases of disclosure moving into the process of recovery, and rebuilding trust in relationships. We have helped many couples rebuild their relationship and grasp and implement the necessary skills for an intimate relationship.

Individual counseling offers a personal treatment plan for successful healing in your life. In just one session a counselor can help you understand how you became stuck and how to move toward freedom.

Partners of sex addicts need an advocate. Feelings of fear, hurt, anger, betrayal, and grief require a compassionate, effective response. We provide that expert guidance and direction. We have helped many partners heal through sessions that get them answers to their many questions including: "How can I trust him again?"

A counseling session today can begin your personal journey toward healing.

3 and 5 Day Intensives
in Colorado Springs, Colorado are available for the following issues:

- Sexual Addiction Couple or Individual
- Intimacy Anorexia
- Partners of Sexual Addicts
- Partner Betrayal Trauma

Attendees of Intensives will receive:

- Personal attention from counselors who specialize in your area of need
- An understanding of how the addiction /anorexia and its consequences came into being
- Three appointments daily
- Daily assignments to increase the productiveness of these daily sessions
- Individuals get effective counseling to recover from the effects of sexual addiction, abuse and anorexia
- Addiction, abuse, anorexia issues are thoroughly addressed for couples and individuals. This includes the effects on the partner or family members of the addict, and how to rebuild intimacy toward a stronger relationship.

A·A·S·A·T

American Association for Sex Addiction Therapy

Sex Addiction Training Set
$1195

Both men and women are seeking to counsel more than ever for sexually addictive behaviors. You can be prepared! Forty-seven hours of topics related to sexual addiction treatment are covered in this training including:
- The Six Types of Sex Addicts
- Neurological Understanding
- Sex and Recovery
- Relapse Strategies

Partner's Recovery Training Set
$995

With this AASAT training, you will gain proven clinical insight into treating the issues facing partners. You can be prepared! Thirty-nine hours of topics related to partners treatment are covered in this training, including:
- Partner Model
- Partner Grief
- Anger
- Boundaries

Intimacy Anorexia Training Set
$995

This growing issue of Intimacy Anorexia will need your competent help in your community. Now, you can be prepared to identify it and treat it. In this training you'll cover topics like:
- Identifying Intimacy Anorexia
- Causes of Intimacy Anorexia
- Treatment Plan
- Relapse Strategies

For more information visit www.aasat.org or call 719.330.2425

Struggling with Trauma, Anxiety, and PTSD?

Trauma, anxiety, and PTSD can imbalance your brain. When your brain is out of balance, or stuck, you don't feel right and it's impossible to function at your highest level. Cereset is a proven technology that's non-invasive and highly effective. Cereset can help your brain free itself, enabling you to achieve higher levels of well-being and balance throughout your life.

Cereset – Garden of the Gods is located at Heart to Heart Counseling Center in Colorado Springs, Colorado and specializes in working with sexual addiction, intimacy anorexia, betrayal trauma, PTSD, anxiety, and more.

Here's what clients had to say about Cereset Garden of the Gods after their sessions:

"Cereset helped save our marriage. My husband and I both did Cereset and with it helping both of us be calmer and sleep better, we respond to each other in a more loving and respectful way. I notice a big change in him, and he says the same about me. After the sessions I noticed a marked improvement in my sleep and my ability to stay calm during moments that would trigger an argument with my spouse prior to Cereset. Before Cereset we felt chaotic and now, afterwards, we both feel more at peace. our household is a is a calm place to be now and we are so grateful!"

"I've noticed a significant improvement in my ability to control and correct my patterns of thought – specifically negative thoughts. I also noticed my reaction to negative events was calmer and more controlled instead of being thrown in a downward spiral. I'm more able to recognize and deal with stress."

View a client testimonial here

Schedule Your Cereset Intensive Today!

The cost for five sessions (one per day) is $1,500.

For more information call us at 719-644-5778